The DevelopMentor Series

Don Box, Editor

Addison-Wesley has joined forces with DevelopMentor, a premiere developer resources company, to produce a series of technical books written by developers for developers. DevelopMentor boasts a prestigious technical staff that includes some of the world's best-known computer science professionals.

*"Works in **The DevelopMentor Series** are practical and informative sources on the tools and techniques for applying component-based technologies to real-world, large-scale distributed systems."*
 —Don Box

Titles in the Series:

Don Box, *Essential COM*, 0-201-63446-5

Don Box, Aaron Skonnard, and John Lam, *Essential XML: Beyond Markup*, 0-201-70914-7

Keith Brown, *Programming Windows Security*, 0-201-60442-6

Matthew Curland, *Advanced Visual Basic 6: Power Techniques for Everyday Programs*, 0-201-70712-8

Doug Dunn, *Java™ Rules*, 0-201-70916-3

Tim Ewald, *Transactional COM+L: Building Scalable Applications*, 0-201-61594-0

Jon Flanders, *ASP Internals*, 0-201-61618-1

Richard Grimes, *Developing Applications with Visual Studio.NET*, 0-201-70852-3

Martin Gudgin, *Essential IDL: Interface Design for COM*, 0-201-61595-9

Stuart Halloway, *Component Development for the Java™ Platform*, 0-201-75306-5

Joe Hummel, Ted Pattison, Justin Gehtland, Doug Turnure, and Brian A. Randell, *Effective Visual Basic: How to Improve Your VB/COM+ Applications*, 0-201-70476-5

Stanley B. Lippman, *C# Primer: A Practical Approach*, 0-201-72955-5

Everett N. McKay and Mike Woodring, *Debugging Windows Programs: Strategies, Tools, and Techniques for Visual C++ Programmers*, 0-201-70238-X

Aaron Skonnard and Martin Gudgin, *Essential XML Quick Reference: A Programmer's Reference to XML, XPath, XSLT, XML Schema, SOAP, and More*, 0-201-74095-8

Watch for future titles in The DevelopMentor Series.

Component Development for the Java™ Platform

Stuart Dabbs Halloway

Addison-Wesley

Boston • San Francisco • New York • Toronto • Montreal
London • Munich • Paris • Madrid
Capetown • Sydney • Tokyo • Singapore • Mexico City

The publisher offers discounts on this book when ordered in quantity for special sales. For more information, please contact:

Pearson Education Corporate Sales Division
201 W. 103rd Street
Indianapolis, IN 46290
(800) 428-5331
corpsales@pearsoned.com

Visit AW on the Web: www.aw.com/cseng/

Library of Congress Cataloging-in-Publication Data

Halloway, Stuart Dabbs.
    Component development for the Java platform / Stuart Dabbs Halloway.
        p. cm. – (DevelopMentor series)
    Includes bibliographical references and index.
    ISBN 0-201-75306-5
    1. Java (Computer programming language) 2. System design. I. Title. II. Series.

QA76.73 J38 H346 2002
005.13'3—dc21   200105379

0-201-75306-5
Text printed on recycled paper
1 2 3 4 5 6 7 8 9 10—MA—0504030201
First printing, December 2001

To Joey

Contents

Foreword

Several years ago, Stu abandoned the world of COM for what he had hoped would be greener pastures. While many of his colleagues felt he had lost his senses, Stu ignored our skepticism and walked away from COM completely. This was especially difficult given the fact that his employer had a tremendous investment in COM and had achieved relatively little traction in the Java world at the time.

Based on this book, I feel the move was beneficial both to Stu and to those who will be influenced by this book.

Stu's view on the Java platform is quite novel. This book portrays the Java Virtual Machine (JVM) as a substrate for component software. Are there languages and compilers that generate these components? Sure, but that isn't the focus of this book. Does the JVM perform a variety of services such as garbage collection and JIT compilation? Absolutely, but again, that isn't the focus of this book either. Rather, Stu focuses the reader on the role the JVM plays in software integration.

I am especially happy to see the book's emphasis on the class loader architecture. After spending over eight years working with COM and now two years with its successor, the Common Language Runtime (CLR), I believe that the key to understanding any component technology is to first look at how component code is discovered, initialized, and scoped during execution. In the JVM, the class loader is responsible for all of these tasks, and Stu gives that devil more than its due.

The JVM (and the Java platform as a whole) has a serious competitor now that Microsoft has more or less subsumed most Java technology into its .NET initiative, most specifically the CLR. It will be interesting to see how Sun adapts to the challenge. In looking at the JVM and CLR side-by-side, the JVM exemplifies the "less is more" philosophy, which I believe is its greatest strength. Hopefully, Sun will remain true to this basic design principle as the pressures of platform warfare pull them in the direction of adding feature upon feature for market positioning rather than aesthetic reasons.

— Don Box,
September 2001
Manhattan Beach, California

Preface

This book is about developing components using the Java platform. In this book, the term *component* has a very specific meaning. A component is an independent unit of production and deployment that is combined with other components to assemble an application.

To elaborate on this definition, consider the difference between objects and components. An object represents an entity in the problem domain, while a component is an atomic[1] piece of the installed solution. The object and component perspectives are complementary, and good designs take account of both.

Modern development platforms such as Java provide the infrastructure that developers need to create classes and components. To support object-oriented programming, Java provides encapsulation, inheritance, and polymorphism. To support components, Java provides loaders and rich type information. This book assumes that you already understand object-oriented programming in Java, and it explains how to use Java's component infrastructure effectively.

Loaders are responsible for locating, bringing into memory, and connecting components at runtime. Using Java's loaders, you can

- Deploy components at fine granularity.
- Load components dynamically as needed.
- Load components from other machines on the network.
- Locate components from custom repositories.
- Create mobile code agents that live across multiple virtual machines.
- Import the services of non-Java components.

---

1. Atomic here means "indivisible," not necessarily "stands alone." Most components will have dependencies on other components.

Loaders manage the binary boundaries between components. In a world of distributed applications and multiple component suppliers, loaders locate and connect compatible components.

Type information describes the capabilities of some unit of code. In some development environments type information is present only in source code. In Java, type information is not merely a source code artifact; it is also an intrinsic part of a compiled class and is available at runtime through a programmatic interface. Because Java type information is never "compiled away," loaders use it to verify linkages between classes at runtime. In application programming, you can use type information to

- Serialize the state of Java objects so that they can be recreated on another virtual machine.
- Create dynamic proxies at runtime, to provide generic services that can decorate any interface.
- Translate data into alternate representations to interoperate with non-Java components.
- Convert method calls into network messages.
- Convert between Java and XML, the new lingua franca of enterprise systems.
- Annotate components with application-specific metadata.

Type information automates many tasks that might otherwise be coded by hand, and it helps to make components forward compatible to platforms of the future.

Who Should Read This Book

You should read this book if you want to design, develop, or deploy substantial applications in Java. Taking a full-lifecycle view of a Java application requires that you consider not just objects, but components. This book is about the core features of Java as a component platform: class loaders, reflection, serialization, and interoperation with other platforms. You should already know the basics of Java syntax and have some experience in object-oriented programming with Java.

This book is not specifically about high-level Java technologies, such as Remote Method Invocation (RMI), Enterprise JavaBeans (EJB), JINI, Java Server Pages (JSP), servlets, or JavaBeans, but understanding the topics in this book is critical to using those technologies effectively. If you learn how to use the component services described here, you will understand how these high-level technologies are built, which is the key to employing them effectively.

Security is also an important aspect of component development and deployment. It is too complex a topic to handle fairly here, and it deserves its own book-length treatment. (See [Gon99] for coverage of security on the Java platform.)

Organization of the Book

The chapters of this book fall into three sections. Chapter 1 introduces components. Chapters 2 through 6 explain loaders and type information on the Java platform. Chapter 7 shows more advanced uses of these services.

Chapter 1 introduces component-oriented programming. Component relationships must be established not only at compile time, but also at deployment and runtime. This chapter asks the key questions of component programming and relates them to the Java platform services discussed in subsequent chapters. Though the other chapters might be read out of order, you should definitely read this chapter first.

Chapter 2 shows how to use and troubleshoot class loaders. Class loaders control the loading of code and create namespace boundaries between code in the same process. With class loaders you can load code dynamically at runtime, even from other machines. Class loader namespaces permit multiple versions of the same class in a single Java virtual machine. You can use class loaders to reload changed classes without ever shutting down the virtual machine. You will see how to use class loaders, how the class loader delegation model creates namespaces, and how to troubleshoot class loading bugs. You will also learn to effectively control the bootclasspath, extensions path, and classpath.

Chapter 3 introduces Java type information. Java preserves type information in the binary class format. This means that even after you compile your

Java programs, you still have access to field names, field types, and method signatures. You can access type information at runtime via reflection, and you can use type information to build generic services that add capability to any object. You will see how to use dynamic invocation, dynamic proxies, package reflection, and custom attributes. Chapter 3 also includes a discussion of reflection performance.

Chapter 4 shows how Java serialization uses reflection. Serialization is a perfect example of a generic service. Without any advance knowledge of a class's layout, serialization can ship both code and state from one virtual machine to another across time or space. You will see how the serialization format embeds its own style of type information and how you can customize that representation. You will also see how to extend default serialization, replace it entirely with custom externalization code, or tune it to handle multiple versions of a class as code evolves. You will then learn how to validate objects being deserialized into your application and how to annotate serialized objects with instructions for finding the correct class loader.

Chapter 5 returns to class loaders and shows you how to implement your own. While the standard class loaders are dominant in most applications, custom class loaders allow you to transform class code as classes are loaded. These transformations could include decryption, adding instrumentation for performance monitoring, or even building new classes on-the-fly at runtime. You will see how to tie your custom class loaders into Java's security architecture, how to write a custom class loader, and how to write protocol handlers that can customize not just how you load classes, but also how you load any other type of resource.

Chapter 6 presents the Java Native Interface (JNI) as a basic means of controlling the boundary between Java code and components written in other environments. JNI provides a set of low-level tools for exposing Java objects to platform native code and native code to Java objects. You will learn to use the JNI application programming interface (API) to translate between Java and native programming styles—which differ markedly in their approach to class loading, type information, resource management, error handling, and array storage.

Understanding the deficiencies of JNI sets the stage for Appendix A, which describes a higher-level approach.

Chapter 7 discusses using Java metadata to automate the creation of source code or bytecode. Generated code is a high-performance strategy for reuse because you generate only the exact code paths that you will need at runtime. The chapter first presents JSP and EJB as examples of existing applications that auto-generate code, and then it introduces some ideas for code generation in your own programs.

Appendix A returns to interoperation. By building on the code generation techniques from Chapter 7, Appendix A shows you how to build an interoperation layer between Java and another component platform: Win32/COM. This chapter uses the open source Jawin library as an example, to show you how to generate Java stubs for Win32 objects, and vice versa.

Sample Code, Website, Feedback...

Unless specifically noted otherwise, all the sample code in this book is open source. You can download sample code from the book's website at http://staff.develop.com/halloway/compsvcs.

Unless otherwise noted, the code in this book is compiled and tested against the Java 2 Software Development Kit (SDK) version 1.3. Most of the code in the book will work identically under SDK versions 1.2, 1.3, and 1.4. Where this is not the case, the text will include a specific reference to the appropriate SDK version.

The author welcomes your comments, corrections, and feedback. Please send email to stu@develop.com.

Acknowledgments

First and foremost, thanks to my wife Joanna. You challenged me to think better, and then actually put up with being around me when I took the challenge. Thanks also to my parents, Ronald and Olive Dabbs, for raising me in an environment that enabled me to find the richly satisfying life I lead today.

Thanks to everyone at DevelopMentor for creating such a fantastic play environment. Thanks to Don Box and Mike Abercrombie for starting it all, and for bringing together such a talented team. Thanks to Brian Maso, whose Intensive Java course materials were the seed of many ideas in this book. Thanks to Simon Horrell, Kevin Jones, and Ted Neward for running an excellent Guerrilla Java class, and for many lengthy conversations on the minutiae of the Java platform.

Thanks to the DevelopMentor folk and other friends who volunteered to review drafts of this book. In addition to Brian, Simon, Kevin, and Ted, these also include Ian Griffiths, Tim Ewald, and Jason Masterman. Thanks to Eric Johnson for reviewing the entire manuscript. Special thanks to Justin Gehtland and Chris Sells, who also reviewed the entire manuscript, despite the fact that their day jobs keep them tied to the other component platform.

Thanks to the excellent group of reviewers provided by Addison-Wesley: Carl Burnham, Joshua Engel, Eric Freeman, Peter Haggar, Howard Lee Harkness, Norman Hensley, Tim Lindholm, and Paul McLachlan. I don't know you all personally, and in some cases do not even have your names, but your contributions to the book were invaluable. Few problems could escape the notice of such an elite group. For any inconsistencies and errors that remain, the fault is mine.

Thanks to Mike Hendrickson and Julie Dinicola, my editors at Addison-Wesley. Thanks also to all the other wonderful people at Addison-Wesley who helped make this book happen: Tyrrell Albaugh, John Fuller, Giaconda Mateu, Patrick Peterson, Tracy Russ, Mary Cotillo, Stephane Thomas, and Ross Venables.

Thanks to the staff of Neo-China restaurant in Durham, North Carolina, for providing a substantial fraction of my caloric intake while I was writing this book.

Chapter 1

From Objects to Components

Well-written Java programs are both object-oriented and component-oriented. This chapter characterizes the differences between object and component perspectives, and then it demonstrates these differences by taking a program design that is object-oriented and modifying it to be component-oriented as well.

Consider an example problem domain of contact management systems. One important facet of this domain is the ability to find contacts based on a variety of different criteria. Listing 1–1 shows a partial listing for the `Contact` and `FindContact` interfaces.

Listing 1–1   Contact and FindContact Interfaces

```
package contacts;
public interface Contact {
  public String getLastName();
  public void setLastName(String ln);
  public String getFirstName();
  public void setFirstName(String fn);
  public String getSSN();
  public void setSSN();
  //etc. for other standard fields
}

//contacts/ContactFinder.java
package contacts;
public interface ContactFinder {
  Contact[] findByLastName(String ln);
  Contact[] findByFirstName(String fn);
  Contact[] findBySSN(String ssn);
  //other more exotic search methods...
}
```

Given these interfaces, it is easy to imagine a variety of client applications that access contact information. Listing 1–2 shows a simple `ListByLastName` console client that lists all the contacts with a given last name. Assuming that the `Contact` and `ContactFinder` interfaces have correctly captured the problem domain, this can be judged an adequate object-oriented (OO) design. Notice the complete separation of interface and implementation. `ListByLastName` uses variables only of interface types such as `Contact` and `ContactFinder`. If future versions use a different implementation, only one line of code needs to change.

Listing 1–2 ListByLastName

```
package contacts.client;

import contacts.*;
import contacts.impl.*;

public class ListByLastName {
  public static void main(String [] args) {
    if (args.length != 1) {
      System.out.println("Usage: ListByLastName lastName");
      System.exit(-1);
    }
    ContactFinder cf = new SimpleContactFinder();
    Contact[] cts = cf.findByLastName(args[0]);
    System.out.println("Contacts named " + args[0] + ":");
    for (int n=0; n<cts.length; n++) {
      System.out.println(cts[n]);
    }
  }
}
```

This design is easily extensible via inheritance. Imagine that each purchaser of the contact management system wants to add a few items of custom data to the basic notion of a `Contact`. They would simply extend the `Contact` interface, creating a different subinterface for each customer. Listing 1–3 shows a sample extension that tracks information of interest to diplomats.

Listing 1–3 A DiplomaticContact

```
package contacts.diplomatic;

import contacts.*;
public interface DiplomaticContact extends Contact {
  public float getSpyProbability();
  public void setSpyProbability(float newProb);
  public Contact[] getKnownAssociates();
  //etc.
}
```

The contact management design shown in Listing 1–3 does a good job of modeling the problem domain while preserving the ability to repair and/or enhance specific implementations. This is no ordinary achievement, and the success of object-oriented languages such as Java derives from their support in accomplishing these objectives. But don't start celebrating yet. The current design does not begin to address the issues of component deployment.

A *component* is an independent unit of production and deployment that is combined with other components to assemble an application. There is some conceptual overlap between objects and components. Objects are instances of classes; in fact, object-oriented design might just as well be called class-oriented design. A component is often just a compiled class, or a group of compiled classes.[1] One might ask, if the most important work product of both paradigms is the class, what is the significant difference between object and component approaches? The object approach emphasizes design and development, while the component approach emphasizes deployment.

Object-oriented design emphasizes the development-time relationships between entities in a system. Component-oriented design extends these relationships to other phases of the application lifecycle, particularly production and deployment. An object-oriented approach leads to questions such as the following:

1. Does the design capture the relevant part of the problem domain?

2. Are the interfaces and classes easy to extend and modify?

---

1. A component might also be some other independent unit of deployment: a text file, a graphic image, a data file, or a script.

A component-oriented approach leads to questions like these:

1. How will a client find implementation classes at runtime?

2. What happens if there is more than one version of the implementation classes available at runtime?

3. How will components locate and load necessary configuration information?

4. What happens if a process or container needs to be shut down temporarily? Can work in progress be saved and restored transparently? Can component instances migrate from one container to another?

5. How does the development and maintenance of one member of a family of products impact the other members?

6. Are components bloated by code unrelated to a particular customer's task?

7. An old component is *almost* a perfect fit for a new system. Can the old component be extended in unanticipated new ways without touching the source code?

8. What happens when part of the system must be implemented on a different software platform and seamlessly interoperate with the rest?

These sound like important questions, so why do components get so much less attention than objects do?

Any particular set of tools encourages some kinds of solutions while it discourages others. The friendly environment of a developer's computer discourages the analysis of deployment issues. At any given time, a development machine has a snapshot of a complex, evolving system. The pieces of the snapshot can be proven to fit together by compilers and other development tools. Configuration information is all in the right place, and even if it is not, there is an expert nearby who can tweak things until they work. Everyone has heard the classic refrain "It works fine on my machine!"

The real world is just the opposite of the developer's machine. Different components and different component versions get jumbled together, and applications are expected to load correctly and sort things out on their own. Configuration information is missing or inaccurate, and systems are expected to function anyway. Applications need to grow and evolve without ever shutting down, and systems must be built from disparate components that were never intended to work together. Programs struggle under the weight of thousands of lines of code that are not related to the task at hand but cannot easily be removed.

Java is not just an OO language; it is also a platform that provides the tools to manage complex deployment. Consider again the component architecture questions raised earlier:

1. *How will a client find implementation classes at runtime?* The class loader architecture (Chapter 2) provides a flexible means for locating classes from different sources. Custom class loaders (Chapter 5) extend this architecture to support arbitrary new strategies for dynamically locating components at runtime.

2. *What happens if there is more than one version of the implementation classes available at runtime?* The class loader delegation model (§2.4.2) defines a search order. Package reflection (§3.6) can discover the version of a loaded class. You can use custom attributes (§5.5) to define a more sophisticated version-reconciliation mechanism.

3. *How will components locate and load necessary configuration information?* Components should rarely load configuration information directly from the file system. Instead, you should use the current class loader (§2.3) or the context class loader (§2.9) to load resources relative to the classes that need them.

4. *What happens if a process or container needs to be shut down temporarily? Can work in progress be saved and restored transparently? Can component instances migrate from one container to another?* Here, you should use Java serialization (Chapter 4) to write a Java instance to a stream and then instantiate an equivalent instance somewhere else. Or, use reflection (Chapter 3) to read and write the state of an object as XML.

5. *How does the development and maintenance of one member of a family of products impact the other members?* Object-oriented design provides inheritance and delegation as mechanisms to share code across a family of products. With a component-oriented approach, you can automate delegation using reflection (§3.2), dynamic proxies (§3.4), or generated code (Chapter 7).

6. *Are components bloated by code unrelated to a particular customer's task?* Straight OO designs may preserve too much flexibility, carrying unneeded code at deployment time or runtime. You can use domain analysis and code

generation (Chapter 7) to generate the exact solution you need, exactly when you need it.

7. *An old component is almost a perfect fit for a new system. Can the old component be extended in unanticipated new ways without touching the source code?* You can use dynamic proxies (§3.4) to transparently layer new functionality over existing interfaces. If you need better performance (§3.5), use reflection to generate static proxies.

8. *What happens when part of the system must be implemented on a different software platform and seamlessly interoperate with the rest?* The Java Native Interface (Chapter 6) is inadequate. You should build a marshalling layer (Appendix A) to encapsulate the details of cross-platform communication.

For those seeking immediate gratification, Listing 1–4 shows a more component-oriented approach to the contact management domain. While this is much more complete than the earlier listings, it leaves plenty of room for improvement. As you read the remaining chapters, consider how you might employ class loaders, reflection, serialization, code generation, and native code to enhance this example.

Listing 1–4   A Component Approach to Contacts

```
package contacts;
import java.io.*;
import java.net.*;
import java.util.*;

/**
 * Factory class for the <code>Contacts</code> package.
 * Use this instead of instantiating classes directly.
 */
public class ContactFactory {
  /**
   * Process administrators should specify the concrete
   * implementation class to use by setting the
   * <code>contacts.impl.SimpleContactFinder</code> property,
   * and specify the class loader to use by setting
   * the context class loader.
   */
  public ContactFinder getDefaultFinder() {
    try {
```

```java
      String className =
             System.getProperty("contacts.FinderClass",
                    "contacts.impl.SimpleContactFinder");
      Class clazz = Class.forName(className, true,
          Thread.currentThread().getContextClassLoader());
      return (ContactFinder) clazz.newInstance();
    }
    catch (Exception e) {
      e.printStackTrace();
      throw new Error("Default Finder not available");
    }
  }
}


//contacts.impl.SimpleContactFinder
package contacts.impl;
import contacts.*;
import java.util.*;
import java.io.*;

public class SimpleContactFinder implements ContactFinder {
  /**
   * Default values for JNDI lookups, database table
   * names, etc.
   */
  private static Properties configProps;

  /**
   * Do not assume that a file system is available.
   * Always load co-located application resources by
   * using the class's own class loader
   */
  static {
    try {
      InputStream is = SimpleContactFinder.class.
                    getClassLoader().
       getResourceAsStream("contacts/impl/config.properties");
      configProps = new Properties();
      configProps.load(is);
    }
    catch (Exception e) {
      e.printStackTrace();
      throw new Error(
            "Could not load contacts.impl.config.properties");
```

```
    }
  }
  //implementation continues…
}

//contacts.impl.SimpleContact.java
package contacts.impl;
import contacts.*;
import java.io.*;

/**
 * Data classes need to be serializable so that instances
 * can be moved from one process to another.
 * If necessary, you can wrap instances in a MarshalledObject
 * to preserve codebase information
 */
public class SimpleContact implements Contact, Serializable {
  private String lastName;
  private String firstName;
  private String ssn;

  public SimpleContact(String lastName, String firstName,
        String ssn) throws ContactsException
  {
    this.lastName = lastName;
    this.firstName = firstName;
    this.ssn = ssn;
    validateNewInstance();
  }

  /**
   * Deserialization must be validated, just like any
   * other "constructor".
   */
  private void readObject(ObjectInputStream ois)
    throws IOException, ClassNotFoundException,
        ContactsException
  {
    ois.defaultReadObject();
    validateNewInstance();
  }

  /**
   * All constructors, plus deserialization (i.e. the
```

```
   * readObject method) share validation code. Throws
   * application-specific ContactException if instance
   * is invalid
   */
  private void validateNewInstance() throws ContactsException
  {
    //check valid ssn
    //check non-null name, etc.
  }
  //implementation continues…
}


;contacts.jar manifest file
;each package is JARred and sealed separately
;all package reflection info is specified
Sealed=true
Implementation-Title=Contacts
Implementation-Version=1.0.0
Implementation-Vendor=Stuart Halloway
Specification-Title=Contacts
Specification-Version=1.0.0
Specification-Vendor=Stuart Halloway
```

Chapter 2

The Class Loader Architecture

This chapter introduces Java's class loader architecture, which provides a dynamic, flexible means for locating resources (both code and data) at runtime. Class loaders allow an application to be built from many disparate resources at runtime, and they provide a namespace mechanism that allows multiple versions of the same resource to coexist in a single virtual machine. Class loaders are also integral to the security architecture because they tell the virtual machine (VM) how and from where classes were loaded.

This chapter will cover finding and loading resources, the class loader delegation model for sharing resources, the standard class loaders provided by the core API, debugging class loading, and some straightforward examples of using class loaders. For information about the relationship between class loaders and the security model and for how to write your own class loaders, see Chapter 5.

2.1 Assembling an Application

Assembling a statically linked, standalone application is easy. In the simplest scenario, all of the binaries that constitute a standalone application are linked into a single file during development. Deploying the application is an all-or-nothing proposition. If you have possession of that single file, then the application is correctly deployed. If you do not have the file, then you do not have the application.

Actual practice is more complex. There are many reasons that you need to split applications into separate components:

- Different applications may share the same components. It is wasteful to deploy a separate copy of a component for each application that uses it.

3. There are two different versions of the `Widget` class, version 1.0 and 1.1. A deployer should be able to automatically access the most recent version or be able to explicitly fall back to older versions when necessary.

4. Finally, the application wants to use some JDBC configuration settings from URL B, *not* the settings that are available locally. A deployer should be able to bypass or ignore local settings.

To make the type resolution process robust, the Java platform provides both reasonable default rules for how resources are located, and a mechanism deployers can use to customize this behavior. Additionally, Java can audit the linking process at runtime and optionally abort if the wrong resource is encountered. These services are the province of class loaders.

The Java class loader architecture provides the services that you need to assemble applications at runtime. Using class loaders, you can find and verify classes, resources, and configuration settings. Class loading services go well beyond support for simple scenarios to handle the challenges of real-world application deployment. For example, you can safely load resources, even code, from untrusted network locations. You can reload changed versions of a component without shutting down your application, or you can even permit multiple versions of a component to coexist at one time.

Unfortunately, most of the details of class loading are hidden from view during application development, and some key services are disabled by default. As a result, many application designs do not make effective use of class loaders. Instead, they rely on abstractions such as the classpath to hide the details of deployment. This approach to deployment leads to applications that cannot evolve and adapt at runtime. Worse yet, they do not even fail gracefully; instead, they terminate with exceptions that are far removed from the actual deployment problems. The remainder of this chapter will explain the class loader architecture and show you how to use and extend it effectively.

2.2 Goals of the Class Loader Architecture

"Design before you code" is a good rule, even when you are merely studying a system already in place. So, before you learn how class loaders work, you need to understand the goals of the architecture. This section serves to justify, in advance, some of the complexity you will see in the class loader code.

The class loader architecture aims to be transparent, extensible, capable, and configurable. Also, it needs to deal sensibly with name conflicts and version incompatibilities without compromising the ability to share resources loaded from different places or in different ways. Finally, it has to define and enforce some notion of security so that there are specific control mechanisms for what dynamically loaded classes can and cannot do.

2.2.1 Transparency

Transparency is critical. Most Java code is, and should continue to be, written with no explicit awareness that class loaders even exist. Consider the `Simplicity` application shown in Listing 2–1. This code makes no mention of class loaders, yet somehow the `Simplicity` class is loaded into the virtual machine, and later the `RocketShip` class is also loaded. This implies that when the virtual machine begins execution, it knows how to find the application main class, and then somehow it infers where to look for additional classes as necessary. This loading happens implicitly, without any specific coding effort. The principle of least surprise also dictates that once the `RocketShip` class is loaded, it continues to be available and doesn't magically change its characteristics in any way. So, the `println` statement in `main` should output `true`.

Listing 2–1 The Simplicity Class

```
public class Simplicity {
  public static void main(String [] args) {
    RocketShip r1 = new RocketShip("Gemini");
    RocketShip r2 = new RocketShip("Apollo");
    System.out.println(r1.getClass() == r2.getClass());
  }
}
```

2.2.2 Extensibility

Class loading must be extensible. No matter what capabilities are built into the system, some particular user will need something different. Exotic class loader designs might inject debugging information, smuggle optimization hints to just-in-time (JIT) compilers, pull binary code from source control systems, or enforce Eiffel-like invariants.[1] The class loader architecture should allow these, and other, extensions to be made without requiring modification to the classes to be loaded.

2.2.3 Capability

Class loading must be capable. Specifically, the core API should include class loaders that meet common needs, such as on-the-fly reloading of code that has changed on the file system, loading code from other nodes on the network, and loading code from compressed archives. Additionally, these facilities must not compromise simplicity by surprising the developer; for example, you should not suddenly discover that your application was unknowingly using code downloaded from http://pureevil.org instead of from your local hard drive.

2.2.4 Configurability

Class loading must be easily configurable. It is not sufficient to provide a class loading API that developers must explicitly code against. All of the standard scenarios above should be available as configuration options of the virtual machine. They should be accessible for modification by system administrators, not just Java developers. Also, it would be nice if there were an obvious system for adding configuration options for custom class loaders created by third parties, such as Java 2 Enterprise Edition (J2EE) container vendors.

2.2.5 Handling Name and Version Conflicts

Class loading must deal sensibly with name conflicts and with version incompatibilities. Java programmers are taught to avoid name conflicts through careful use of package names. The naming rule is that any classes that you ship must have package names that begin with your dotted domain name in reverse, followed by whatever internal package scheme your organization uses. For example, my company website is http://www.develop.com, so my packages begin with `com.develop`.

---

1. The Eiffel programming language provides constructs to specify *invariants*—conditions that must be true—at the beginning or end of a method's exeuction. Programs that encode invariants tend to be more readable and have fewer bugs. See [Mey00] for details.

The naming rule is a good start, but it is insufficient in a dynamic system because it relies on the goodwill and competence of all parties involved. In practice, the naming rule will fail in two ways:

1. Organizations have internal name collisions. Without a very strict top-down policy, this is more difficult to avoid than it might at first seem. Consider a company whose U.S. and European branches each define an interface named `com.myco.FootballPlayer`, for example. Worse still, some organizations might place code in the default package.

2. Organizations need to deploy multiple versions of the same class simultaneously. Consider a mission critical server that needs 24/7 availability. When a new version of a class becomes available, that class should be used to service new clients. Unfortunately, bugs happen and some clients may discover that they have an unintended dependency on an older version. A server should be able to continue to serve the old version of the class to those clients until the problem can be solved.

The runtime must be able to load multiple classes with the exact same name and keep track of them so that developers using the classes are never unpleasantly surprised. Moreover, it is inefficient to create a new virtual machine every time this situation occurs. Classes that change dynamically should be able to share the code from classes that change less frequently.

2.2.6 Security

Finally, the entire architecture must make some security guarantees. This is not often a major problem for monolithic applications where the entire application is viewed as a single whole. Dynamic class loading opens the possibility of multiple classes that do not trust each other, coexisting uneasily in the same virtual machine. The Java class loader architecture is supplemented by a security architecture that provides flexible, administrative security for code loaded from different sources.

2.3 Explicit and Implicit Class Loading

The simplest class loading API is provided by the `ClassLoader` class shown in Listing 2–2.

Listing 2–2   Explict Loading with ClassLoader

```
package java.lang;
public class ClassLoader {
 public Class loadClass(String n)
        throws ClassNotFoundException;
 //remainder omitted for clarity
 }
```

This is fairly straightforward. You pass in the full name of the class, delimiting packages with dots, and you get back a distinguished `Class` object that represents the loaded class. If the class loader fails, it throws the checked `Class-NotFoundException`.

2.3.1   Explicit Loading with URLClassLoader

The easiest way to see `loadClass` in action is to use a concrete `Class-Loader` implementation provided by the core API. By far, the most common and useful standard class loader is `java.net.URLClassLoader`. The class constructor takes an array of URLs, and it can find classes that reside at any of those URLs. The simplest type of URL is a file URL, which simply points to a location on the file system. Consider Listing 2–3.

Listing 2–3   Explicitly Loading from a URL

```
import java.net.*;
public class LoaderDemo {
  public static void main(String [] args) throws Exception {
    URL url = new URL("file:subdir/");
    URL[] urls = new URL[]{url};
    URLClassLoader loader = new URLClassLoader(urls);
    Class cls = loader.loadClass("LoadMe");
    Object o = cls.newInstance();
  }
}
public class LoadMe {
  static {
    System.out.println(LoadMe.class + " loaded.");
  }
}
```

Compile the `LoaderDemo` into one directory, and then compile `LoadMe` into a subdirectory named `subdir`. Navigate to the directory that contains Loader-Demo.class, and run `LoaderDemo` with the command line

```
java -classpath . LoaderDemo
```

The dot is shorthand for the current directory, so the Java launcher should be able to load `LoaderDemo`. Also, you will see that `LoaderDemo` successfully loads `LoadMe`, even though the LoadMe.class file is not on the classpath. Try deleting the LoadMe.class file, and run `LoaderDemo` again. This time you will see a `ClassNotFoundException`. In a real application, you could catch this exception and possibly continue execution, even with some classes missing.

The ability to load classes dynamically via a `URLClassLoader` is so powerful that more than 95 percent of all Java application classes are probably loaded by `URLClassLoader` and its subclasses. However, you will rarely call `load-Class` explicitly as shown above. *Explicit* class loading, in any form, runs counter to one of the primary goals of the class loader architecture: transparency. Explicit class loading requires work by the programmer for each class to be loaded, and it is too tedious for general use.

2.3.2 Implicit Class Loading

Java provides an intuitive mechanism for *implicit* class loading. Every Java class maintains a reference to the class loader that loaded it, accessible via the `get-ClassLoader()` method. Whenever a class *refers* to another class, the referent is loaded implicitly, using the same class loader that loaded the referring class. Listing 2–4 shows some examples of references.

Listing 2–4   Referenced Classes Are Loaded Implicitly

```
//reference to LoadMeBase
public class LoadMe extends LoadMeBase {
  //reference to LoadMeToo
  static LoadMeToo lmt = new LoadMeToo();
  //reference to LoadMeAlso
  static LoadMeAlso lma;
  static ClassLoader ldr = getSomeLoader();
  //Neither of these refer to LoadMeThree!
```

```
static Class cls = ldr.loadClass("LoadMeThree");
static Object o = cls.newInstance();
}
```

This new version of the `LoadMe` class refers to several other classes, all of which will be loaded implicitly when needed. First, `LoadMe` extends another class `LoadMeBase`. In order to verify that `LoadMe` is a legal extension of `Load-MeBase`, the `LoadMeBase` class must be loaded. Whenever a virtual machine loads `LoadMe`, it will attempt to load `LoadMeBase` using the same class loader.

`LoadMe` also has static references to objects of type `LoadMeToo` and `LoadMeAlso`. The virtual machine will load these classes only when they are actually needed to initialize a reference. Since the `LoadMeAlso` reference is initialized only to `null`, the virtual machine will not bother loading this class at all.[2]

2.3.3 Reference Type versus Referenced Class

Notice that `LoadMeThree` is *not* referenced by `LoadMe`, even though the class will be loaded when the code runs. The difference is that the references `cls` and `obj`, which are used to manipulate `LoadMeThree`, are statically typed as `java.lang.Class` and `java.lang.Object`, respectively. It is the compile-time type of a reference that triggers implicit class loading; so while `Class` and `Object` are *implicitly* loaded, the `LoadMeThree` class object is *explicitly* loaded by `someOtherLoader`. The subtle distinction between reference type and referent class allows implicit and explicit class loading to coexist.

Most Java code uses implicit references, all of which will be transparently loaded by a single `ClassLoader`. On rare occasions, a developer breaks this chain by using explicit class loading and assigning the result to some base-class reference type. Then, life continues as before. If `LoadMeThree` itself makes references, they will be loaded implicitly by the class loader that loaded `Load-MeThree`, that is, `someOtherLoader`.[3]

---

2. As an optimization, a virtual machine can preload classes that are not needed yet. However, it cannot make the effects of loading these classes visible to the program. So, if preloading a class caused an exception, that exception would not be thrown until the point in the code where the class was actually first used.
3. This is not completely true but will have to do for now. The delegation mechanism makes things a little more complex, as you will see momentarily.

2.3.4 ClassLoader.loadClass versus Class.forName

The `loadClass` method shown in Listing 2–2 is actually one of a family of methods in the `Class` and `ClassLoader` classes. The complete list is shown in Listing 2–5. All the methods look similar, so which should you use?

Listing 2–5 Explict Class Loading APIs

```
//all methods listed throw ClassNotFoundException
package java.lang;

public class Class {
  public Class forName(String name);
  public Class forName(String name, boolean resolve,
                       ClassLoader cl);
  //remainder omitted for clarity
}

public class ClassLoader {
  public Class loadClass(String name);
  public Class loadClass(String name, boolean resolve);
  //remainder omitted for clarity
}
```

The various explicit loading APIs differ in three ways:

1. The APIs that take a `resolve` parameter allow the user to pass `in false` to postpone linking the class. Since the virtual machine will have to link the class before it is used anyway, this option is rarely needed. For more on linking see [Ven99].

2. The single-argument version of `forName` is a shortcut for using the caller's class loader.

3. Some implementations of the `loadClass` method will not load arrays that are not already loaded into the virtual machine. The API docs do not make clear whether this is a bug, but it is "fixed" in SDK version 1.3.

Because of `loadClass`'s odd history of mishandling arrays, `Class.forName` is probably the better choice.

2.3.5 Loading Nonclass Resources

In addition to loading classes, class loaders can also load arbitrary resources. The relevant methods are demonstrated in Listing 2–6.

Listing 2–6   Loading Resources

```
import java.io.*;
import java.net.*;
import java.util.*;
public class LoadResources {
  public static final String res = "config.props";
  public static void main(String [] args)
    throws IOException
  {
    ClassLoader cl = LoadResources.class.getClassLoader();
    System.out.println("All resources at " + res);
    Enumeration enum = cl.getResources(res);
    while (enum.hasMoreElements()) {
      System.out.println(enum.nextElement());
    }
    URL url = cl.getResource(res);
    System.out.println("First resource at " + res);
    System.out.println(url);
    InputStream is = cl.getResourceAsStream(res);
    Properties props = new Properties();
    props.load(is);
    System.out.println("Properties from " + res);
    props.list(System.out);
  }
}
```

The call to getResources returns an enumeration of URLs for all the resources found at the specified path. More than one match is possible since a class loader can search multiple locations. The call to getResource returns only the first matching URL. The convenience method getResourceAsStream uses getResource to locate a URL, then connects to the URL and opens an InputStream on the data.

The resource loading functions are typically used to load data needed by an application class, such as configuration information or images for a graphical application. By using a class loader instead of talking directly to a file system, you simplify deployment of applications. If you place application resources in the same location as your application classes, you do not have to worry about finding resources.

While standard class loaders such as `URLClassLoader` implement the resource loading methods correctly, custom class loaders (discussed in Chapter 5) may ignore these methods or throw an exception. If you rely on class loaders to load resources, make sure that the class loaders in your application are resource-aware.

2.4 The Class Loader Rules

Implicit class loading provides simplicity, and explicit class loading provides flexibility. However, these mechanisms must have some additional properties to deal with the tricky issue of class visibility. What communication should be possible between classes loaded by two different class loaders? The simple answers to this question have undesirable properties: If there is no communication across class loader boundaries, then there is no real benefit to dynamic class loading, and separate class loaders might just as well be separate virtual machines. On the other hand, complete visibility between class loaders leads to chaos, as there is no way to hide conflicting names or versions from each other. So, the class loader architecture adopts a middle path characterized by the following three rules:

1. The consistency rule: Class loaders never load the same class more than once.

2. The delegation rule: Class loaders always consult a parent class loader before loading a class.

3. The visibility rule: Classes can only "see" other classes loaded by their class loader's *delegation*, the recursive set of a class's loader and all its parent loaders.

In combination, these three rules provide a workable solution to all of the design problems listed above.

2.4.1 The Consistency Rule

The consistency rule is the easiest to understand. Once a class is loaded, any future attempts to load the same class from the same class loader must return the already-loaded class. This rule is necessary to prevent nasty surprises for developers and for the virtual machine. It is also easy to implement; class loaders simply keep a `HashMap` or other data structure of already-loaded classes and consult that structure before attempting to load the class again.

The consequences of breaking the consistency rule are dire:

1. Implicit class loading no longer makes any sense. If more than one version of a class is loaded, you have no way to know which one is used when an implicit reference is made.

2. The integrity of developer code is endangered. For example, imagine that your code assumes that class `Foo` has a field named `bar`. What happens when that field suddenly disappears because a new version of `Foo` has been loaded?

3. The integrity of the virtual machine is endangered. Virtual machine implementations are built based on the assumption that class loaders never reload the same class, and their behavior is undefined if this actually occurs. This is even worse than compromising developer code because a damaged virtual machine might crash, corrupt data, or open a security hole.

Given that following the consistency rule is easy, and the consequences of breaking it are so dire, you may wonder why I belabor the point. The problem is that breaking the consistency rule appears to be a simple way of replacing classes at runtime. On some virtual machines, this can even appear to work for a while. Do not be fooled. The correct way to replace classes on-the-fly (§2.5) has nothing to do with reloading classes into the same `ClassLoader` instance. The delegation and visibility rules provide the necessary framework for replacing classes on-the-fly. When implemented correctly, dynamic replacement is portable to all legal VMs, and it has none of the liabilities associated with trying to shoehorn new classes into old class loaders.

2.4.2 The Delegation Rule
The delegation rule states that class loaders always consult a parent class loader before loading a class. `ClassLoader`'s constructor takes a single argument of type `ClassLoader`, which is the parent of the new class loader. The

parent is available to application code via the `getParent()` method.[4] The set of a class loader and all of its ancestors is called a class loader *delegation*. Because each class loader checks with its parent, the entire delegation will be checked recursively before a specific class loader is allowed to load a class.

The overall effect of the delegation rule is to allow limited sharing of classes between class loaders. Consider Figure 2–2, which shows a class loading scenario that might occur in a web browser. The browser will provide applets from different domains with unique `URLClassLoader`s to load their own specific classes. However, the applet class loaders must consult their delegations before loading any class. So, when an applet refers to system classes such as `java.lang.Object` or `java.net.URL`, it will get the versions provided by the system class loader. All applets are forced to share the same version of these core classes. As you will see later, this point is critical to security since the core classes include security classes such as `java.lang.SecurityManager`, not to mention classes that can access your hard drive such as `java.io.FileOutputStream`.

2.4.3 The Visibility Rule

The visibility rule states that classes can only see other classes loaded by their class loader's delegation. Consider Figure 2–2 again. Both good.org and pure-evil.org have a class with the same name, `org.good.Main`. Assuming that you browse to good.org first, the following sequence of events ensues:

1. The browser creates a class loader CL_{good} for good.org.
2. CL_{good} is asked to load `Main`.
3. CL_{good} first delegates to the system class loader.
4. The system class loader fails to find `Main`.
5. CL_{good} loads `Main` from good.org. Any classes that `Main` refers to will be implicitly loaded by CL_{good}'s delegation.
6. The browser creates a class loader CL_{evil} for pureevil.org.

---

4. `ClassLoader` also has a convenience constructor that takes no arguments. If you use this version, then the new class loader will take the result of `ClassLoader.getSystemClass-Loader()` as its parent. The system class loader finds classes from various locations including the classpath and is discussed in detail shortly.

7. CL$_{evil}$ executes steps 2 through 4 again.

8. CL$_{evil}$ loads `Main` from pureevil.org. As far as the VM is concerned, this class is *entirely different* from the class of the same name loaded in step 5.

The fact that pureevil.org introduces its own private version of `org.good.Main` has no effect on the execution of the "real" `org.good.Main` loaded from good.org. Each applet gets its own copy of any application-specific classes. This helps to guarantee that applets do not accidentally or maliciously manipulate code loaded by other applets. At the same time, delegation guarantees that all applets share the core API classes such as `java.lang.String` and `java.io.FileOutputStream`. This helps to protect the integrity of the core API and is far more efficient than loading multiple copies of exactly the same code.

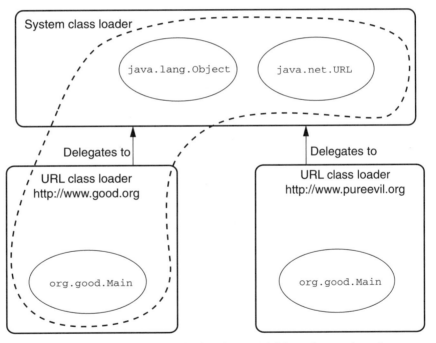

The dotted line surrounds the classes visible to the version of org.good.Main loaded from http://www.good.org.

Figure 2–2   Class loader delegations

COMPONENT DEVELOPMENT FOR THE JAVA™ PLATFORM

2.4.4 Delegations as Namespaces

The class loading rules have several surprising implications. The first is that a class loader delegation forms a namespace. The Java language already has namespaces in the form of packages; for example, `com.develop.String` is a totally different class than `java.lang.String`. Once you factor in class loading, the idea of namespace includes not only a class's package name, but also which class loader loaded the class. This fact is easily verified by executing Listing 2–7.

Listing 2–7 The Same Binary Class Loaded by Two Different Loaders

```
import java.net.*;
public class LoaderDemo2 {
  public static void main(String [] args) throws Exception {
    URL url = new URL("file:subdir/");
    URL[] urls = new URL[]{url};
    URLClassLoader loader = new URLClassLoader(urls);
    URLClassLoader loader2 = new URLClassLoader(urls);
    Class cls = loader.loadClass("LoadMe");
    Class cls2 = loader2.loadClass("LoadMe");
    Object o = cls.newInstance();
    //cls == cls2 is false
    System.out.println("(cls == cls2) is " + (cls == cls2));
  }
}
```

As far as the VM is concerned, `cls` and `cls2` are just as different as classes with different names. In this example, the classes happen to be loaded from the same location, so the bytecodes are exactly the same.[5] However, the classes might just as well have been loaded from different locations, or at different times. The classes might contain different fields, different method signatures, or different method implementations. Since the VM considers the classes to be totally different anyway, it does not have to know, or care.

The delegation model introduces another wrinkle into the namespace issue. Try running the `LoaderDemo` example, but this time, install the `LoadMe` class

---

5. The one exception to this is if the LoadMe.class file is replaced while this program is running. In this case, it is possible that two different files would be loaded. This is discussed in more detail later in this chapter in the Hot Deployment example.

into the same directory instead of into `subdir`. Now, you will see a totally different result—`LoaderDemo` will report that `cls` and `cls2` are the same, even though different loaders were asked to load each. What has happened? Both `loader` and `loader2` implicitly delegate to the system class loader. When you moved `LoadMe` into the same directory as `LoaderDemo`, you made `LoadMe` visible to the system class loader. Neither `loader` nor `loader2` actually loads the `LoadMe` class. So, the first run reported that

$$LoadMe_{loader} \text{ != } LoadMe_{loader2}$$

and the second run reported that

$$LoadMe_{system} \text{ == } LoadMe_{system}$$

Though this delegation behavior is efficient and allows controlled sharing of code, it is also the cause of most class loading errors. The bugs all follow this general pattern: A developer designs a class to be loaded dynamically. Then, the class is unintentionally copied onto the classpath. Because all class loaders delegate to the system class loader,[6] the classpath version of the class is always the one found. The symptom of this bug is that dynamic class loading does not occur. If the purpose of dynamic class loading was to centralize deployment to a website, new versions of the class never seem to work on client machines. This bug is difficult to detect because no exception is thrown. The virtual machine succeeds in finding a class, but it loads the "wrong" version of the class that is visible to a parent class loader.

2.4.5 Static Fields Are Not Singletons

The singleton design pattern models an entity that appears only a single time in a system. A simple approach to implementing the singleton pattern in Java is to create a class with a private constructor to prevent accidental creation of multiple instances. Then, the class can provide a static method that returns the single instance of the class, as shown in Listing 2–8.

---

6. This is an example of being economical with the truth. It is possible to use the single-argument ClassLoader constructor to deliberately bypass the classpath, but this usage is very rare in practice.

Listing 2–8 A Naive Singleton Implementation

```
public class NaiveSingleton {
  private static NaiveSingleton onlyOne;
  private NaiveSingleton() {}
  static {
    onlyOne = new NaiveSingleton();
  }
  public NaiveSingleton getInstance() { return onlyOne; }
}
```

Dynamic class loading thwarts this approach because over time, multiple versions of a class might be loaded, each with its own copy of the static field. As a result, designing a singleton in Java requires some additional thought about how to maintain the singleton identity in a dynamic environment. Some solutions include keeping the singleton in a class that is not loaded dynamically, or storing the singleton state outside of a particular Java instance using JDBC or EJB.

2.4.6 Implicit Loading Hides Most Details

"Normal" code that relies on implicit class loading will never see any of these issues. Implicit class loading is kept simple by the consistency and visibility rules. The consistency rule says that there will be only one version of a class loaded by a particular class loader, and the visibility rule says that the class loader delegation defines the set of all visible classes. So, there may be multiple different versions of classes floating around your VM, but unless you explicitly use class loaders, you will only ever see one of them.

Even when you do make explicit use of class loaders, you can use abstraction to hide this complexity from the bulk of your code. The next section will show you how to divide your application into two distinct parts, a simple client part that doesn't worry about class loader issues, and a server that does the grunt work to provide a useful service based on class loaders.

2.5 Hot Deployment

Class loaders can be used to load multiple versions of a class from different locations in space, but they can also be used to load different versions of a class from the same location at different times. This ability, often called *hot deployment*, is useful for redeploying incremental changes to a class without having to shut down the virtual machine. In the example that follows, client code[7] will use multiple versions of a class, without writing any explicit class loading code. The server code will instantiate new class loaders as necessary to load new versions of the class.

The example will use that classic OO staple, the two-dimensional Point, as seen in Listing 2–9.

Listing 2–9   The Point Interface

```
public interface Point {
  public int getX();
  public int getY();
  public void move(int dx, int dy);
}
```

The initial PointImpl implementation is defective, as shown in Listing 2–10. It will later be replaced without shutting down the VM.

Listing 2–10   A Defective PointImpl

```
public class PointImpl implements Point {
  private int x;
  private int y;
  public int getX() { return x; }
  public int getY() { return y; }
  public void move(int dx, int dy) {
    x += dx;
    //oops! forgot to move y
  }
  public String toString() {
    return "Point at " + x + ", " + y;
  }
}
```

The client code is a PointClient class that creates a Point and moves it around. However, PointClient should not reference the PointImpl implementation class through a variable of type PointImpl. If it does, the rules of implicit class loading will take over, and the PointImpl class will be loaded by

---

7. Throughout the book, I will use the terms "client" and "server" in their most generic sense. Client code is code that utilizes some service provided by server code.

the same class loader that loads `PointClient`. This defeats the purpose of the example. A single version of `PointClient` should be able to load and use new versions of `PointImpl`. This is impossible if `PointClient` is loaded from the same loader because the consistency rule forbids unloading and reloading `PointImpl` from a single loader. Therefore, the creation of `PointImpl` is hidden behind a `PointServer` object that handles the details of explicitly loading new versions of `PointImpl`, as shown in Listing 2–11.

Listing 2–11 The PointServer Class

```java
import java.net.*;
public class PointServer {
  static ClassLoader cl;
  static Class ptClass;
  public static synchronized Point
        createPoint(Point template) throws Exception
  {
    if (ptClass == null) reloadImpl();
    Point newPt = (Point) ptClass.newInstance();
    if (template != null) {
      newPt.move(template.getX(), template.getY());
    }
    return newPt;
  }
  public static synchronized void reloadImpl()
                      throws Exception
  {
    URL[] serverURLs = new URL[]{new URL("file:subdir/")};
    cl = new URLClassLoader(serverURLs);
    ptClass = cl.loadClass("PointImpl");
  }
}
```

The `PointServer` object acts as a factory, providing a `createPoint` method that returns a `Point`. The `template` parameter can be used to initialize the new `Point` to match an existing `Point`. If `templatePoint` is `null` the new `Point` will start at the origin. `PointServer` also provides the helper method `reloadImpl` to load a new version of `PointImpl`.

The `PointClient` class provides a simple command-line interface to move a `Point` or reload the `PointImpl` implementation, as shown in Listing 2–12.

Listing 2–12 PointClient

```java
import java.io.*;
public class PointClient {
  static Point pt;
  public static void main(String [] args) throws Exception
  {
    BufferedReader br = new BufferedReader(
          new InputStreamReader(System.in));
    pt = PointServer.createPoint(null);
    System.out.println(pt);
    while (true) {
      System.out.println("MOVE1, RELOAD, or EXIT");
      String cmdRead = br.readLine();
      String cmd = cmdRead.toUpperCase();
      if (cmd.equals("EXIT")) {
        return;
      } else if (cmd.equals("RELOAD")) {
        PointServer.reloadImpl();
        pt = PointServer.createPoint(pt);
      System.out.println(pt);
      } else if (cmd.equals("MOVE1")) {
        pt.move(1,1);
        System.out.println(pt);
      }
    }
  }
}
```

In order to run this example, you will need to compile the `PointImpl` class into a directory named `subdir`, and you will need to compile `Point`, `Point-Client`, and `PointServer` into your top-level directory. Then, when you run the application and enter the appropriate commands, you will see a session similar to Listing 2–13.

Listing 2–13 A Session with PointClient

```
Point at 0, 0
MOVE1, RELOAD, or EXIT
MOVE1
Point at 1, 0
MOVE1, RELOAD, or EXIT
RELOAD
```

```
Point at 1, 0
MOVE1, RELOAD, or EXIT
MOVE1
Point at 2, 0
MOVE1, RELOAD, or EXIT
```

The `move` implementation is broken; although the `PointClient` is trying to increment both `x` and `y`, only `x` is changing. Simply reloading the class doesn't fix the problem. Even though the `PointServer` is loading a new version of `PointImpl`, it contains the same defective code as the original. You need to repair the bug in Java and then recompile the fixed version. Make sure that you leave the `PointClient` process running while you make these changes. Fix and recompile `PointImpl` to correctly increment `y`. Now, try again to reload and move the `Point`.

Listing 2–14   Moving the Corrected PointImpl

```
RELOAD
Point at 2, 0
MOVE1, RELOAD, or EXIT
MOVE1
Point at 3, 1
MOVE1, RELOAD, or EXIT
EXIT
```

Listing 2–14 shows that after you reload the changed `PointImpl`, the move operation now works correctly. You can use this technique to replace code in the field without forcing clients to shut down their applications.

2.5.1   Using Hot Deployment

There are several points to remember when you apply hot deployment in your own applications. The first three have to do with how the classes get loaded. First, clients must not reference the type that will need to be dynamically replaced. If they do, one of two bad things will happen: The client will implicitly load the classes with its class loader, or it will fail to load the classes at all. Either way, there will be no way to get a new version of the server class without shutting down the client.

The second point is implied by the first one. Clients cannot use a reference of the implementation type; they must use a reference of a base class or interface type. As the `PointClient` example shows, the client uses a reference of type `Point`. This base interface is loaded implicitly by the client's class loader. Of course, this does imply that you have to shut down the client if you want to change the *interface* that the client is programming against. This is reasonable since the client would have to write some new code to use a new interface anyway.

The third point is that the implementation class must be able to find the same version of the base interface that the client is using. In other words, the implementation's class loader must delegate to the client's class loader. This is implicit in the `Point` example because the `PointClient` is loaded by the system class loader, which is the default parent for new class loaders.

The remaining issues deal with the relationship between old and new versions of a class. The VM recognizes no relationship between old and new versions of a class, so you must manufacture any necessary relationship in your code. In the example, the `PointServer` class manages the relationship between old and new versions of `PointImpl`. When a new `PointImpl` is instantiated, the `PointServer` uses the old `PointImpl` as a template, thereby maintaining the state that the client had already accumulated. This requires two specific actions on the part of the client. First, the client must make the state of the original object available to the server factory so that it can correctly instantiate the new version. Second, the client must drop any references to the old version of the `PointImpl`, both to preserve resources and to take advantage of the new version of the code. The client executes both of these actions via the single line of code[8]

```
pt = PointServer.createPoint(pt)
```

8. With one more level of indirection, you could hide these details from the client as well. The server gives the client a forwarding proxy to the actual object, which allows the server to control the object itself and swap it out at any time, possibly without consent or even awareness on the part of the client.

2.6 Unloading Classes

Once you switch all of your applications to use dynamic class loading, what happens to old versions of classes that nobody is using anymore? Class loaders and classes require a noticeable amount of memory, and if this memory is not reclaimed, your highly available server application will eventually fail. Of course, in Java you cannot explicitly destroy an object. The absence of an explicit `delete` operator is one of the primary safety features of the language. So, class loaders and classes must be reclaimed just like any other object, by the garbage collector (GC).

The VM specification does not make any special distinction about how class or class loader objects will be collected. This means that virtual machines may garbage collect these objects exactly like they would recover any other Java objects. On the other hand, the spec does not *prevent* a VM from handling these objects separately or even from refusing to unload them from memory.

The SDK implementation of Java treats classes and class loaders slightly differently from other objects. The SDK garbage collector defaults to treating classes and loaders just like any other objects, and it can collect them when there are no existing references. You can disable this behavior with the non-standard launcher flag `-Xnoclassgc`. You will need to check the documentation, or possibly even write test cases, to determine the behavior of other virtual machines.

2.6.1 Making Sure Classes Are Collectable

If you are writing server applications, it is probable that you will deploy them on a VM that can garbage collect classes. The only thing you have to worry about is making sure that your code drops all references to classes that you want the GC to reclaim. This is easier said than done. Unintended references are one of the major memory problems in Java, and they can strike any kind of code.

The consequences of unintended references are particularly severe when class loaders are involved. Consider these facts. Every instance of a class maintains a reference to its `Class` object, accessible through the `getClass()` method. Moreover, every instance of `Class` maintains a reference to its `ClassLoader`, accessible via `getClassLoader()`. In turn, class loaders hold a cache of every `Class` that they have ever loaded. The net result of all of these references is that *a single instance of any class loaded by a class loader will keep the class loader, and every class that it loaded, in memory.*

In a simple example like the `PointClient`, references are easy to track down. The three references that might keep an old class loader in memory are `PointClient.pt`, `PointServer.cl`, and `PointServer.ptClass`. Each of these references is reset whenever a new version is loaded, so there is no danger that an unintended reference will hold the old classes in memory. In a larger application, it is important to keep track of these "problem" references during the design phase to make sure that none of them cause trouble later.

2.7 Bootclasspath, Extensions Path, and Classpath

Java provides several mechanisms for configuring how classes are loaded, which do not require any explicit class loader code. One of these mechanisms, the classpath, is the only interaction with class loaders that some Java applications will ever need. The classpath provides a simple mechanism to specify a set of locations where your code can be found. Despite its simplicity, the classpath is the source of a great many headaches, even for experienced Java developers. By understanding the classpath in terms of the class loader architecture, though, you can avoid these problems or quickly troubleshoot them when they occur.

The classpath is only one part of Java's class loader configuration options. When you run an application with the standard Java launcher `java`, your application begins life with a set of three class loaders already in place: the bootstrap, extensions, and system class loaders, as is shown in Figure 2–3. The bootstrap class loader loads the core system packages from the bootclasspath, the extensions class loader loads extensions to the core API from the extensions path, and the system class loader loads application code from the classpath. The three loaders are often treated as a single loader named the system class loader.[9] This three-tiered design accomplishes two objectives: simplicity for the

---

9. It is confusing that the term "system class loader" can be used to mean either (1) the loaders that consult the classpath, or (2) the loader plus its delegation. In practice, this distinction rarely matters. The API call `ClassLoader.getSystemClassLoader()` returns the classpath class loader, but because of the delegation model this loader can also load bootstrap or extensions classes.

common case, and great flexibility for the rare cases where you need to make sweeping changes to deployment, security, or how the core classes are loaded.

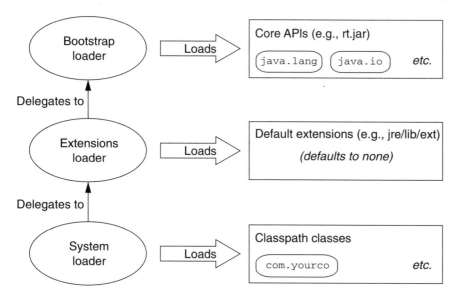

Figure 2–3 The three standard class loaders

2.7.1 The Classpath

The common case mentioned previously involves only the system class loader. This class loader is variously called the application class loader, the classpath class loader, or the system class loader. Although "classpath loader" is the most informative, the API functions that deal with this loader use the term "system," therefore, system will be preferred here. Regardless of how you name this loader, it simply loads classes from directories and Java Archive (JAR) files listed on the classpath.

There are several ways to control the initial setting of the classpath. In the absence of any other information, the classpath is set to ".", the directory from which the java launcher is run. This setting can be overridden by specifying a CLASSPATH environment variable. The environment variable, in turn, can be overridden via a command-line switch. The java launcher recognizes either −cp or −classpath, but note that many other Java SDK command-line tools recognize only the longer —classpath form. Finally, the —classpath command-line switch can be overridden by yet another command-line switch, —jar. If you use the —jar switch, then user classes will only be loaded from a single specified JAR file. These options are summarized in Table 2–1.

Time and experience have proven that using the command line is the cleanest, most reliable way to set the classpath. If you set the CLASSPATH environment variable, then you always run the chance of another application or user resetting it to point somewhere else. Similarly, you cannot rely on the implicit use of the current directory because if any other actor on your system has set the CLASSPATH, the current directory will be ignored. When you set the classpath from the command line, you have complete control. The command line is the one place to look in case of problems, and changes elsewhere on the machine will not cause mysterious failures loading classes. For this reason, choose the command-line method of setting the classpath over any other method whenever you are using the java launcher.

The value of the classpath is a delimited list of directories or JAR files. The delimiter is platform specific, and it is available on each platform as the constant java.io.File.pathSeparatorChar. Examples in the text will use a semicolon, which is the delimiter for Win32 operating systems. If a class is not in the default package, then the class's package name must be combined with the classpath to locate the class. For instance, the command line

```
java -cp MyJar.jar;MyClasses com.develop.Test
```

Table 2–1   Setting the Classpath

Setting	Comments
—jar switch	Lst only a single JAR
—cp switch	List a mix of JARs and directories
CLASSPATH environment variable	Not recommended
Current directory	Not recommended

will only be able to locate the file Test.class if it is located in the

```
MyClasses/com/develop/
```

directory, or if it is stored in MyJar.jar with directory information included, as

```
com/develop/Test.class
```

The conversion of the package name into a directory hierarchy is necessary to distinguish classes with the same base name but different package names.

The launcher's command-line processing is relatively forgiving. The launcher accepts relative paths and forgives your choice of a directory delimiter; for example, the names `MyClasses`, `MyClasses/`, and `MyClasses\` all correctly locate classes in the MyClasses subdirectory of the current directory. However, there are other places in the Java world where the only legal choice is the '/' delimiter, including a trailing '/' at the end of a string specifying a directory. If you develop the habit of using `foo/` to specify a directory name on the command line, you will be using a consistent syntax that will also work in other places such as file URLs.

2.7.2 The Extensions Path

The system class loader delegates to the extensions class loader. The extensions class loader loads *installed optional packages*, which the Java Extension Mechanism [Ext] defines as "packages housed in one or more JAR files that implement an API that extends the Java platform […] in the sense that the virtual machine can load them without their being on the class path, much as if they were classes in the platform's core API." This characterization implies that the extensions class loader should be used to share packages that are common to a large number of applications for which it would be inconvenient to repeatedly specify locations on the classpath. Examples of such packages include XML tools and custom security providers.

In short, installed optional packages are JAR files that are placed in a set of well-known directories and made available to all applications. Placing classes on the extensions path differs from placing classes on the classpath in two major ways:

1. It is easy to specify a large number of JAR files at once.
2. Extensions pass all security checks.

Directories in the extensions path are automatically scanned for JAR files. Directories in the classpath are not scanned, so you must list each JAR file individually. Note, however, that the extensions loader loads *only* from JAR files, never from class files. The reason for this is the assumption that the code for common libraries should be deployed as JAR files. When they are deployed this way the danger of loading mismatched versions of classes is minimized.

By default, installed optional packages are loaded as needed from the

```
${JAVA_HOME}/lib/ext
```

directory. It is possible to override this by setting the `java.ext.dirs` property on the command line. For example,

```
java -Djava.ext.dirs=myext1;myext2 MyMainClass
```

would allow any JAR files under the myext1 or myext2 directories to be loaded as installed optional packages. In practice, you are unlikely to override the location of the extensions directory. Since the purpose of extensions is to be omnipresent, it usually makes little sense to override the extensions path on a per-application basis.

Some developers use the extensions path in place of the classpath because they like the convenience of not listing each JAR individually. I would discourage this practice if you are concerned about security, however, because it operates against the intention that extensions are exempt from security checks. Per-application class settings are better accomplished by setting a command-line classpath.

The second major difference between installed optional packages and classpath classes has to do with security. When Java 2 security is enabled, like it is with the `-Djava.security.manager` launcher flag, installed optional packages default to being *completely* trusted by the virtual machine. This high level of trust is enabled by the following entry in the default `java.policy` file, which resides at ${JAVA_HOME}/lib/security/java.policy:

```
grant codeBase "file:${java.home}/lib/ext/*" {
    permission java.security.AllPermission;
};
```

On the other hand, classes loaded from the classpath run with a minimal set of permissions, which does not include general access to the network, local files, or critical virtual machine subsystems. Both the classpath and extensions security settings can be changed, augmented, or replaced on a per-VM basis with custom policies. Nevertheless, the design assumes that classes in installed optional packages will normally be trusted parts of the system and that application classes from the classpath will not.

2.7.3 The Bootclasspath

The extensions class loader delegates to the bootstrap class loader, sometimes also known as the primordial class loader. The bootstrap class loader checks the bootclasspath and loads the core API packages such as `java.lang`, `java.io`, and `java.util`, usually from a file named rt.jar. The bootstrap class loader is almost certain to be implemented in native code, and unlike all other class loaders, it does not present itself as a Java identity. When you call `get-ClassLoader()` for a bootstrap class, the result will be `null`.

The bootstrap class loader has two significant properties that separate it from all other class loaders; both are related to security:

1. Classes loaded by the bootstrap class loader are not verified, that is, the virtual machine assumes that they are well-formed binary classes.

2. Classes loaded by the bootstrap loader are not subject to security checks. This is subtly different from installed optional packages loaded by the extensions class loader: Bootstrap classes are never even *asked* for their permissions, while installed optional packages are asked but default to having all permissions anyway.

You will rarely want to place your own classes on the bootclasspath. There is no need to do so for security reasons or to make deployment convenient because installed optional packages work well for these purposes. There are only two situations in which it makes sense to deploy on the bootclasspath: if you wish to replace the core classes with custom versions, or if the core API classes need to have direct access to your code.

Replacing core classes is a useful debugging trick. In its simplest form, you might want to recompile the core classes with the `javac -g` flag to generate debugging information, which the default rt.jar lacks. Many Java integrated development environments (IDEs) include an rtd.jar file, which has debugging information included, and they automatically set the bootclasspath to this version of the core API when they start a debugging session by calling

```
java -Xbootclasspath:rtd.jar {vmArgs} YourMainClass
```

You might also want to recompile a subset of the core classes to insert debugging information. In this case, you can use the

```
-Xbootclasspath/a: or -Xbootclasspath/p:
```

flags, which append or prepend your classpath to the normal bootclasspath, respectively. The following section (§2.8) demonstrates one use of this technique.

The other situation that demands changes to the bootclasspath is when the core API classes need direct access to your code. The only case where this might occur is when the core API provides a factory method for installing some service that you define. In this situation, your service class must be visible to the class loader expected by the factory method.

One situation that requires changes to the bootclasspath is loading a custom security policy. The security policy implements the mapping between a class and the security permissions that are granted to that class. The exact details of how the policy works are unimportant here; suffice it to say that you can configure the virtual machine to replace its standard policy with a class of your own choosing.

However, there is a hitch. Look at Listing 2–15, which shows pseudocode for loading a custom policy. Notice the single-argument version of `Class.for-Name`, which relies on implicit class loading. Since the system code resides in rt.jar, it is loaded by the bootstrap class loader. In order to be visible, a custom policy implementation must also be loaded by the bootstrap loader. If you write a custom policy, you will need to set the bootclasspath to point to your custom policy class.

Listing 2–15   Loading a Custom Security Policy

```
String custPolicy = System.getProperty(
                    "java.security.policy");
Class cls = Class.forName(custPolicy);
Object o = cls.newInstance();
Policy.setPolicy((java.security.Policy) o);
```

Taken together, the bootstrap, extensions, and system loaders provide a large variety of options for deployment and security settings on a single machine. This is often sufficient for configuring simple applications. If you want to dynamically deploy and redeploy classes, the standard class loaders won't help you. You, or some other code in your process, will need to install some additional class loader instances, probably of `java.net.URLClassLoader`.

2.8   Debugging Class Loading

The flexibility of the class loader architecture creates the potential for extreme confusion when something goes wrong. Consider the simple situation of an application failing with a `ClassNotFoundError` for class `Foo`. This could be caused by the Foo.class file being in the wrong directory, by an incorrect `-cp` parameter on the command line, by a problem with the `CLASSPATH` environment variable, or by any of the bootclasspath or extensions path settings. Even worse, the failure to load `Foo` could be the result of a chain reaction caused by some other class `Quux` being loaded from an unexpected location. Once `Quux` is loaded, all of the classes that `Quux` references are implicitly loaded from `Quux`'s class loader delegation, so if `Quux` is in an unexpected place (but still visible), it may cause bizarre loading failures at distant locations in the code.

All of these problems can happen even with the standard class loaders. When you start instantiating your own class loaders, the situation becomes even more bewildering. This section will show you three tricks for debugging class loading problems:

1. Instrumenting your application
2. Using the –verbose:class flag
3. Instrumenting the core API

2.8.1 Instrumenting an Application

You can often diagnose class loading problems by instrumenting your application near the trouble spot. For example, consider Listing 2–16, which you might use to troubleshoot the case of class Quux being unable to implicitly load class Foo.

Listing 2–16 Instrumenting an Application

```java
public class Quux {
  public void useFoo() {
    //assume this call is failing, and you don't know why
    Foo f = new Foo();
  }
  //add this static block to tell where Quux is coming from
  static {
    ClassLoader cl = Quux.class.getClassLoader();
    System.out.println("Delegation for Quux");
    while (cl != null) {
      System.out.println(cl);
      cl = cl.getParent();
    }
    System.out.println("{bootstrap loader}");
  }
}
```

The static block added to the Quux class simply logs the entire delegation for Quux by recursively calling getParent() until the bootstrap loader is reached. If Quux came from the classpath, you would see output similar to this:

```
sun.misc.Launcher$AppClassLoader@404536
sun.misc.Launcher$ExtClassLoader@7d8483
{bootstrap loader}
```

Here you can see the three installed class loaders in action. The instance of the nested class `sun.misc.Launcher.AppClassLoader` is the system class loader, and the instance of `sun.misc.Launcher.ExtClassLoader` is the extensions loader. By inserting a block of code like this near the site of a class loading failure, you will be able to verify that the classes that *did* load came from the right place.

2.8.2 Using –verbose:class

You can obtain similar logging without writing any code by running the virtual machine with the `–verbose:class` flag for tracing class loading. Listing 2–17 shows a partial example of the output from running the `LoaderDemo` example (see Listing 2–2) with the `–verbose:class` flag.

Listing 2–17 Output from -verbose:class

```
[Opened d:\java\jdk1.3\jre\lib\rt.jar]
[Opened d:\java\jdk1.3\jre\lib\i18n.jar]
[Opened d:\java\jdk1.3\jre\lib\sunrsasign.jar]
[Loaded java.lang.Object from d:\java\jdk1.3\jre\lib\rt.jar]
[Loaded java.io.Serializable from d:\java\jdk1.3\jre\lib\rt.jar]
[Loaded java.lang.Comparable from d:\java\jdk1.3\jre\lib\rt.jar]
   {more lines like this }
[Loaded LoaderDemo]
[Loaded sun.misc.URLClassPath$JarLoader from
d:\java\jdk1.3\jre\lib\rt.jar]
   {more lines again }
[Loaded LoadMe]
```

The output shows the order in which classes are loaded, and for the core API classes, it also shows the JAR file they were loaded from. The complete listing of loaded classes from an application run can be very helpful in many debugging scenarios. In addition to helping with class loading problems, it also gives some hints as to what the application was doing. This information can also help you tune the application footprint. Sometimes a single class can pull in a large number of other classes via implicit class loading. The `–verbose:class` output makes this situation painfully clear, and it gives you the opportunity to locate and perhaps discontinue using classes that incur this hidden expense.

2.8.3 Instrumenting the Core API

The `-verbose:class` feature is easy to use, but the format and quantity of output is controlled by the virtual machine. In some situations, you might want to log even more information, such as failure to load classes or the order in which loaders are consulted to load a class. If you control the source code for the class loaders used in an application, you can create a special logging subclass for each class loader. If you do not control the source code, your only recourse may be to modify the core API classes to add custom logging.

The Java SDK provides a nonstandard flag that makes it easy to replace core API classes. To take advantage of this, specify an alternate location that is consulted before the normal bootclasspath via the `-Xbootclasspath/p:` flag. Even if a VM does not support this nonstandard flag, you can still replace core classes by building a version of rt.jar that contains the modified classes. The VM flag simply makes experimentation easier by eliminating the need to keep track of multiple custom versions of rt.jar.

Listing 2–18 shows a modified version of `URLClassLoader` that logs class loader creation, classes found, and classes not found. The `logConstructor` method logs the creation of all `URLClassLoaders`, including the URLs that the loader will consult and the parent loader. The log output also includes the `this` reference, which you can use to cross-reference with the class loading portion of the log to determine which specific instance loaded a class. The `logConstructor` method also logs the call stack at the time the loader was created by instantiating an `Exception` and then extracting its stack trace (without ever throwing the `Exception`). This is a common trick for logging call stacks.[10]

Listing 2–18   Adding Logging to URLClassLoader

```
//extract java.net.URLClassLoader from src.jar in your SDK
//directory to a "boot" directory. Insert the following
//methods adding other code as instructed in the comments:
/**
 * add a call to logConstructor after the call to super
```

---

10. You could also use `Thread.dumpStack()`, which does the same trick internally. I prefer the direct instantiation of an exception because the `printStackTrace` can be redirected to a `PrintStream` other than `out`.

```
 * in each URLClassLoader constructor
 */
private void logConstructor(URL[] urls, ClassLoader parent) {
  if (parent == null) {
    parent = getSystemClassLoader();
  }
  System.out.println("Created URLClassLoader " + this);
  System.out.println("\tparent: " + parent);
  for (int n=0; n<urls.length; n++) {
    System.out.println("\turl: " + urls[n]);
  }
  System.out.println("created at ");
  new Exception().printStackTrace();
  System.out.println();
}

protected Class loadClass(String name, boolean resolve)
    throws ClassNotFoundException
{
  Class cls = null;
  try {
    cls = super.loadClass(name, resolve);
    return cls;
  }
  finally {
    System.out.print("Class " + name);
    if (cls == null) {
      System.out.println(" could not be loaded by " + this);
    } else {
    ClassLoader cl = cls.getClassLoader();
    if (cl == this) {
      System.out.println(" loaded by " + cl);
    } else {
      System.out.println(" requested by " + this +
                            ", loaded by " + cl);
    }
    }
  }
}
```

The `loadClass` method logs whether class loading was successful and the identity of both the requesting loader and the loader that was actually used. (Remember that the delegation model implies that the requesting loader may delegate instead of doing the loading itself.) If you compile this version of `URLClassLoader` to a boot directory and then prepend that directory to the bootclasspath, you will get quite a large output, similar to Listing 2–19.

Listing 2–19 Output from the Logging Version of URLClassLoader

```
{Note: this output has been drastically clipped to show only a few
classes being loaded}
>java -Xbootclasspath/p:boot -cp classes LoaderDemo
Created URLClassLoader sun.misc.Launcher$ExtClassLoader@100d7a
   parent: null
created at {stack trace omitted}
Created URLClassLoader sun.misc.Launcher$AppClassLoader@ac738
   parent: sun.misc.Launcher$ExtClassLoader@100d7a
   url: file:/D:/halloway/JavaCode/v1tests/classes/
created at {stack trace omitted}
Class LoaderDemo could not be loaded by
      sun.misc.Launcher$ExtClassLoader@100d7a
Class LoaderDemo loaded by
      sun.misc.Launcher$AppClassLoader@ac738
Created URLClassLoader java.net.URLClassLoader@3179c3
   parent: sun.misc.Launcher$AppClassLoader@ac738
   url: file:subdir/
created at {stack trace omitted}
Class LoadMe could not be loaded by
      sun.misc.Launcher$ExtClassLoader@100d7a
Class LoadMe could not be loaded by
      sun.misc.Launcher$AppClassLoader@ac738
Class LoadMe loaded by java.net.URLClassLoader@3179c3
```

This output demonstrates many of the points made in this chapter. First, the VM creates the extensions class loader, which delegates to the bootstrap class loader. Then, the VM creates the system class loader, which delegates to the extensions class loader. The log output clearly shows that both the system and extensions class loaders are implemented as subclasses of `URLClassLoader`. When `LoaderDemo` creates an instance of `URLClassLoader`, it does not specify a parent, but you can see that it implicitly delegates to the classpath class loader. Finally, you can see that `LoaderDemo` is loaded from the classpath but that `LoadMe` is loaded by the `URLClassLoader` that points to `file:subdir/`.

You will find that replacing `java.net.URLClassLoader` is far more useful for debugging than either using the `-verbose:class` flag or adding ad hoc code to your own classes. Of course, you may not like the specific information generated by the `URLClassLoader` modifications listed above. Good! The entire point of replacing the class is to generate exactly the output you want, so start with the example code and tweak it to meet your needs.

Replacing core classes is a trick for in-house debugging only. You should never *ship* a custom version of a core API class to customers without specifically verifying that what you are doing does not violate the license agreement. For more information see the LICENSE file that is in the root directory of your SDK installation.

You might find similar approaches useful in logging Swing, or Remote Method Invocation (RMI), or just about any Java technology. In theory, any core API class is fair game. In practice, you need to be very careful not to break anything. If you are not exactly sure what you are doing, you may introduce catastrophic bugs. Even simply adding logging code could cause concurrency problems and deadlocks. Modifying the core APIs is like recompiling your operating system. It can be entertaining and highly educational, but you should not do it in a production environment.

2.9 Inversion and the Context Class Loader

Thanks to the delegation model, one class can reference another without both classes having to come from the same class loader. In particular, a class A can reference any class B that is visible to A's class loader's delegation. More concretely, an application class `Main` can refer to `java.lang.String` even though `Main` comes from the classpath class loader and `String` comes from the bootstrap loader. However, this relationship is *not* bidirectional. The `String` class cannot refer to the application `Main` class, because the classpath class loader is not part of the bootstrap loader's delegation. The problem is one of *inversion*—a class from a parent loader cannot reference a class from a child loader. Some legal permutations that do not cause inversion are listed in Table 2–2.

Table 2–2 Legal and Illegal References across Class Loaders

Relationship between Classes A and B	Legal Class Loader Relationships
No relationship	Any
A has field/variable of type B	CL_A equals/descends from CL_B
A extends B	CL_A equals/descends from CL_B
A has field/variable of type B *and* B has field/variable of type A	CL_A *must* equal CL_B

In most situations, inversion problems are easily avoided. Simply put base classes, superinterfaces, and referenced classes *at least as high* in the class loader hierarchy as the classes that reference them. This is trivially accomplished by placing all of your application code on the classpath. For hot deployment scenarios, install interfaces on the classpath and load implementations with URLClassLoaders that are children of the classpath loader.

Sometimes code that is very high in the class loader hierarchy will need to access code that is an arbitrary distance lower in the class hierarchy. Consider the hypothetical StuffedAnimal API (a.k.a. SAPI) in Listing 2–20. The API consists of two classes, StuffedAnimal and StuffedAnimalFactory. The StuffedAnimal interface defines the contract between the client and the implementation, and the StuffedAnimalFactory provides a configurable way for clients to request a StuffedAnimal implementation.

Listing 2–20 The StuffedAnimal API (SAPI)

```java
public interface StuffedAnimal {
  public void snuggle();
  public void sleep();
  public void getMisplaced();
}

public class StuffedAnimalFactory {
  public static StuffedAnimal newAnimal() {
    String name = System.getProperty("stuffed.animal");
    if (name == null) {
      throw new Error("stuffed.animal not specified");
    }
```

```
      //see StuffedAnimalFactory3 for better approach
      try {
        Class cls = Class.forName(name);
        return (StuffedAnimal) cls.newInstance();
      } catch (Exception e) {
        e.printStackTrace();
        throw new Error("Unable to create " + name);
      }
    }
  }
```

Listing 2–21 A StuffedAnimal Provider

```
public class TeddyBear implements StuffedAnimal {
  public void snuggle() {
    System.out.println("I love you");
  }
  public void sleep() {
    System.out.println("ZZZ");
  }
  public void getMisplaced() {
    throw new Error("child very unhappy");
  }
}
```

Listing 2–22 A StuffedAnimal Client

```
public class StuffedAnimalClient {
  public static void main(String [] args) {
    StuffedAnimal sa = StuffedAnimalFactory.newAnimal();
    sa.snuggle();
    sa.sleep();
  }
}
```

Imagine that StuffedAnimals become so popular that almost all Java applications want to use them. Because the API is stable and widely used, you can make the SAPI available to all. Simply add StuffedAnimal and StuffedAnimalFactory to a SAPI.jar file in the extensions directory. Now, assume that the StuffedAnimalClient wants to define and use a particular TeddyBear provider implementation as shown in Listings 2–21 and 2–22. Assuming that the client and provider code are in the classes subdirectory, the `java` command line would look like this:

```
java -cp classes/ -Dstuffed.animal=TeddyBear \
StuffedAnimalClient
```

This usage has several advantages:

1. The client does not have to worry about the location of the API code because it is picked up automatically from the extensions directory.

2. The API definition, client, and server are all free from worrying about explicit class loading—none of the code even mentions a class loader.

3. The client is the deployer. Clients can select different implementations without changing a line of code by setting the `stuffed.animal` property.

In fact, the only problem with this example is that it simply doesn't work. The API is loaded as an extension, but the server code (Teddy Bear) is on the classpath. The API's reference to the server code is a class loader inversion and the factory's call to `Class.forName` is unable to see the `TeddyBear` class.

There are a couple of workarounds to this problem that you should avoid. Obviously, you could dodge the issue by installing *all* the classes under the same class loader, either the extensions or the system loader. Application architectures that take this approach often end up installing classes in several different places just to make sure things load. Never do this. This haphazard approach defeats the purpose of having a *hierarchy* of different loaders, and it almost guarantees deployment problems.

A slightly better idea would be to add a `ClassLoader` argument where necessary in the API, as shown in Listing 2–23. This version of SAPI allows the client to specify a class loader on each call to the factory, and it uses the three-argument version of `Class.forName` to reach the correct class loader. This explicit approach will work, but it is tedious to ask the client to pass in a class loader every time. This strategy becomes even more tedious if the class loader must be passed through dozens of intermediate methods before it needs to be used.

Listing 2–23   SAPI with Explicit Class Loading

```
public class StuffedAnimalFactory2 {
    public static StuffedAnimal newAnimal(ClassLoader cl) {
```

```
      String name = System.getProperty("stuffed.animal");
      if (name == null) {
        throw new Error("stuffed.animal not specified");
      }
      //see StuffedAnimalFactory3 for best approach
      try {
        Class cls = Class.forName(name, true, cl);
        return (StuffedAnimal) cls.newInstance();
      } catch (Exception e) {
        e.printStackTrace();
        throw new Error("Unable to create " + name);
      }
    }
}

public class StuffedAnimalClient2 {
  public static void main(String [] args) {
    Class cls = StuffedAnimalClient2.class;
    ClassLoader cl = cls.getClassLoader();
    StuffedAnimal sa = StuffedAnimalFactory2.newAnimal(cl);
    sa.snuggle();
    sa.sleep();
  }
}
```

An easier approach than using an explicit argument is to define a *context class loader* to use in potential inversion situations. A context loader is not passed as an explicit parameter; instead, it is available at any time through a special API.

The thread context class loader is designed precisely for this purpose. New as of SDK version 1.2, the context loader is implemented by a pair of methods on the thread class, shown in Listing 2–24. Functionally, the context class loader methods are simply a wrapper around a single object reference kept in thread local storage. When you write a provider API, such as the StuffedAnimal API, you should use the thread-specific context loader on each thread, thereby avoiding the need to pollute your API with extra class loader parameters. This is particularly important if your code is going to execute in a container environment, such as a J2EE implementation, in which the instantiation of class loaders is typically controlled by the J2EE container vendor, not the application author.

Listing 2–24   The Context Class Loader API

```
package java.lang;
public class Thread implements Runnable {
  public void setContextClassLoader(ClassLoader cl);
  public ClassLoader getContextClassLoader();
  //rest of class omitted for clarity
}
```

Listing 2–25 shows a version of SAPI that uses the thread context class loader. In this listing, the context loader is used only once, so the code is actually a little longer than the explicit version shown in Listing 2–23. In a larger application, setting the context loader in a centralized location would greatly reduce the amount of class loader–related code.

Listing 2–25   SAPI Using the Thread Context Class Loader

```
public class StuffedAnimalFactory3 {
  public static StuffedAnimal newAnimal() {
    String name = System.getProperty("stuffed.animal");
    if (name == null) {
      throw new Error("stuffed.animal not specified");
    }
    ClassLoader cl = Thread.currentThread()
                    .getContextClassLoader();
    try {
      Class cls = Class.forName(name, true, cl);
      return (StuffedAnimal) cls.newInstance();
    } catch (Exception e) {
      e.printStackTrace();
      throw new Error("Unable to create " + name);
    }
  }
}

public class StuffedAnimalClient3 {
  public static void main(String [] args) {
    Class cls = StuffedAnimalClient2.class;
    ClassLoader cl = cls.getClassLoader();
    Thread.currentThread().setContextClassLoader(cl);
    StuffedAnimal sa = StuffedAnimalFactory3.newAnimal();
    sa.snuggle();
    sa.sleep();
  }
}
```

In the versions of the `StuffedAnimalClient` that set a class loader, I chose the class loader using the code

```
ClassLoader cl = StuffedAnimalClient.class.getClassLoader();
```

instead of the arguably simpler

```
ClassLoader cl = ClassLoader.getSystemClassLoader();
```

These two formulations mean entirely different things. The former says "Give me the class loader that loaded `StuffedAnimal`," while the latter says "Give me the class loader that loads from the classpath." It is a coincidence that these evaluate to the same loader in this example. If you used the latter formulation and later switched to using hot deployment, someone besides the system loader might load the `StuffedAnimalClient` and `TeddyBear`, and you would have another inversion problem. Do not make assumptions about what class loader will load your class. Always query for your class's actual loader at runtime with `YourClass.class.getClassLoader`.

2.10 Onward

Class loaders enable flexible, dynamic deployment of Java applications. Classes can be loaded from a variety of different sources, which are selected at runtime. Class loaders provide controlled sharing of code. The delegation model of class loading allows some classes to be shared widely, while other classes are kept local to class loaders far down the delegation hierarchy.

Class loading is often felt but not seen. Most Java code takes no explicit account of class loading, allowing implicit class loading to deal with many common loading scenarios. The core API provides a set of built-in class loaders: the bootstrap, extensions, and system class loaders. These loaders provide for different levels of security and different policies of sharing between and within applications. The combination of implicit class loading and the configuration options for the standard class loaders meets many class loading needs without requiring any explicit class loading code.

You can gain additional flexibility by instantiating your own class loaders to explicitly load classes. The `java.net.URLClassLoader` class can load classes from any supported URL protocol. One use of `URLClassLoader` is hot deployment, whereby old and new versions of a class can coexist in the same process. Debugging class loading can be tricky, but with the `-verbose:class` flag and customized implementations of `URLClassLoader`, you can quickly eliminate most problems.

The context class loader is a thread local class loader reference. Use the context loader as an out-of-band mechanism to communicate which class loader needs to be used when related components are loaded by different class loaders.

2.11 Resources

If you want to learn more about the topics covered in this chapter, the following references may prove useful. [New00] covers class loading in detail, with an emphasis on how to use class loading to support different deployment strategies. [JavaGeeks] includes several free white papers related to class loading. "Understanding Class.forName()" has a good explanation of the thread context class loader, and "Using the BootClasspath" discusses replacing the core classes. [Ven99] explains the class loading process, with an emphasis on the actual structure of class files and how the virtual machine loads and verifies classes.

Chapter 3

Type Information and Reflection

Java classes preserve a wealth of information about programmer intent. Rather than just containing a jumble of executable instructions, binary classes[1] also contain large amounts of *metadata*—data that describes the structure of the binary class. Most of this metadata is *type information* enumerating the base class, superinterfaces, fields, and methods of the class. Type information is used to make the dynamic linking of code more reliable by verifying at runtime that clients and servers share a common view of the classes they use to communicate.

The presence of type information also enables dynamic styles of programming. You can *introspect* against a binary class to discover its fields and methods at runtime. Using this information, you can write generic services to add capabilities to classes that have not even been written yet.

The binary class format is a simple data structure that you could parse to perform introspection yourself. Rather than going to this trouble, you can use the Java Reflection API instead. Reflection provides programmatic access to most of the metadata in the binary class format. It also provides not only the ability to introspect classes for metadata, but also the ability to dynamically access fields and methods. Reflective invocation is critical for writing generic object services. As of SDK version 1.3, reflection also includes the ability to manufacture classes called dynamic proxies at runtime. This chapter introduces

---

1. [LY99] uses the term "class file" instead. This usage encourages the mistaken assumption that classes *must* live in files, and it will probably be replaced in a future edition of the spec. Throughout this book, I will use the more generic term "binary class."

the binary class format, the uses of metadata, the Reflection API, dynamic proxies, and custom metadata.

3.1 The Binary Class Format

The binary class format means different things to different people. To an application developer, the binary class is the compiled output of a Java class. Most of the time, you can treat the class format as a black box—a detail that is thankfully hidden by the compiler. The binary class is also the unit of executable code recognized by the virtual machine. Virtual machine developers see the binary class as a data structure that can be loaded, interpreted, and manipulated by virtual machines and by Java development tools. The binary class is also the unit of granularity for dynamic class loading. Authors of custom class loaders take this view and may use their knowledge of the binary class format to generate custom classes at runtime. But most importantly, the binary class is a well-defined format for conveying class code and class metadata.

Most of the existing literature on the binary class format targets compiler and virtual machine developers. For example, the virtual machine specification provides a wealth of detail about the exact format of a binary class, plus a specific explanation of extensions that can legally be added to that format. For a Java developer, such detail is overkill. However, hidden in that detail is information that the virtual machine uses to provide valuable services, such as security, versioning, type-safe runtime linkage, and runtime type information. The availability and quality of these services is of great concern to all Java developers. The remainder of Section 3.1 will describe the information in the binary class format, and how that information is used by the virtual machine. Subsequent sections show you how you can use this information from your own programs.

3.1.1 Binary Compatibility

A clear example of the power of class metadata is Java's enforcement of binary compatibility at runtime. Consider the `MadScientist` class and its client class `BMovie`, shown in Listing 3–1. If you compile the two classes and then execute the `BMovie` class, you will see that the `threaten` method executes as expected. Now, imagine that you decide to ship a modified version of `Mad-Scientist` with the `threaten` method removed. What happens if an old version of `BMovie` tries to use this new version of `MadScientist`?

In a language that does not use metadata to link methods at runtime, the outcome is poorly defined. In this particular case, the old version of `BMovie` probably would link to the first method in the object. Since `threaten` is no longer part of the class, `blowUpWorld` is now the first method. This program error would literally be devastating to the caller.

Listing 3–1   The MadScientist Class

```
public class MadScientist {
  public void threaten() {
    System.out.println("I plan to blow up the world");
  }
  public void blowUpWorld() {
    throw new Error("The world is destroyed. Bwa ha ha ha!");
  }
}
public class BMovie {
  public static void main(String [] args) {
    MadScientist ms = new MadScientist();
    ms.threaten();
  }
}
```

As bad as this looks, an obvious failure is actually one of the *best* possible outcomes for version mismatches in a language without adequate metadata. Consider what might happen in a systems programming language, such as C++, that encodes assumptions about other modules as numeric locations or offsets. If these assumptions turn out to be incorrect at runtime, the resulting behavior is undefined. Instead of the desired behavior, some random method may be called, or some random class may be loaded. If the random method does not cause an immediate failure, the symptoms of this problem can be incredibly difficult to track down. Another possibility is that the code execution will transfer to some location in memory that is not a method at all. Hackers may exploit this situation to inject their own malicious code into a process.

Compare all the potential problems above with the actual behavior of the Java language. If you remove the `threaten` method, and recompile only the `MadScientist` class, you will see the following result:

```
>java BMovie
java.lang.NoSuchMethodError
    at BMovie.main(BMovie.java:4)
```

If a class makes a reference to a nonexistent or invalid entity in some other class, that reference will trigger some subclass of `IncompatibleClass-ChangeError`, such as the `NoSuchMethodError` shown above. All of these exception types indirectly extend `Error`, so they do not have to be checked and may occur at any time. Java assumes fallible programmers, incomplete compile-time knowledge, and partial installations of code that change over time. As a result, the language makes runtime metadata checks to ensure that references are resolved correctly. Systems languages, on the other hand, tend to assume expert programmers, complete compile-time knowledge, and full control of the installation processes. The code that results from these may load a little faster than Java code, but it will be unacceptably fragile in a distributed environment.

In the earlier example, the missing method `threaten` caused the new version of `MadScientist` to be incompatible with the original version of `BMovie`. This is an obvious example of incompatibility, but some other incompatibilities are a little less obvious. The exact rules for binary class compatibility are enumerated in [LY99], but you will rarely need to consult the rules at this level. The rules all support a single, common-sense objective: no mysterious failures. A reference either resolves to the exact thing the caller expects, or an error is thrown; "exactness" is limited by what the caller is looking for. Consider these examples:

- You cannot reference a class, method, or field that does not exist. For fields and methods, both names and types must match.
- You cannot reference a class, method, or field that is invisible to you, for example, a private method of some other class.
- Because private members are invisible to other classes anyway, changes to private members will *not* cause incompatibilities with other classes. A

similar argument holds for package-private members *if* you always update the entire package as a unit.

- You cannot instantiate an abstract class, invoke an abstract method, subclass a `final` class, or override a `final` method.

- Compatibility is in the eye of the beholder. If some class adds or removes methods that you never call anyway, you will not perceive any incompatibility when loading different versions of that class.

Another way to view all these rules is to remember that changes to invisible implementation details will never break binary compatibility, but changes to visible relationships between classes will.

3.1.1.1 *Declared Exceptions and Binary Compatibility*

One of the few oddities of binary compatibility is that you *can* refer to a method or constructor that declares checked exceptions that you do not expect. This is less strict than the corresponding compile-time rule, which states that the caller must handle all checked exceptions. Consider the versions of `Rocket` and `Client` shown in Listing 3–2. You can only compile `Client` against version 1 of the `Rocket` since the client does not handle the exception thrown by version 2. At runtime, a `Client` could successfully reference and use either version because exception types are not checked for binary compatibility.

This loophole in the binary compatibility rules may be surprising, but it does not compromise the primary objective of preventing inexplicable failures. Consider what happens if your `Client` encounters the second version of `Rocket`. If and when the `InadequateNationalInfrastructure` exception is thrown, your code will not be expecting it, and the thread will probably terminate. Even though this may be highly irritating, the behavior is clearly defined, and the stack trace makes it easy to detect the problem and add an appropriate handler.

Listing 3–2 Checked Exceptions Are Not Enforced by the VM.

```
public class Client {
  Rocket r = new Rocket();
}
public class Rocket { //version 1
  public Rocket() { … }
```

```
}
public class Rocket { //version 2
  public Rocket()
  throws InadequateNationalInfrastructure { … }
}
```

3.1.1.2 *Some Incompatible Changes Cannot Be Detected*

The Java compiler enforces the rules of binary compatibility at compile time, and the virtual machine enforces them again at runtime. The runtime enforcement of these rules goes a long way toward preventing the accidental use of the wrong class. However, these rules do not protect you from bad decisions when you are shipping a new version of a class. You can still find clever ways to write new versions of classes that explode when called by old clients.

Listing 3–3 shows an unsafe change to a class that Java cannot prevent. Clients of the original version of `Rocket` expect to simply call `launch`. The second version of `Rocket` changes the rules by adding a mandatory `preLaunchSafetyCheck`. This does not create any structural incompatibilities with the version 1 clients, who can still find all the methods that they expect to call. As a result, old versions of the client might launch new rockets without the necessary safety check. If you want to rely on the virtual machine to protect the new version of `Rocket` from old clients, then you must deliberately introduce an incompatibility that will break the linkage. For example, your new version could implement a new and different `Rocket2` interface.[2]

Listing 3–3 Some Legal Changes to a Class May Still Be Dangerous.

```
public interface Rocket {   //version 1
  public void launch();
}
public interface Rocket { //version 2
  public void mandatoryPreLaunchSafetyCheck();
  public void launch();
}
```

---

2. Package reflection, discussed later in this chapter, provides another approach to preventing this problem.

3.1.2 Binary Class Metadata

[LY99] documents the exact format of a binary class. My purpose here is not to reproduce this information but to show what kinds of metadata the binary class includes. Figure 3–1 shows the relevant data structures that you can traverse in the binary class format. The constant pool is a shared data structure that contains elements, such as class constants, method names, and field names, that are referenced by index elsewhere in the class file. The other structures in the class file do not hold their own data; instead, they hold indexes into the constant pool. This keeps the overall size of the class file small by avoiding the repetition of similar data structures.

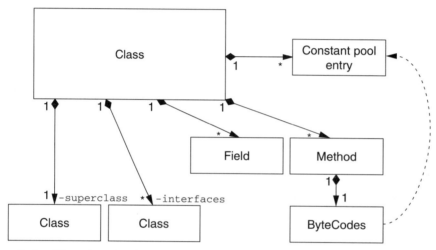

Figure 3–1 Metadata in the binary class format

The -superclass and -interfaces references contain indices into the constant pool. After a few levels of indirection, these indices eventually lead to the actual string names of the class's base class and superinterfaces. The use of actual string names makes it possible to verify *at runtime* that the class meets the contractual expectations of its clients.

Note that the class name format used by the virtual machine is different from the dotted notation used in Java code. The VM uses the "/" character as a package delimiter. Also, it often uses the "L" and ";" characters to delimit class names if the class name appears inside a stream where other types of data might also appear. So, the class `java.lang.String` will appear as either `java/lang/String` or `Ljava/lang/String;` in the class file's constant pool.

The fields and methods arrays also contain indices into the constant pool. Again, these constant pool entries lead to the actual string names of the referenced types, plus the string names of the methods and fields. If the referenced type is a primitive, the VM uses a special single-character string encoding for the type, as shown in Table 3–1. A method also contains a reference to the Java bytecodes that implement the method. Whenever these bytecodes refer to another class, they do so through a constant pool index that resolves to the string name of the referenced class. Throughout the virtual machine, types are referred to by their full, package qualified string names. Fields and methods are also referenced by their string names.

Table 3–1   Virtual Machine Type Names

Java Type	Virtual Machine Name
int	I
float	F
long	J
double	D
byte	B
boolean	Z
short	S
char	C
type[]	*[type*
package.SomeClass	*Lpackage.SomeClass;*

3.1.2.1   *Analyzing Classes with javap*

The details of binary class data structures are of interest to VM writers, and they are covered in detail in the virtual machine specification [LY99]. Fortunately, there are a large number of tools that will display information from the binary class format in a human-friendly form. The `javap` tool that ships with the SDK is a simple class decompiler. Consider the simple `Echo1` class:

```
public class Echo1 {
  private static final String prefix = "You said: ";
  public static void main(String [] args) {
    System.out.println(prefix + args[0]);
  }
}
```

If you run `javap` on the compiled `Echo1` class, you will see output similar to Listing 3–4. As you can see, the class format contains the class names, the method names, and the parameter type names. The `javap` utility has a variety of more verbose options as well, including the –c flag to display the actual byte-codes that implement each method, shown in Listing 3–5. Without worrying about what specific bytecodes do, you can easily see that the bytecode instructions refer to classes, fields, and members by name. The #10, #5, #1, and #8 in the output are the indices into the constant pool; `javap` helpfully resolves these indices so that you can see the actual strings being referenced.

Listing 3–4 Standard javap Output

```
>javap Echo
Compiled from Echo1.java
public class Echo1 extends java.lang.Object {
    public Echo1();
    public static void main(java.lang.String[]);
}
```

Listing 3–5 Javap Output with Bytecodes Included

```
>javap -c Echo1
  {output clipped for brevity}
Method void main(java.lang.String[])
   0 getstatic #10 <Field java.io.PrintStream out>
   3 new #5 <Class java.lang.StringBuffer>
   6 dup
   7 ldc #1 <String "You said: ">
   9 invokespecial #8 <Method
         java.lang.StringBuffer(java.lang.String)>
   etc...
```

3.1.3 From Binary Classes to Reflection

Java class binaries always contain metadata, including the string names for classes, fields, field types, methods, and method parameter types. This metadata is used implicitly to verify that cross-class references are compatible. Both metadata and the notion of class compatibility are built into the bones of the Java language, so there is no subterranean level where you can avoid their presence. By themselves, the binary compatibility checks provided by the virtual machine would be sufficient to justify the cost of creating, storing, and processing class metadata. In reality, these uses only scratch the surface. You can access the same metadata directly from within your Java programs using the Reflection API.

3.2 Reflection

The Java Reflection API presents a Java interface to the metadata contained in the binary class format. You can use reflection to dynamically discover the characteristics of a Java class: its base class, superinterfaces, method signatures, and field types. Better yet, you can use reflection to dynamically instantiate objects, invoke methods, and mutate fields. These features make it possible to write generic object services that do not rely on, or even have advance knowledge of, the specific classes they will be working on.

Reflection makes it straightforward to serialize an instance to a stream, generate relational database tables that correspond to a class's fields, or create a user interface that can manipulate instances of any arbitrary class. Reflection can also be used to automatically generate source or compiled code that forwards method calls for a set of interfaces to a generic handler. This feature is invaluable for adding layers of code for logging, auditing, or security. Reflection allows you to write service layers that do not require compile-time knowledge of the specific systems they will support.

Some examples of reflection in the core API include serialization and Java-Beans. Java can serialize class instances by writing their state into an opaque stream to be reloaded in some other time or place. Java serialization works even for classes that have not been written yet, because the serialization API uses reflection to access class fields.

At the bare minimum, a JavaBean is a serializable class with a default constructor. However, bean-aware tools can use reflection to discover the properties and events associated with a bean. This means that tools can deal with classes that they have never seen simply by reflecting against them.

Serialization and JavaBeans are powerful idioms, but they are still just idioms. Their underlying architecture is reflection. If you understand reflection you can develop your own idioms, more suited to your particular problem domain.

Most of the Reflection API lives in the `java.lang.reflect` package, but the central class in reflection is the `java.lang.Class` class. A `Class` represents a single binary class, loaded by a particular class loader, within the virtual machine. By using a `Class` instance as a starting point, you can discover all type information about a class. For example, you might want to know all of a class's superclasses and superinterfaces. The `ListBaseTypes` class shown in Listing 3–6 uses the `Class` methods `getInterfaces` and `getSuperclass` to return a class's superinterfaces and superclass, and then it follows these recursively back to the beginning, which is defined to be `java.lang.Object` for classes and `null` for interfaces. Sample output for `ListBaseTypes` is shown in Listing 3–7.

Listing 3–6   The ListBaseTypes Class

```java
public class ListBaseTypes {
  public static void main(String [] args) throws Exception
  {
    Class cls = Class.forName(args[0]);
    System.out.println("Base types for " + args[0]);
    listBaseTypes(cls, "");
  }
  public static void listBaseTypes(Class cls, String pref) {
    if (cls == Object.class) return;
    Class[] itfs = cls.getInterfaces();
    for (int n=0; n<itfs.length; n++) {
      System.out.println(pref + "implements " + itfs[n]);
      listBaseTypes(itfs[n], pref+"\t");
    }
    Class base = cls.getSuperclass();
    if (base == null) return;
    System.out.println(pref + "extends " + base);
    listBaseTypes(base, pref+"\t");
  }
}
```

Listing 3–7 Sample Output from ListBaseTypes

```
Base types for java.io.ObjectOutputStream
implements interface java.io.ObjectOutput
    implements interface java.io.DataOutput
implements interface java.io.ObjectStreamConstants
extends class java.io.OutputStream
    extends class java.lang.Object
```

3.2.1 Reflecting on Fields

A more interesting use of reflection is to discover the fields of a class. Fields are represented by the `java.lang.reflect.Field` class. As Listing 3–8 shows, the `Field` class contains all of the information from the original source code declaration of a field: the field's name, type, and modifiers. The `Class` class provides several methods for retrieving a class's fields, shown in Listing 3–9.

Listing 3–8 Type Information in the Field Class

```
package java.lang.reflect;
public class Field {
  public String getName();
  public int getModifiers();
  public Class getType();
}//remainder omitted for clarity
```

Listing 3–9 Class Methods for Accessing Fields

```
package java.lang;
public class Class {
  public Field[] getDeclaredFields();
  public Field[] getFields();
  public Field getDeclaredField(String name)
    throws NoSuchFieldException;
  public Field getField(String name)
    throws NoSuchFieldException;
  //remainder omitted for clarity
}
```

3.2.2 The Difference between get and getDeclared

The `Field` methods of `Class` exhibit a pattern that occurs throughout the Reflection API: an accessor method named `getXXX`, plus a similar accessor named `getDeclaredXXX`. These method forms differ in two ways. The getxxx methods return only public members of a class, but they will return members from a class and all of its base classes. The getDeclaredxxx methods will return all members of a class, regardless of protection modifier; however, they will *not* recurse to base classes. There is no compelling reason for or against this convention; you simply must memorize it. The combination of get-Fields and getDeclaredFields is not sufficient to access nonpublic base class fields. As shown in Figure 3–2, in order to list all fields of a class and its base classes, you need to use the getDeclaredField form and then also recurse to base classes using getSuperclass.

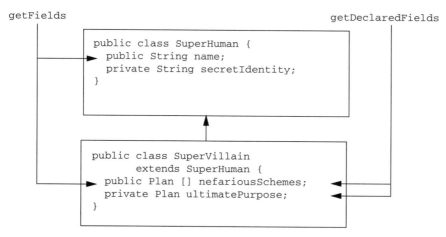

Figure 3–2   The difference between get and getDeclared

If you run ListMostFields (Listing 3–10) against String, you will see a list of nine fields (on the Java 2 SDK1.3, anyway). This surprisingly large list is due to the fact that the field APIs return static fields as well as instance fields. In order to distinguish static from instance fields, or to discover any other field modifiers, you must call getModifiers.

Listing 3–10   ListMostFields

```
import java.lang.reflect.*;
/**
 * lists all fields except superinterface fields
 * and fields from Object
 */
```

```
public class ListMostFields {
  public static void main(String [] args) throws Exception
  {
    Class cls = Class.forName(args[0]);
    System.out.println("Fields for " + args[0]);
    listMostFields(cls);
  }
  public static void listMostFields(Class cls) {
    if (cls == Object.class) return;
    Field[] fields = cls.getDeclaredFields();
    for (int n=0; n<fields.length; n++) {
      System.out.println(fields[n]);
    }
    Class base = cls.getSuperclass();
    if (base == null) return;
    System.out.println("extends " + base);
    listMostFields(base);
  }
}
```

The `getModifiers` call is one of the few places where Java thoroughly shows its nuts-and-bolts C language heritage. Instead of returning a `Modifiers` object, `getModifiers` returns an `int` that is a collection of bit flags. There actually is a `java.lang.reflect.Modifiers` class, but all it does is provide constants and static methods to interpret the bit flags. So, you can determine whether a `Field` is static by calling a static method on the `Modifiers` class but not through an instance of `Field` itself, as shown here:

```
//this is correct
Modifiers.isStatic(f.getModifiers());

//These are intuitive possibilities, but will not compile!
f.isStatic();
f.getModifiers().hasStatic();
```

3.2.3 Type Errors Occur at Runtime

The `getField` and `getDeclaredFields` of `Class` request a particular `Field` by name. These APIs introduce another wrinkle that recurs throughout reflection—the possibility that any call may fail at runtime. With "normal" nonreflective code, you get substantial feedback at compile time. If you reference a field that does not exist, the compiler will simply refuse to compile the class. With reflection, you are querying for the existence of a field at runtime, and you must be prepared for the possibility of failure at runtime. The `getField` and `getDeclaredField` methods remind you of this possibility by throwing the checked exception `NoSuchFieldException`. This is the blessing and curse of reflective programming. You can use reflection to refer to classes that do not even exist at compile time, but you must remember that the compiler is powerless to protect you from misusing such classes.

Listing 3–11   Type Information in the Method and Constructor Classes

```
//these methods appear in both
//java.lang.reflect.Method and
//java.lang.reflect.Constructor
public String getName();
public int getModifiers();
public Class getReturnType();
public Class[] getParameterTypes();
public Class[] getExceptionTypes();
```

3.2.4   Reflecting on Methods

You can use reflection to access methods in a fashion very similar to accessing fields. Methods are represented by the `java.lang.reflect.Method` class, which preserves the information from the method signature in the original Java source code file, as shown in Listing 3–11. Finding `Method` objects is slightly more complex than finding `Field` objects because `Method` names can be overloaded. The `Class` APIs for `Methods`, shown in Listing 3–12, require that you specify argument types in addition to the method name. In addition to argument types, the `Method` class also lets you access the return type and checked exceptions thrown by a method.

Listing 3–12   Class Methods for Accessing Methods and Constructors

```
//java.lang.Class methods for accessing Methods
//versions that take a name throw NoSuchMethodException
public Method getDeclaredMethod(String name, Class[]
                                 parameterTypes);
public Method getMethod(String name,
                         Class[] parameterTypes);
```

```
public Method[] getDeclaredMethods();
public Method[] getMethods();
//methods for accessing Constructors
public Constructor getDeclaredConstructor(Class[]
                    parameterTypes);
public Constructor getMethod(Class[] parameterTypes);
public Constructor[] getDeclaredConstructors();
public Constructor[] getConstructors();
```

The rules for `Methods` are exactly the same as for `Fields`—the `getDeclared` versions of the APIs ignore protection modifiers, while the `get` versions return public members for the class and its base classes. The `Constructor` APIs work almost exactly like the `Method` APIs, but since the name of a constructor is implicit, the name parameter is absent from the `Constructor`-related methods.

3.3 Reflective Invocation

The Reflection API's ability to report the fields, methods, and constructors of a class is a very useful feature for the authors of Java development environments. For example, Java IDE wizards can automatically generate empty implementations of an interface for you to fill in. Java reflection makes this simple, whereas with many other languages, the development environment must build its own custom metadata representation to provide these services. While reflective reporting is a nifty parlor trick, the real power of reflection lies elsewhere, in the invocation APIs. With reflective invocation, you can access or change the value of a field and you can even invoke a method without any compile-time knowledge of the classes involved.

The invocation portion of the Reflection API uses the `Field`, `Method`, and `Constructor` classes to query and modify the state of Java classes and instances at runtime. This ability can be used to emulate function pointers, which do not exist in Java. Invocation can also be used as a substitute for inheritance. Instead of casting an object to a known interface type, you simply reflect against the class to see if it implements a particular method. Reflective invocation is also critical in crossing class loader boundaries. If you have a reference to a type that is not visible to your class loader delegation, you can use reflection to access that type's fields, constructors, and methods.

The reflective invocation APIs share several common elements. Because they are invoked on instances of `Field`, `Method`, or `Constructor`, they do not have an implicit `this` reference to the actual type being modified, and they must specify the `this` reference as an explicit parameter. Because reflective invocation APIs do not know the parameter types in advance, parameters are specified as `Object` or arrays of `Object`. Similarly, return types are always of type `Object`. Finally, reflective invocation cannot know in advance what checked exceptions might be thrown by a method, so all exceptions are caught by the APIs and rethrown as some wrapper type. The key reflective invocation APIs are summarized in Listing 3–13.

Listing 3–13 Key Reflective Invocation APIs

```
//all invocation APIs may throw
//IllegalArgumentException, IllegalAccessException

//from java.lang.reflect.Field
public Object get(Object this);
public void set(Object this, Object value);

//from java.lang.reflect.Method
public Object invoke(Object this, Object[] args)
      throws InvocationTargetException

//from java.lang.reflect.Constructor
public Object newInstance(Object[] args)
      throws InstantiationException,
              InvocationTargetException
```

3.3.1 A Reflective Launcher

As an example of a situation in which the Reflection API is essential, consider the `RunFromURL` class shown in Listing 3–14. `RunFromURL` is very similar to the Java launcher except that it loads a class from a URL passed on the command line instead of from the classpath. The meat of the code is the `run` method, which uses `getMethod` to find a method with the signature `main(String[] args)` and then invokes that method with a `null` reference for `this` (since the method is assumed to be static)[3] and an array of arguments from the command line. `RunFromURL` can execute the main method of any arbitrary class. Moreover, reflection is the only way this can be accomplished. `RunFromURL` cannot directly reference the class to be loaded. If `RunFromURL` referenced the class directly, implicit class loading would cause the class to be loaded from the classpath, which would defeat `RunFromURL`'s ability to dynamically load classes from a location chosen at runtime.

Listing 3–14   RunFromURL

```
//imports, error checking removed for brevity
public class RunFromURL {
  public static void run(String url, String clsName,
                         String[] args) throws Exception
  {
    URLClassLoader ucl = new URLClassLoader(new URL[]
                         {new URL(url)});
    Class cls = ucl.loadClass(clsName);
    Class argClass = String[].class;
    Method mainMeth = cls.getMethod("main",
                      new Class[]{argClass});
    mainMeth.invoke(null, new Object[]{args});
  }
  public static void main(String [] args) throws Exception
  {
    int argCount = args.length-2;
    String[] newArgs = new String[args.length-2];
    for (int n=0; n<argCount; n++) {
      newArgs[n] = args[n+2];
    }
    run(args[0], args[1], newArgs);
  }
}
```

3.3.2   Wrapping Primitive Types

The syntax shown so far works fine for object types, but what about methods and fields that utilize primitive types? Java includes a set of primitive types (`short`, `long`, `byte`, `boolean`, `double`, `float`, `int`, and `char`) that can be

---

3. A production version should use the `Modifiers` class to make sure the method actually is static.

represented directly in memory without the overhead of extending `Object`. These types pose a problem for reflection because the invocation APIs have generic signatures based on `Object` and `Object[]`. To enable the use of primitive types in reflective invocation, each primitive type in Java has a corresponding immutable class in the `java.lang` package. If you want to use reflection to call a method that takes a primitive type, you must use an instance of one of the wrapper classes instead. So for a hypothetical method

```
int add(int n1, int n2);
```

you would use the following reflective syntax:

```
//to reflectively add ints n1 and n2
Object[] args = new Object[]{new Integer(n1),
                                new Integer(n2)};
Integer temp = (Integer) addMethod.invoke(args);
int result = temp.intValue();
```

Before calling `add`, you must "box" the `int` parameters as `Integer`s. Then, you must take the result of the call, cast it to `Integer`, and then "unbox" it to an `int`. This is inconvenient but necessary given the dual nature of numeric types in Java.

A related issue is the process of requesting a method with primitive types in its signature. Given that reflective invocation must use `Integer` wherever `int` was originally specified, how can `getMethod` distinguish between the two signatures shown in Listing 3–15? Even though both of these methods would be reflectively invoked with the same argument types, there is a way to distinguish between them to `getMethod` and related methods. `Integer`, like any other Java class, can be represented by its corresponding pseudo-literal, in this case `Integer.class`. For reflection purposes, the primitive types, such as `int`, have a special `Class` representation that is the static `TYPE` constant of the corresponding wrapper class. So, you should use `Integer.class` to request an `Integer` but `Integer.TYPE` to request an `int`, as Listing 3–15 demonstrates.

Listing 3–15   Finding Methods That Use Primitive Types

```
//two methods differing only in wrapper vs. primitive
public Integer add(Integer n1, Integer n2);
public int add(int n1, int n2);
```

```
//to access the wrapper version
Class[] wcls = new Class[]{Integer.class,Integer.class};
Method methWrapper = cls.getMethod("add", wcls);

//to access the primitive version
Class[] pcls = new Class[]{Integer.TYPE,Integer.TYPE};
Method primitiveWrapper = cls.getMethod("add", pcls);
```

3.3.3 Bypassing Language Access Rules

The rules for dealing with primitive types are arbitrary but raise no interesting design questions. A more challenging design issue is deciding how to enforce language access rules during reflective invocation. In normal Java programming, member access is controlled by the `public`, `private`, and `protected` keywords, plus the implied package-private setting if no keyword is specified. If you attempt to access a member whose access is restricted, compilation will fail. With reflective invocation, there is no way to know the protection modifier of a method at compile time. At runtime, the virtual machine can use class metadata to determine the protection modifier, and it can possibly prevent the operation being attempted.

If a piece of code attempts to use reflection to access a member that it would not have been allowed to access from compiled Java code, should the operation be allowed to proceed? The initial intuition is "no!" There are at least two good reasons to enforce the language protection rules during reflective invocation. First, reflection should not act as a back door to compromise encapsulation. It is both a design flaw and a security risk to open private members to code outside of a class. Second, reflection should obey the common-sense rule of least surprise. If the language works a certain way during normal method invocation, reflective invocation should mimic that behavior to the extent possible.

3.3.3.1 Using setAccessible

Despite these arguments in favor of limiting reflection, reflective code sometimes needs to bypass Java's protection modifiers in order to implement low-level subsystems that provide services for arbitrary Java classes. For example, one use of the Reflection API is for generic persistence services for instances. A generic persistence layer that did not persist the entire state of an object, including private members, would not be very generic. However, the design of the Reflection API also addresses the concerns raised previously about blithely accessing private data. The rules for language-level access checks provide something for everybody:

1. By default, reflective invocation does *not* bypass language access checks. If you attempt to access a private, package-private, or protected member that you could not access normally, reflection will fail with an `IllegalAccessException`. This preserves the rule of least surprise.

2. If you want to bypass language-level access checks, you can request this ability by calling `setAccessible(true)` on an `AccessibleObject` (see Listing 3–16). The reflection classes `Field`, `Method`, and `Constructor` all extend `AccessibleObject`. This allows a service like an XML serializer to gain access to all of an object's state.

Listing 3–16   AccessibleObject

```
// from java.lang.reflect.AccessibleObject
package java.lang.reflect;
public class AccessibleObject {
  //request permission to bypass access checks
  public void setAccessible(boolean flag)
            throws SecurityException;
  //bypass access checks for several items in one shot
  public static void setAccessible(AccessibleObject[]
                    arr, boolean flag);
  //remainder omitted for clarity
}
```

You can control which code is allowed to call `setAccessible` by installing a `SecurityManager` for a process.[4] The `setAccessible` method provides a convenient chokepoint for a security check, and the default security implementation will prevent application code from calling `setAccessible`, while allowing system code to do so.

To see these rules in action, consider a `Reporter`'s attempts to discover a `Superhero`'s secret identity, shown in Listing 3–17. The `Reporter` wants to

---

4. See [Gon99] for a detailed treatment of Java 2 Platform Security.

retrieve the `Superhero`'s `secretIdentity` field via reflection, thus bypassing the fact that the field is private. If you execute this code as is, it will fail with an `IllegalAccessException`. In order to bypass the language check, add a call to `secret.setAccessible(true)` before the call to `secret.get(s)`. With this call in place, reflection will bypass the language access check and return the private field. However, if you turn security on with the `java.security.manager` flag, the call to `setAccessible` will fail with an `AccessControlException` as it does here:

```
>java -cp classes -Djava.security.manager Reporter
java.security.AccessControlException: access denied
(java.lang.reflect.ReflectPermission suppressAccessChecks)
```

Listing 3–17   Misusing Reflection to Access a Private Field

```java
public class Superhero {
public class Superhero {
  public final String name;
  private final String secretIdentity;
  public Superhero(String name, String secretIdentity) {
    this.name = name;
    this.secretIdentity = secretIdentity;
  }
}
public class Reporter {
  public static void main(String [] args)
        throws Exception {
    Superhero s = new Superhero("ReflectionMan",
                              "Brian Maso");
    hackIdentity(s);
  }
  public static void hackIdentity(Superhero s)
                  throws Exception {
    Field secret = Superhero.class.
                 getDeclaredField("secretIdentity");
    System.out.println("Identity is " + secret.get(s));
  }
}
```

To call `setAccessible` when security is enabled, you must have the `suppressAccessChecks` permission. By default, code that is in the core API or the extensions directory will have the `suppressAccessChecks` permission and be able to perform services such as serializing an object's private state. Application code loaded from the classpath or via a `URLClassLoader` will not have this permission, and therefore, it will be unable to inadvertently manipulate an object's implementation details.

3.3.3.2 Reflective Modification of Final Fields

Given that reflection sometimes has a legitimate reason to modify `private` fields, it is also logical to consider whether reflection might need to modify `final` fields. Before you look at how Java actually handles this today, consider the problem. Imagine a `Person` class that wanted to have some immutable fields:

```
public class Person {
   private final String name;
   private final String socialSecurityNo;
   //etc...
}
```

Now consider what would happen if you wanted to write a generic mechanism to instantiate `Person` from a row in a database. There are three approaches that might work:

1. You could use reflection to instantiate a `Person` and then assign its fields. However, since some of the fields are final, this would require that the reflection APIs be designed with the ability to modify final fields. Many people argue that this ability is counter to the very definition of `final`.

2. You could use a native method to instantiate a `Person` and then assign its fields. The Java Native Interface (JNI) includes APIs to do all sorts of things that would be illegal in Java, including instantiating objects without running their constructors and modifying final fields. The major downside to this approach is that you have to develop and deploy native code.

3. You could require that the `Person` class provide an "all-fields constructor" that would simply pass through an initial value for every single field in the object. Generic services, such as the hypothetical database code, would use reflection to invoke this special constructor. The constructor probably would not be used during normal operation, and in fact, you could mark it `private` to guarantee this. This approach has neither of the disadvantages of

the first two. Because constructors are allowed to set final fields, reflection does not need the ability to subvert final semantics. Also, no native code is required. The problem with this approach is that it requires the author of a class to explicitly write a special constructor in order to use serialization. The first two approaches simply leverage metadata and require no assistance from the classes that want generic services.

None of these solutions is ideal, and the Java language is still evolving in this area. Prior to SDK version 1.3, the first approach was used. The `setAccessible` method gave permission to modify `final` fields, and APIs such as serialization leveraged reflection. This led to some very confusing situations, as demonstrated in Listing 3–18.

Listing 3–18 Reflectively Modifying final Fields Is a Bad Idea.

```
import java.lang.reflect.*;
public class LimitedInt {
  public static void main(String[] args) throws Exception
  {
    System.out.println("Integer.MAX_VALUE=" +
                       Integer.MAX_VALUE);
    Field mv = Integer.class.getField("MAX_VALUE");
    mv.setAccessible(true);
    mv.set(null, new Integer(42));
    System.out.println("Retest: MAX_VALUE=" +
                       Integer.MAX_VALUE);
    System.out.println("Reflective: MAX_VALUE=" +
                       mv.get(null));
  }
}
```

Prior to SDK 1.3, `setAccessible` worked for `final` fields, and it was actually possible to change `Integer.MAX_VALUE`! This was made doubly confusing because Java compilers typically optimize `static final` primitive type declarations by inlining any access. So, even though you could change the value of `MAX_VALUE` seen by reflection, you could not change the value of `MAX_VALUE` where that constant was referenced in a class. On SDK 1.2, the code in Listing 3–18 prints the following:

```
Integer.MAX_VALUE=2147483647
Retest: MAX_VALUE=2147483647
Reflective: MAX_VALUE=42
```

SDK 1.3 removed reflection's ability to change `final` fields. In the case of `static final` fields, this was definitely a step in the right direction. However, this also broke the approach to serialization that leveraged reflection to populate instance fields for classes like `Person`. In order to get around this new limitation, services like serialization switched to the second approach detailed earlier, using native methods to populate fields. This is not likely to be the final word on the subject. The proposed changes to Java's memory model would remove even the ability of native code to modify `final` fields (see [JMM] for details). If the new model is adopted, then the third approach might become necessary; this would require class authors to provide a special constructor for serializable classes that have `final` fields.

3.3.4 Exceptions Caused by Reflective Invocation

As mentioned above, attempts to bypass language restrictions without calling `setAccessible(true)` will generate an `IllegalAccessException`. `IllegalAccessException` is one of several exceptions that reflective invocation throws to indicate a problem that normal code would catch at compile time. Another example is `IllegalArgumentException`, used to indicate that a method argument is invalid. This will occur if one of the `Objects` in the array passed to `invoke` cannot be converted to the correct type for the underlying method. If you try to use reflection to instantiate an abstract class, `Class` will throw an `InstantiationException`.

Taken together, these three exception types are the reflection equivalent of the compiler's enforcement of language rules. While `setAccessible` can bypass the access rules, there is no way to get around the situations that cause an `IllegalArgumentException` or an `InstantiationException`. You must always pass arguments of the correct type, and you can never instantiate abstract classes.

Another situation where reflection may throw an exception is if the underlying method or constructor throws an exception. If this occurs, one of three things will happen:

1. If a method throws an unchecked exception, such as an `Error` or `RuntimeException`, then this exception will be passed unmodified through the reflection layer to the caller. This behavior is no different from ordinary method invocation, where unchecked exceptions do not require an explicit catch block.

2. A method may throw a declared checked exception. This is a problem for reflection because checked exceptions must be declared in a method signature, and reflection does not know a method's signature at compile time. The reflection APIs catch checked exceptions and convert them into a checked type `InvocationTargetException` that is declared in the signature of `Method.invoke`. This situation occurs frequently and leads to a special idiom on the part of the caller, as shown in Listing 3–19. `InvocationTargetException` is a reflection-provided wrapper class that can access the original exception via `getTargetException`. A client is typically more interested in the original exception, which indicates what went wrong, than it is in the `InvocationTargetException`, which only indicates that reflection was involved. As the sample shows, reflective clients will frequently catch `InvocationTargetException`, extract the original exception, cast it to some type expected by the caller, and rethrow.

3. A method may throw a checked type that it did *not* declare. If this happens, `invoke` will convert the exception into the unchecked type `UndeclaredThrowableException`. This situation is extremely rare since the compiler will prevent a class from compiling if it tries to throw a checked exception that it did not declare. `UndeclaredThrowableException` indicates either a version mismatch caused by a partial recompile, or a corrupted binary class.

Listing 3–19 Extracting the "Real" Exception

```
//invokes some I/O method unknown at compile time
public void reflectiveIO(Method m, Object this,
            String fileName) throws IOException
{
  try {
    m.invoke(this, new Object[]{filename});
```

```
  }
  catch (InvocationTargetException ite) {
    throw (IOException) ite.getTargetException();
  }
}
```

3.4   Dynamic Proxies

Dynamic proxies, available since SDK 1.3, are the exact opposite of reflective invocation. With reflective invocation, a client uses a generic API to call methods
(on a server class) that are not known at compile time. With dynamic proxies, a
server uses a generic API to implement methods on a server class that is manufactured at runtime to meet a client's specification. Dynamic proxies are chame-
leons that take the shape of any set of interfaces desired by the client. When
combined with reflective invocation, dynamic proxies can implement *generic interceptors*. An *interceptor* is a piece of code that sits between a client and a
server and adds an additional service, such as transaction enlistment, auditing,
security checking, or parameter marshalling. A *generic interceptor* requires no
compile-time knowledge of the client or server APIs being intercepted.

3.4.1   Delegation instead of Implementation Inheritance

Generic interception makes it possible to use an object-oriented style based not
just on inheritance, but also on delegation. Consider an entity class that accesses employee information from a database. If you wanted to use inheritance
to layer in transaction enlistment, auditing, and security checks, you would need
to use multiple inheritance. After pointing out that multiple implementation inheritance does not exist in Java, you might also object to the fact that this design
would require eight different concrete subclasses of `Employee`, one each for
every possible service being turned on or off, as shown in Figure 3–3. In general, adding another service doubles the number of concrete subclasses you
need.

   With delegation, each new service adds only one class, and classes are simply chained together to provide the exact mix of services needed, as shown in
Figure 3–4.

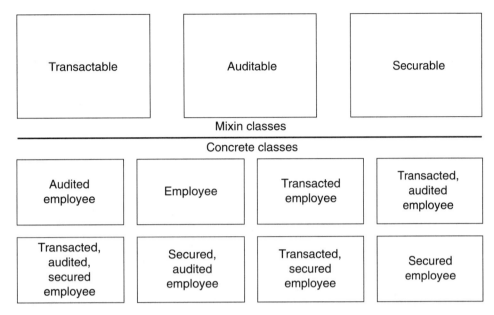

Figure 3–3   Implementation inheritance causes class proliferation.

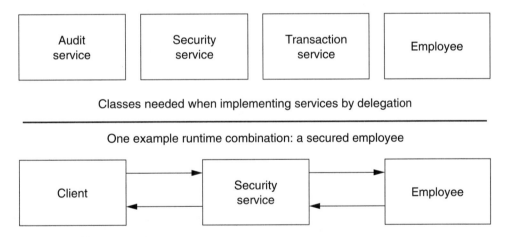

Figure 3–4   Delegation requires only one class per service.

3.4.2   Dynamic Proxies Make Delegation Generic

Historically, the problem with the delegation model was how to make each service generic. For example, an `Audit` class would need to implement `EmployeeItf` when it was dealing with an `Employee` entity, but it would need to

COMPONENT DEVELOPMENT FOR THE JAVA™ PLATFORM

implement `InventoryItf` when it was dealing with the `Inventory` entity. Also, the service classes would need to implement interfaces that had not even been designed yet. Dynamic proxies neatly solve this problem by allowing the transaction class to manufacture an implementation of whatever interface the client expects at runtime.

To manufacture a dynamic proxy, you need only call `Proxy.newProxyInstance`, passing in an implementation of the `InvocationHandler` interface. Summaries of these classes appear in Listing 3–20. The `newProxyInstance` method manufactures a new binary class in memory. This special class implements all the interfaces passed in the `itfs` array by forwarding every single method to an instance of `InvocationHandler`. Then, the new class is loaded into the virtual machine by the class loader specified by `ldr`, and it is used to construct a proxy instance that forwards to `handler`.

Listing 3–20 Key Elements of Proxy and InvocationHandler

```
package java.lang.reflect;
public class Proxy {
    static Object newProxyInstance(ClassLoader ldr,
            Class[] itfs, InvocationHandler handler)
                throws IllegalArgumentException;
    //remainder omitted for clarity
}
public interface InvocationHandler {
    public Object invoke(Object proxy, Method method,
                    Object[] args) throws Throwable;
}
```

3.4.3 Implementing InvocationHandler

Dynamic proxies allow you to implement a single `invoke` method on the invocation handler and then use it to service any interface you choose at runtime. For example, consider an `InvocationHandler` that logs method calls, shown in Listing 3–21. This `LoggingHandler` class provides a trivial implementation of any interface that simply logs method calls as they are made. `DemoLogging` demonstrates using the `LoggingHandler` to log calls to `DataOutput`. One possible use for `LoggingHandler` is during development, when you need to stub out an interface that you have not yet implemented.

Notice that the toString method is treated specially. In addition to any interface methods, dynamic proxies always forward the Object methods toString, hashCode, and equals to the handler. In this case, the proxy's toString method is invoked by the handler's call to System.out.println. If the toString method were not special-cased, the call to toString would trigger the invoke method of LoggingHandler, which triggers another call to toString, and so on, recursing until the stack overflowed.

Listing 3–21 LoggingHandler

```
import java.lang.reflect.*;
public class LoggingHandler implements InvocationHandler {
  public Object invoke(Object proxy, Method method,
                       Object[] args) throws Throwable
  {
    if (method.getName().equals("toString")) {
      return super.toString();
    }
    System.out.println("Method " + method +
                       " called on " + proxy);
    return null;
  }
}
import java.lang.reflect.*;
import java.io.*;
public class DemoLogging {
  public static void main(String [] args)
    throws IOException
  {
    ClassLoader cl = DemoLogging.class.getClassLoader();
    DataOutput d = (DataOutput) Proxy.newProxyInstance(cl,
                               new Class[] {DataOutput.class},
                               new LoggingHandler());
    d.writeChar('a');
    d.writeUTF("stitch in time");
  }
}
```

3.4.4 Implementing a Forwarding Handler

Although "standalone" dynamic proxies such as LoggingHandler are useful, they suffer from a major limitation in dealing with return values. Because they are totally generic, InvocationHandlers have no idea how to generate a legitimate return value for a method call. LoggingHandler finesses this issue by always returning null, which the generated proxy class will coerce to the return type of the interface method. In Listing 3–21, the DataOutput methods happen to return void, so the generated proxy simply ignores the return from LoggingHandler's invoke method. This coincidence will not hold up in more complex cases, those in which methods might return any type, and the compile-time type might need to be further constrained at runtime in accordance with the documented semantics of the method. In order to reasonably mimic any arbitrary interface, a dynamic proxy will either need to know the semantics of the interface, or it will need to forward the method call to some other object that does. Since the raison d'être of a proxy is to be generic, knowing the specifics on an interface is not an option. Instead, most dynamic proxies are used to forward calls to other objects.

The strength of dynamic proxies is method call forwarding. A dynamic proxy can intercept a method call, examine or modify the parameters, pass the call to some other object, examine or modify the result, and return that result to the caller. When correctly configured, dynamic proxies work transparently without the knowledge of either the client or server code.

Figure 3–5 shows how a dynamic proxy enables generic services. A generic service implements only one method, InvocationHandler.invoke, and forwards the call using only one method, Method.invoke. Without changing, or even reading, any existing implementation code, you can insert a dynamic proxy between two objects to inject some additional service.

3.4.5 The InvocationHandler as Generic Service

To appreciate the power and simplicity of this model for reuse, imagine the following scenario: A large server application has been ported to Java and continues to access legacy code through a bridge that presents the legacy code as a set of Java interfaces. Unfortunately, the legacy code was written in a pointer-based language and experiences occasional memory corruption. The specific symptom is that methods sometimes return the java.util.Date

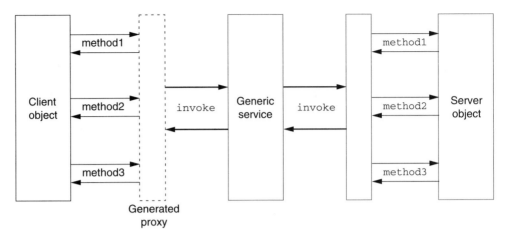

Figure 3–5 Dynamic proxies enable generic services.

"Thu Dec 25 07:42:41 EST 1969."[5] Your task is to guarantee that this bug does not introduce corrupt data into the application.

With dynamic proxies, you can add an interceptor that traps all attempts to return the offending value, as is shown in Listing 3–22. Here, a `TrappingHandler` forwards all method calls to its `delegate`. If the `delegate` functions unexceptionally and returns an object, the handler checks to see if it is a `Date` instance indicative of the memory corruption bug. If it is, then the handler might throw an error, as the example shows, or it might take whatever other action may be necessary.

Listing 3–22 TrappingHandler

```
import java.lang.reflect.*;
import java.util.*;
public class TrappingHandler implements InvocationHandler {
  //BAD_DATE is "Thu Dec 25 07:42:41 EST 1969"
  //This value corresponds to an error code on some systems
  public static final Date BAD_DATE = new Date(-559038737);
  private Object delegate;
  public TrappingHandler(Object delegate) {
    this.delegate = delegate;
  }
```

---

5. Bonus points will be awarded for figuring out why this particular date value is likely to indicate memory corruption.

COMPONENT DEVELOPMENT FOR THE JAVA™ PLATFORM

```
    public Object invoke(Object proxy, Method method,
                 Object[] args) throws Throwable {
      Object result = null;
      try {
        result = method.invoke(delegate, args);
      } catch (InvocationTargetException e) {
        throw e.getTargetException();
      }
      if (result instanceof Date) {
        Date d = (Date) result;
        if (d.equals(BAD_DATE)) {
          throw new Error("Corrupted date " + d);
        }
      }
      return result;
    }
  }
```

3.4.6   Handling Exceptions in an InvocationHandler

It is important to code carefully against the possibility that the `delegate` will itself throw an exception. Because the handler is generic, you have no compile-
time knowledge of what particular exceptions the `delegate` might throw. However, since the `delegate`'s methods are invoked via reflection, any exception
will be wrapped by an `InvocationTargetException`. You should not let this
exception percolate out of the dynamic proxy code.

The dynamic proxy provides some help here. Since a proxy wants to be
transparent to the client, it will only permit exceptions that the client expects. To
enforce this, a proxy compares any thrown exception to the list of checked exceptions for the current method. If an exception is not in the list, a proxy will
wrap it in an `UndeclaredThrowableException`, which is a `RuntimeEx-`
`ception` subclass that signals a programmer error.

To complete the illusion of transparency, your `InvocationHandler` must
not give the proxy any reason to throw an `UndeclaredThrowable Excep-`
`tion`. Therefore, the canonical implementation of a forwarding proxy includes a
try/catch block that catches the `InvocationTargetException` and then extracts and throws the underlying exception, which is the one the client expects.
Refer back to Listing 3–22, which demonstrates this.

3.4.7 Either Client or Server Can Install a Proxy

Either the client or the server code can wrap suspicious objects with the Trap-pingHandler before using them. In the TestTrappingHandler example (Listing 3–23), the client wraps an instance of the Test interface. If either get-GoodDateValue or getBadDateValue of the Test interface return a bad date, the handler will protect the client by throwing an exception. More importantly, the same TrappingHandler can be used throughout a system to protect any number of different interfaces and implementation classes.

You could make the proxy code transparent to both client and server by using an object factory to hide the details of connecting client and server code.

Listing 3–23   Testing a TrappingHandler

```java
//Test.java
import java.util.*;
interface Test {
  Date getGoodDateValue();
  Date getBadDateValue();
}


//TestTrappingHandler.java
import java.lang.reflect.*;
import java.util.*;

public class TestTrappingHandler implements Test {
  public static void main(String [] args) {
    TestTrappingHandler t = new TestTrappingHandler();
    System.out.println("Testing unwrapped object.\n" +
                        "This should permit date value " +
                        TrappingHandler.BAD_DATE);
    executeTests(t);
    Test wrap = (Test)Proxy.newProxyInstance(
    TestTrappingHandler.class.getClassLoader(),
    new Class[]{Test.class}, new TrappingHandler(t));
    System.out.println("Testing wrapped object.\n" +
                        "This should reject date value " +
                        TrappingHandler.BAD_DATE);
    executeTests(wrap);
  }
```

```
    public Date getGoodDateValue() {
      return new Date();
    }
    public Date getBadDateValue() {
      return TrappingHandler.BAD_DATE;
    }
    public static void executeTests(Test t) {
      System.out.println(t.getGoodDateValue());
      System.out.println(t.getBadDateValue());
    }
  }
```

3.4.8 Advantages of Dynamic Proxies

Dynamic proxies do not provide any service that you could not provide yourself by hand-coding a custom delegator class for every different interface. The advantage of dynamic proxies over hand-rolled delegators is twofold. First, you do not have to write dynamic proxies. Second, they can be generated on-the-fly at runtime to handle new interfaces as they appear. Because dynamic proxies are generic, they tend to be used for services that do not rely on any specific knowledge of the interface or method being forwarded:

- Parameter validation or modification, where a parameter value is of interest regardless of where it appears, as in the example above

- Security checks, some of which can be made based on the identity of the user or the source of the code, not the particular method being called

- Propagation of "implicit" or "context" parameters, such as the transaction ID, which is automatically handled by an EJB container and does not appear in any interface declaration

- Auditing, tracing, or debugging of method calls

- Marshalling a Java method call to some other process, machine, or language

Like any generic tool, dynamic proxies may be inefficient compared to a solution hand-tuned to a particular problem. Situations in which performance considerations may rule out the use of dynamic proxies are discussed in §3.5.

3.5 Reflection Performance

Reflective invocation is slower than direct method invocation. Similarly, using dynamic proxies as a generic forwarding device results in slower code than manually crafting interface-specific delegation code does. When is the performance penalty acceptable? Programmers who are used to dynamic, interpreted runtime environments are already accustomed to dynamic programming styles and see uses for reflection everywhere. On the other hand, programmers who are used to the performance of a strongly typed, compiled language often laugh at the slow speed of reflection and reject it outright.

The truth lies somewhere in between. Reflection is best suited for writing "glue"—code that sits at the boundaries between disparate classes, packages, and subsystems. If your task description includes words such as "adapter" or "decorator," then reflection may be a good fit. But reflection is not well suited for code on the critical path in an application. If your task vocabulary tends more toward "inner loop" or "heavy recursion," avoid reflection. This section presents some order-of-magnitude estimates of reflection performance, and then it gives some specific examples of where it should and should not be used.

Before directing your attention to some performance numbers, I must begin with some major caveats about their use. Evaluating a system's performance is a tricky task. Many factors impact the execution speed of even a simple Java application: virtual machine, processor speed, available memory, memory speed, OS, OS version, and other applications that are also running.

Because of these complexities, measurement is essential. Do not rely on intuition. Programmers' intuitions about performance are reliable only to within about six orders of magnitude. If you need better precision than that, you must measure. In Java, even measurement can be tricky. The virtual machine introduces yet another layer of indirection between you and the Platonic ones and zeroes. As of SDK version 1.3, the virtual machine (HotSpot) is adaptive over time, so short-run tests can grossly misrepresent long-run behaviors.

Fortunately, there is some value even in very rough measurements. For the purpose of deciding where reflection might fit into a program design, it is sufficient to have some order-of-magnitude, relative measurements. The test harness used to make the following measurements is the `Timer` class from the `com.develop.benchmark` package, which is included in the sample code for this book [Hal01].

Table 3–2   Rough Estimate of Reflection Performance

Operation Tested	Time (Nearest Power of 10 nsec)
Increment integer field	10^0
Invoke a virtual method	10^1
Invoke through a manual delegate	10^1–10^2
Reflective method invocation[*]	10^4–10^5
Invoke through a proxy delegate	10^4–10^5
Reflectively increment integer field	10^4–10^5
RMI call on a local machine	10^5
Open, write, close a file	10^6
Light travels 3000km	10^7

[*]Reflective method invocation actually involves three steps: getting a `Method` object with a call to `get-Method`, boxing the arguments into an array of `Object`, and calling `invoke`. Many reflection-based systems make only a single call to `getMethod` followed by many calls to `invoke`, so it may not always be appropriate to include the `getMethod` overhead in the per-call timings. In my tests, the costs with `getMethod` included were closer to 10^5 nsec, and the costs just for boxing the arguments and calling the method were closer to 10^4 nsec.

Table 3–2 lists order-of-magnitude comparisons for reflective and nonreflective tasks. These tests were made on the HotSpot 1.3 client virtual machine, with JIT enabled, on a Pentium2-450 running Windows NT 4.0 server. However, the conclusions I plan to draw are very limited, and they should hold for a wide variety of virtual machines and hardware. First, notice that direct access to a field and direct invocation of a virtual method are very fast, in the ones and tens of nanoseconds respectively. This is getting reasonably close to a single operation per processor tick since the P450's clock ticks in a little over two nanoseconds. When you switch to reflective field access, reflective method invocation, or invocation through a dynamic proxy, you will notice that they all impose a stiff penalty, taking in the tens of microseconds to execute. This is the statistic that causes systems programmers to scoff and abandon reflection.

When you look a little further down the table, you will see some reasons for a more optimistic assessment. Though reflection may be slow compared to direct access to class members, it is quite fast compared to many other common programming tasks. A simple, cross-process method invocation on a local machine is an order of magnitude slower than a reflective invocation. Opening, writing, and closing a file is another order of magnitude slower than that. Hundreds of reflective operations could transpire in the time it takes light to travel 3,000km, which in turn, is likely faster than the time in which network packets can travel between your computer and some location on the Internet. A single online transaction involves several of these expensive operations: invoking methods cross-process, reading and writing files, and routing packets around the Internet. A single reflective method call would have a negligible impact on an Internet-based transaction.

The performance numbers could vary wildly on different virtual machines, and they are not intended to guide optimization decisions other than at the broadest level. What they do show, however, is that reflective access is not onerous if it is used sparingly in an application that is also doing interesting work. Moreover, reflection performance should improve substantially in the 1.4 SDK release. If you can easily make your design work without resorting to reflection, then do so. But do not be alarmed about performance if reflection appears to be the most convenient glue between subsystems in your application.

3.6 Package Reflection

Most of the Reflection API deals with class-level metadata. However, version information is another form of metadata, and it plays a critical role as code evolves; it makes sure that client code accesses only compatible versions of needed classes. Version metadata is also useful when you need to know the exact version of software that caused a problem. In Java, version information is typically tracked at the level of a package, and it is stored at the level of the JAR file. This is reasonable because the next smaller unit, the class file, is typically too small to be the standard unit of versioning or deployment. Version information is embedded in JAR files, added to the virtual machine by a class loader, and accessed programmatically via the `java.lang.Package` class.

3.6.1 Setting Package Metadata

In order to use the version metadata currently provided by Java, you must deploy your code as a JAR file instead of as separate class files. Adding version information to a JAR file is a simple matter of adding name/value pairs to the manifest file. For example, Listing 3–24 specifies all the possible version fields for a hypothetical `com.develop.hello` package.

Listing 3–24   Manifest Entries for Package Versioning

```
Manifest-version: 1.0
Name: com/develop/hello/
Specification-Title: Hello World
Specification-Version: 1.0.0
Specification-Vendor: DevelopMentor
Implementation-Title: com.develop.hello
Implementation-Version: build1
Implementation-Vendor: DevelopMentor
```

The manifest information is added to the JAR file with the −m switch. Assuming the file above is named hellov1.mf, you might create a JAR file with the command

```
jar -cmf hellov1.mf hellov1.jar com/develop/hello/Main.class
```

When a `URLClassLoader` loads classes from a JAR file that includes version information, it registers the version information with the virtual machine by calling the `definePackage` method defined by the `ClassLoader` class, shown in Listing 3–25. This method takes the name of the package, the six well-known version information strings, and the `sealBase` (more on sealing in §3.6.3).

Listing 3–25   The definePackage Method

```
package java.lang;
public class ClassLoader {
protected Package definePackage(
                String name, String specTitle,
                String specVersion, String specVendor,
                String implTitle, String implVersion,
                String implVendor, URL sealBase);
//other methods omitted for clarity
}
```

3.6.2 Accessing Package Metadata

The virtual machine makes package metadata available to code at runtime through the `Package` class. Included in the `Package` class are accessor methods for the six version info strings, plus two methods for looking up the packages known to the virtual machine, as shown in Listing 3–26.

Listing 3–26 Querying Package Metadata

```
package java.lang;
public class Package {
  public String getSpecificationTitle();
  public String getSpecificationVersion();
  public String getSpecificationVendor();
  public String getImplementationTitle();
  public String getImplementationVersion();
  public String getImplementationVendor();
  public static Package getPackage(String packageName);
  public static Package[] getPackages();
  public Boolean isCompatibleWith(String desired);
  //additional methods omitted for clarity
}
```

The version strings provide a minimal infrastructure you can use as a starting point when you are developing versioning semantics for your applications. All six well-known version strings can be set to any arbitrary String value; none has any semantics that are enforced by the current version of the SDK.

One of the six version strings provides a documented semantic. If you set the `specVersion` value to a dotted string, such as 1.0.2, you can use the `isCompatibleWith` API to see if a package is compatible with a particular version number. The specification version should be a dotted number such as 1.0.5, and the compatibility check uses a simple definition of compatibility, in which higher-numbered versions are always compatible with lower numbered ones. Although this usage of `specVersion` is documented, it is not enforced by the platform. For the other version strings, no semantics are even documented, and you can define any semantic that is convenient for you.

3.6.3 Sealing Packages

JAR files also support the process of *sealing* a package. When you seal a package, you guarantee that all the code from that package must come from the same location. This is valuable for versioning and security because it allows you to guarantee that your packages are not polluted by invalid or malicious versions of any classes. To seal a package, you add a `Sealed: true` pair to the metadata, somewhere after a package's `Name` field and before the next blank line, like so:

```
Name: com/develop/hello/
Sealed: true
```

You can also seal all packages in a JAR file by adding the `Sealed` entry to the main section of the manifest. For package sealing to take effect, you must use a class loader that honors the metadata in the JAR file, such as your good friend `URLClassLoader`.

Sealing all of your packages is a *very good idea*. Consider the following, all-too-common scenario. Version 2.0 of an application modifies several classes from version 1.0 while it also adds some new classes. Unfortunately, JAR files for both version 1.0 and version 2.0 are on the classpath. As a result, the virtual machine loads a mix of version 1.0 and version 2.0 classes, a sure recipe for trouble and confusion. If either version had sealed its packages, this configuration problem would have triggered an easily diagnosed error. Unless you specifically want to load package code from more than one JAR, always seal all application packages.

3.6.4 Weaknesses of the Versioning Mechanism

There are several problems with the versioning mechanism as it exists today. First, though the class loaders provided with the core API correctly propagate version information as described above, they do not automatically reject incompatible versions of a package, nor do they seek out compatible ones. Second, the `URLClassLoader` and subclasses do not load package information until *after* the first class in a particular package is loaded, so you have to load at least one class in a package before you can find out whether the package version actually meets your needs. Third, the text format for the manifest is not adequately validated; so for example, a spelling error in the name of a version field silently obliterates that field's information. The 1.4 version of Java is slated to have a built-in XML parser, which would permit a more structured manifest format. For the other problems, you will have to wait a while longer or address them in your own code. (§5.5.1 presents a more robust approach to versioning based on custom class loaders.)

3.7 Custom Metadata

The type information stored in a Java class file is very thorough, as far as it goes. When you first move to Java from a nonreflective programming environment, the new possibilities seem limitless. Knowing the names and types of all methods and fields makes it easy to implement all sorts of runtime services for your Java objects: XML views, object/relational mappings, generic user interfaces, and on and on. Nevertheless, it is possible to imagine wanting even *more* metadata.

Consider the hypothetical `LaunchVehicle` interface shown in Listing 3–27. As a human reader, you can infer several important details about how to use this interface. For example, you know to use liters when you `addFuel`. From your knowledge of the problem domain, you know that you should always `countdown` before you `launch`. These are important, contractual elements of the interface, but they do not have a standard language representation and are not part of the class metadata. You cannot count on clients always getting these details correct. Even if you could, some other important details of the design are *not* obvious to the reader. What units are to be used when calling `thrust`? Is it acceptable to `addFuel` during the `countdown`? This example illustrates the need for two kinds of metadata not available to the Java language: the correct units for numeric arguments, and tables of state transitions allowed by an interface. If these metadata elements were added to Java, the virtual machine could enforce the rules for you, eliminating two more sources of program errors.

Listing 3–27 The LaunchVehicle Interface

```
public interface LaunchVehicle {
  public void addFuel(int liters);
  public void countdown(int seconds);
  public void launch(int thrust);
  //etc.
}
```

It would be unreasonable to expect a Java virtual machine to support every possible flavor of useful class metadata. Virtual machines would need to be far more complex than they are today, and classes would carry around enormous amounts of metadata not useful to their problem domain. It was good design to limit the scope of the virtual machine's responsibilities; the line had to be drawn somewhere.

Fortunately, the virtual machine specification offers a hook for customization by permitting the addition of custom *attributes* to the class file format. Attributes can be any binary data, and they are housed in a data structure called an `attribute_info`. The `attribute_info` structure, shown in Listing 3–28, contains a constant pool index to a string that names the attribute, plus an opaque array of bytes containing the attribute's data. You can attach attributes to classes, methods, fields, or even to the bytecodes that implement a method.

Listing 3–28 The attribute_info Structure

```
//pseudocode from the JVM spec
attribute_info {
  u2 attribute_name_index;  //reference to constant pool
  u4 attribute_length;
  u1 info[attribute_length]; //custom data
}
```

Figure 3–6 is an expanded view of the binary class format diagram, originally presented in Figure 3–1, with custom attributes shown below the solid line. The virtual machine spec already defines some standard attributes for its own use. The bytecodes that implement a method are stored as an attribute, which can in turn have custom subattributes. The standard attributes defined by the specification are listed in Table 3–3.

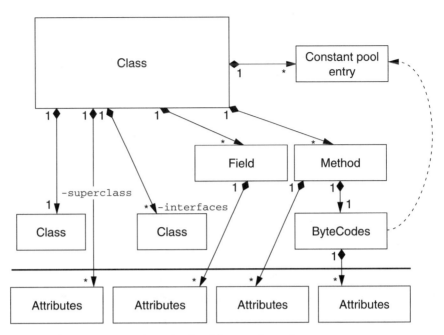

Figure 3–6   Custom metadata in the binary class format

Table 3–3   Attributes Defined by the Virtual Machine Specification

Attribute Name	Attibute Purpose
Code	Holds bytecodes that implement a method
ConstantValue	Holds value used to initialize a constant field
Exceptions	Lists checked exceptions a method may throw
InnerClasses	Links nested classes and outer classes
Synthetic	Marks methods not present in original source file
SourceFile	Holds name of original source file
LineNumberTable	Maps bytecode offsets to source line numbers
LocalVariableTable	Maps variables to source variable names
Deprecated	Marks deprecated class, field, or method

The Code, ConstantValue, and Exceptions attributes contribute to the documented semantics of class files and must be understood by conformant virtual machine implementations. The InnerClass and Synthetic attributes contribute to the semantics of the core API libraries and will therefore also be understood by compliant virtual machines.

The remaining standard attributes provide useful information, but they are not essential for the correct functioning of the language. For example, the SourceFile, LineNumberTable, and LocalVariableTable attributes enable source-level debuggers. Because these attributes are optional, they can be silently ignored by virtual machines that do not understand them. Any custom attributes that you develop must also be optional.

If a custom attribute were necessary for a class to function correctly, then a standard virtual machine would be unable to load a class that relied on the custom attribute. Such a custom attribute would encourage developers to write non-portable Java classes, defeating the write-once, run-anywhere nature of the language. It is legal to write custom tools that manipulate or even mandate custom attributes, but virtual machine implementations must silently ignore attributes that they do not recognize. The rules limit custom attributes to *optional* data that adds value when it is recognized by the virtual machine but does not break functionality when it is not. Even when they are operating within this constraint, custom attributes have many uses. They can store domain-specific metadata, debugging information, profiling information, documentation, and JIT optimization hints or hints that support interoperation with other programming environments.

Standard Java compilers will not emit your custom attributes, and the Reflection API provides no support for accessing them. If you want to define and use custom attributes, you will need to develop a development tool that injects attributes, a custom class loader that tracks attributes as classes are loaded, and extensions to reflection that can access these attributes at runtime.

Custom attributes are not in wide use today because they receive only limited support from the standard Java tools. Java compilers typically do not emit custom attributes, which is not surprising since there is no Java syntax for defining them. Programmers who want to add custom attributes must write their own tools to crack the class file format and inject attributes. Such tools are easy to write, and many are freely available, but none have the blessing of being standardized.

You are also on your own for extracting custom attributes. The Reflection API currently does not define methods for extracting custom attributes, although such methods are easy to design and add. Listing 3–29 shows part of the Java Class File Editor (JCFE). JCFE is an open source library developed by the author for manipulating custom attributes; see [JCFE] for details. The ClassEx augments the standard java.lang.Class class to include access to custom attributes, and the Attribute base class (not shown here) can be used as a subclass for different custom attributes that you design.

Listing 3–29 JCFE Methods for Custom Attributes

```
package com.develop.reflect;
public class ClassEx {
   public void addAttribute(Attribute ca);
   public Attribute[] getAttributes(String name);
   public Attribute[] getAttributes();
}
```

In order to access custom attributes at runtime, you need a custom class loader to extract them. A class loader sees the class file as a byte array during findClass, which provides a hook for manually parsing the class file and remembering any custom metadata. §5.5 develops a full example of this technique, using custom attributes and a custom class loader to automatically locate the correct version of a Java class.

Because the virtual machine must already parse the binary class format, parsing the class file a second time in a custom loader is inefficient. In an ideal world, access to custom attributes belongs in the platform, not in custom loaders. Hopefully a future version of Java will move custom attribute support into the core API.

3.8   Onward

Java reflection preserves name and type information in the compiled class format. This is an evolution from many pointer-based programming languages, which make compile-time assumptions about name and type that might fail to be true at runtime. The availability of class metadata makes the dynamic linking of code more reliable.

Most of the metadata in the class file is also exposed programmatically, via the Reflection API. Reflection includes both discovery and invocation. Reflective invocation can be used to write generic services that adapt themselves to the types they discover at runtime. Dynamic proxies extend the notion of a generic service further by allowing service classes to be manufactured at runtime. While reflective access is noticeably slower than direct access, it is fast enough to be used as the glue code between component, process, or network boundaries.

3.9   Resources

For more information on the binary class format, you should go straight to the source, and read the most recent version of the Java Virtual Machine Specification, which is [LY99] at the time of this writing. Although the virtual machine spec is most valuable for virtual machine developers, it is an invaluable read for all Java programmers.

To the author's knowledge, there are no books providing a treatment of the Reflection API that is complementary to the material presented here. There are, however, several tools that read and manipulate the binary class format, including [JCFE] and [CFParse].

Chapter 4

Serialization

Java serialization allows you to take the state of a Java object and write it into a byte stream. From the stream, you can later create a second Java object that has a state that is equivalent to the state of the original. This facility allows you to persist an instance to a file, transfer an object to another machine on the network, move an object from one class loader to another, or re-create the state of an object against a newer version of the code. In short, serialization lets you make components that are mobile. Several high-level Java technologies build on the backbone of serialization, including Remote Method Invocation (RMI), Java-Beans, Enterprise JavaBeans (EJB), and JINI.

4.1 Serialization and Metadata

Metadata plays two critical roles in serialization. First, serialization relies on class metadata and reflection to extract the state of an instance. In the common case, reflection does all the heavy lifting, and developers do not have to write any per-class serialization code. Unfortunately, the simplicity of basic serialization is deceptive. Java is designed to support dynamic, changing systems, which makes serialization more complex than it appears at first brush. In a dynamic system, it is possible for the receiver of a serialized object to not have the appropriate class. If this is the case, the receiver will need to know what sort of class loader it needs to create to access the class.

What is even worse than not having the class at all is the possibility that the receiver may have a different version of the class. If this occurs, the serialization architecture allows the developer to salvage the information in the stream, even if it does not correspond to the local definition of the class. Real applications may also need to customize an object's serialized format for performance, or to choose between pass-by-value and pass-by-reference semantics when they are passing objects from one virtual machine to another.

The second role that metadata plays is ensuring that the stream matches the receiver's expectations for a class. The serialization binary format defines its own metadata, which can be compared to the metadata in the binary class format. The serialization binary format makes it possible to recover an object's state, even if the code for a class is no longer available, or has changed. The serialization format also includes a number of hooks for customizing how objects are transmitted. This chapter will show you the basics of serialization, and then it will show you how to tweak serialization to improve performance, protect invariants, discover the location of necessary class files at runtime, and recover data if class files have changed since an object was serialized.

4.2 Serialization Basics

Not all Java classes are serializable. To indicate that you want a class to be serializable, you must implement the `java.io.Serializable` interface. This interface has no methods; rather, it simply acts as a marker interface indicating a class's willingness to have its instances serialized. In Listing 4–1, the `Person` class is serializable, but the `Humanoid` class is not. When an instance of `Person` is written to a stream, the serialization architecture uses reflection to extract the field values and write them to the stream.

Listing 4–1   The Humanoid and Person Classes

```
public abstract class Humanoid {
  protected int noOfHeads;
  private static int totalHeads;
  public Humanoid() {
    this(1);
  }
  public Humanoid(int noOfHeads) {
    if (noOfHeads > 10)
      throw new Error("Be serious. More than 10 heads?!");
    this.noOfHeads = noOfHeads;
    synchronized (Humanoid.class) {
```

```
      totalHeads += noOfHeads;
    }
  }
  public int getHeadCount() {
    return totalHeads;
  }
}
import java.io.*;
public class Person extends Humanoid
                    implements java.io.Serializable {
  private String lastName;
  private String firstName;
  private transient Thread workerThread;
  private static int population;
  public Person(String lastName, String firstName) {
    this.lastName = lastName;
    this.firstName = firstName;
    synchronized (Person.class) {
      population++;
    }
  }
  public String toString() {
    return "Person " + firstName + " " + lastName;
  }
  static synchronized public int getPopulation() {
    return population;
  }
}
```

Given that reflective access can work on *any* field of *any* object, there was no mechanical limitation that prevented the language designers from making all classes serializable. They did not do so for two reasons. First, some classes' instances contain resources that are local to a VM, process, or machine. Such classes wrap threads, files, sockets, database connections, and so on. There is no well-defined way to create a new instance from one of these objects that has state that is "equivalent" to the original object.

The second reason has to do with security. Some classes take the privateness of their private fields very seriously. Serialization provides a back door through which these fields can be accessed by writing them into a serialization stream and analyzing the stream's contents. Rather than force developers to worry about these issues for every class, the Java language simply considers objects *not* serializable by default.

To write a serializable object to a stream, you need to create an instance of `java.io.ObjectOutputStream`. `ObjectOutputStream` is a wrapper stream; its constructor takes an `OutputStream` argument that will actually receive data. This wrapper architecture makes it easy to use the same `ObjectOutputStream` class, regardless of whether you are serializing an object to a file, socket, or other destination.

The `WriteInstance` class in Listing 4–2 writes a `Person` to a file specified on the command line. The meat of this example is the call to `os.writeObject(p)`. It is that simple. If the object referenced by `p` were not serializable, the call would throw a `java.io.NotSerializableException`. Since the object referenced by `p` is of a serializable type, the object's state is extracted via reflection and written to `oos`, which in turn writes the state to a file specified on the command line. To verify that this works, you can read the object back in later using `ReadInstance`. You should see output showing that the state "Julius Drabbih" was recovered correctly.

Listing 4–2 The WriteInstance and ReadInstance Classes

```
import java.io.*;
public class WriteInstance {
  public static void main(String [] args) throws Exception
  {
    if (args.length != 1) {
      System.out.println("usage: java WriteInstance file");
      System.exit(-1);
    }
    FileOutputStream fos = new FileOutputStream(args[0]);
    ObjectOutputStream oos = new ObjectOutputStream(fos);
    Person p = new Person("Drabbih", "Julius");
    oos.writeObject(p);
  }
}
import java.io.*;
public class ReadInstance {
  public static void main(String [] args) throws Exception
  {
    if (args.length != 1) {
```

```
      System.out.println("usage: java ReadInstance filename");
      System.exit(-1);
    }
    FileInputStream fis = new FileInputStream(args[0]);
    ObjectInputStream ois = new ObjectInputStream(fis);
    Object o = ois.readObject();
    System.out.println("read object " + o);
  }
}
```

4.2.1 Serialization Skips Some Fields

Serialization does not necessarily read and write *all* class fields to the stream. There are three exceptions, all of which can be seen in Listing 4–1.

1. Base class fields are only handled if the base class itself is serializable. This is in keeping with the idea that a class should only be serializable if the class's author specifically makes it so. In our example, this has the odd consequence of making our `Person` forget how many heads he has. The `noOfHeads` field is part of a nonserializable base class, so serialization ignores it.[1]

2. Second, serialization ignores static fields because they are not part of any particular instance's state.[2] So, `Person`'s `population` field is not written to the stream.

3. You can use the `transient` keyword to disable serialization for specific fields. Normally, you will use `transient` if some of your class's instance fields do not have a logical serialized form. In the `Person` example, `workerThread` is marked transient because there is no standard notion of moving a thread from one VM or process to another. Note that even though `workerThread` is not written to the stream, it will still have a well-defined value of `null` when a `Person` is deserialized. When the Java virtual machine instantiates an object, object reference fields are initialized to `null`, numeric primitive fields to zero, and Boolean fields to `false`. This happens prior to any constructors or serialization code, guaranteeing that objects will have a well-defined initial state.

---

1. You can modify the default behavior and capture the fields from nonserializable base classes. (See §4.3).

2. Even if you wrote a static field during serialization, then what? When you read back in two different instances of a class, which one gets to set the one and only copy of the static field? Serialization doesn't happen for static fields because it does not have clear semantics.

4.2.2 Serialization and Class Constructors

An intriguing aspect of serialization is its relationship to constructors. It is an article of faith among Java programmers that Java objects are never created without a constructor invocation. This is essential for security because otherwise maleficent code could create invalid instances of core system classes in an attempt to destabilize the VM. Additionally, the promise that constructors will run is important to guarantee class invariants. Many constructors include checks to make sure that the object's state is valid, and later methods assume a valid state because they know that a constructor ran.

However sacred constructors may be, serialization does not always invoke them. You can verify this by adding a call to `System.out.println()` to the constructors for the `Humanoid` and `Person` classes used in Listing 4–1. If you do this and then rerun `WriteInstance` and `ReadInstance`, your session should look like Listing 4–3.

Listing 4–3 Deserialization Does Not Invoke Constructors

```
>java -cp classes WriteInstance Person.ser
Humanoid constructor ran
Person constructor called
>java -cp classes ReadInstance Person.ser
Humanoid constructor ran
read object Person Julius Drabbih
```

When `WriteInstance` uses `new` to create a `Person` object, the `Humanoid` and `Person` constructors both run, as expected. However, when `ReadInstance` reads the `Person` from the file, only the `Humanoid` constructor fires. What happened to `Person`'s constructor?

The answer is that serialization does not need to invoke `Person`'s constructor because it plans to assign `Person`'s fields from the stream anyway. Running a constructor for `Person` would be redundant at best. Moreover, notice that `Person` has no default constructor. How would deserialization synthesize arguments for a nondefault constructor?[3] If there were more than one constructor, which one would deserialization choose? Serialization avoids these pitfalls by

---

3. In this case it would be easy, but in general it would not.

skipping the constructor step altogether. It is able to do this without using an invalid bytecode sequence because it creates the object from native code, where the bytecode rules do not apply.

Note that Humanoid's constructor is still invoked because Humanoid is not serializable. Since serialization has no way to assign Humanoid's fields, it relies on Humanoid's default constructor. This implies one of the rules of serialization: If you mark a class Serializable, any nonserializable base classes of your class must have a default constructor.

In the simplest case, you would not worry about the various fields that serialization skips or the constructor behavior. This is because the goal of the architecture is to let developers simply mark their classes Serializable and then forget about them. However, the Person class demonstrates how quickly one can run afoul of the details. When a Person class is read from a serialized stream, there are two semantic problems that default serialization does not solve:

1. Humanoid's default constructor sets the number of heads the Person has to one. This defect might not manifest as a bug for quite a long time since most people do in fact have only one head. However, if and when the bug occurs it would be very confusing.

2. Person's population field is supposed to track the total number of people instantiated in a particular VM. Serialization bypasses Person's constructor, so population is not incremented.

Both of these problems necessitate some ability to customize the serialization process. Most of the rest of this chapter will be spent looking at various customization hooks, starting with one that can be used to solve the population problem.

4.3 Using readObject and writeObject

If a class wishes to add some custom code that runs when an object is read from serialization, it can implement the readObject method:

```
private void readObject(ObjectInputStream stream)
            throws IOException, ClassNotFoundException
```

Before it reads an object's state from the stream, `ObjectInputStream` uses reflection to check to see if the object's class implements `readObject`. If it does, `ObjectInputStream` simply calls `readObject` instead of executing normal deserialization.

When you implement `readObject`, you normally do two things:

1. Call back to `ObjectInputStream` and ask it to read the fields as in normal serialization.

2. Execute any custom steps that you wish to add to the deserialization process.

Listing 4–4 shows how to use `readObject` to deal with the `population` problem.

Listing 4–4   Using readObject as a Deserialization Constructor

```
import java.io.*;
public class Person extends Humanoid
                    implements java.io.Serializable {
  //repeat all code from original version of Person, plus:
  private void readObject(ObjectInputStream ois)
    throws IOException, ClassNotFoundException
  {
    ois.defaultReadObject();
    synchronized (Person.class) {
      population++;
    }
    System.out.println("Adjusting population in readObject");
  }
}
```

The call to `ois.defaultReadObject()` causes `ObjectInputStream` to read the field values from the stream and then to use reflection to assign the field values to the object. The call to increment `population` correctly tracks that a new instance of `Person` is alive in this VM.

You should add any per-instance validation code after the call to `default-ReadObject`. You should also use `readObject` to initialize any transient fields if Java's default values of `null/zero/false` are inappropriate for your object. Any invariant that you would check in a constructor should also be checked by `readObject`. In short, *treat readObject like a public constructor.*

4.4 Matching Streams with Classes

Serialization may involve loading classes if the instance being deserialized is of a type not already present in the virtual machine. The design for how classes are loaded is simple. The common case works without any special effort on the part of the programmer; the current class loader is simply asked to load the class whose name matches the class name in the serialization stream.

When deserialization triggers class loading, there are two problem cases to worry about. When the runtime attempts to load a class to deserialize an object, it might find a different version of the class than the one that serialized the object, or it might not find the class at all. This section will cover the former problem; the problem of finding classes is covered in §4.9.

Fortunately, the common case is handled trivially by the basic class loader architecture. When deserialization needs to load a class, it leverages implicit class loading; so, when `ReadInstance` needs to load `Person`, the virtual machine finds the class loader that loaded `ReadInstance` and tries to load `Person` with the same loader.

You can verify this using the custom version of `URLClassLoader` from §2.8.3. Listing 4–5 shows a run of `ReadInstance` with class loader logging turned on; note that the same loader loads `ReadInstance`, `Person`, and `Humanoid`. You might also try to read in the `Person` after deleting the Person.class file. If you do, deserialization will fail with a `ClassNotFoundException`. This proves that the default serialization mechanism does not embed the actual class file in the stream. If the receiver does not already have the binary class, it will not be able to deserialize the object.

Listing 4–5 Deserialization Leverages Implicit Class Loading.

```
{output clipped to show only relevant details}
>java -Xbootclasspath/p:boot/ -cp classes ReadInstance
>Person.ser
ReadInstance loaded by sun.misc.Launcher$AppClassLoader@ac738
Humanoid loaded by sun.misc.Launcher$AppClassLoader@ac738
Person loaded by sun.misc.Launcher$AppClassLoader@ac738
```

The serialized stream does not contain the entire binary format of the object's class. Nevertheless, there needs to be some way to detect if the class file that the sender used is the same as the one the receiver is using. The classes might have different fields, different methods, or different semantics, and in any of these situations, the receiver may be unable to deserialize a valid instance. This could be a fatal flaw in the architecture since the problems caused by such an invalid instance might percolate to distant parts of the system and be difficult to track down.

4.4.1 The serialVersionUID

To avoid this problem, serialization sends a fingerprint as part of the class metadata in the serialized stream. This fingerprint takes the form of a 64-bit value called the stream unique identifier, or serialVersionUID (SUID). The run-time calculates a SUID for a class using several pieces of class metadata, including the class name, class modifiers, superinterfaces, and the signatures of most fields, constructors, and methods. All of this metadata is written into a `java.io.DataOutputStream`, which is then hashed using the Secure Hash Algorithm (SHA-1). (This is an abridged version of what happens; the exact details are in the serialization spec. See [Ser] for details.) The important point is this: Almost any change to a class, other than editing a method's implementation, will cause the class's SUID to change. If the SUID for a class does not match the SUID from the stream, then deserialization will fail.

You can retrieve the SUID of a class with the command-line tool `serialver` as follows:

```
>serialver Person
Person: static final long serialVersionUID =
3880321542343815834L;
```

Now, try adding a new field to the `Person` class as demonstrated here:

```
private int age;
```

If you attempt to read in the old version of Person.ser using this changed `Person` class, you will get an exception like the one shown here:

```
java.io.InvalidClassException: Person;
  Local class incompatible:
  stream classdesc serialVersionUID=3880321542343815834
  local class serialVersionUID=8695226918703748744
```

The old version of the object does not have a value for age, and the `ObjectInputStream` would have no way to decide a reasonable value for age, so it rejects the attempt to deserialize a `Person`.

The last argument attributes too much intelligence to `ObjectInputStream`. The serialization architecture does not actually know that one version of the class had an `age` field and one did not; all it knows is that the SUIDs are different. This implies that even an innocuous change will break serialization. To see the problem, remove the `age` field from Person.java, and add the following method instead:

```
public void innocuousMethod() {}
```

This method does nothing at all; nevertheless, the SUID changes, and you can no longer read old versions of the class. The SUID is inexpensive, costing only 64 bits in the stream, but it is also a brute-force approach. From the perspective of the SUID, all changes are significant changes, and they all break serialization.[4]

It is interesting to compare serialization versioning to the class compatibility rules for class loading. When it is loading classes, the virtual machine uses the name and type information in the class file format to verify the linkage between classes. If there is a version mismatch, the error information can be quite precise, pinpointing the field or method that is missing. The SUID is another variant of this same idea, but it is compressed for efficient transmission. Because the metadata is hashed down to a single 64-bit value, serialization can only tell you that two classes are different—not what the difference is.

4.4.2 Overriding the Default SUID

If you make a change to a class that you know to be innocuous, you can assert its compatibility with older versions of the class by assigning an explicit `serialVersionUID` field. If you add a field with this signature

```
private static final long serialVersionUID = {somevalue}L;[5]
```

---

4. To be fair, there is a roughly 1 in 2^{64} chance that changing a class will *not* change the serialVersionUID, but don't hold your breath waiting for this.

5. The serialization specification states that the `serialVersionUID` field should be `private`, `static`, and `final`. However, the `serialver` tool omits the `private` keyword, and the implementation only verifies that the field is `static` and `final`.

to a class, the runtime will use this value instead of calculating the hash code. So, all you have to do to read a different version of a class is discover that class's SUID and set a `serialVersionUID` field to match. Discovering the original SUID is a snap because it is in the serialization stream, and it is also contained in the text of the `InvalidClassException` that is thrown when deserialization fails.

Armed with this information, you can create a new version of `Person` that is capable of reading the original version, as is shown in Listing 4–6. This version of `Person` has seen several changes from the original. The static and transient fields are gone, and the instance field `age` has been added. Nevertheless, this version of `Person` can be used to read the original `Person` from a stream because the matching `serialVersionUID` has been added.

Listing 4–6   Using an Explicit serialVersionUID

```
public class Person extends Humanoid
                    implements java.io.Serializable {
  static final long serialVersionUID=3880321542343815834L;
  private String lastName;
  private String firstName;
  private int age;  //this field is new to this version!
  public Person(String lastName, String firstName, int age) {
    this.lastName = lastName;
    this.firstName = firstName;
  }
  public String toString() {
    return "Person " + firstName + " " + lastName +
          " aged " + age;
  }
}
```

As soon as you deploy a second version of any serializable class, you will need to set the `serialVersionUID`. In fact, it is a good idea to manually set the `serialVersionUID` in the *first* version of a serializable class; you do this by running the `serialver` tool and pasting the result back into your source code. Calculating the SUID is expensive, and by setting it yourself, you can pay this cost once, at development time, instead of paying it the first time the class is serialized in each runtime.

4.4.3 Compatible and Incompatible Changes

Once you set the `serialVersionUID`, you are on your own to make sure that the old and new versions of the class are truly compatible. You have traded one problem for its opposite. Instead of all changes being considered bad, all changes are now considered OK. To add some order to this chaos, the serialization spec groups possible changes to a class into two categories: compatible and incompatible changes. *Compatible changes* include adding new serializable fields or adding or removing classes from the inheritance hierarchy. *Incompatible changes* include deleting fields, juggling the order of classes in the inheritance hierarchy, or changing the type of a primitive field. The two types of changes are summarized in Table 4–1.

Table 4–1 Compatible and Incompatible Changes

Type of Change	Examples
Compatible change	Adding fields, adding/removing classes, adding/removing `writeObject`/`readObject`, adding `Serializable`, changing access modifier, removing `static`/`transient` from a field
Incompatible change	Deleting fields, moving classes in a hierarchy, adding `static`/`transient` to a field, changing type of a primitive, switching between `Serializable` or `Externalizable`, removing `Serializable`/`Externalizable`, changing whether `readObject`/`writeObject` handles default field data, adding `writeReplace` or `readResolve` that produces objects incompatible with older versions

When you make a compatible change to a class, the runtime does the best job it can with the data it finds in the stream. For example, if you add a class to the inheritance hierarchy after serializing an instance, there will be no data in the stream for that class's data members. So, when you deserialize the object, the new class's members will be initialized to the default value appropriate to their type: `false` for Booleans, zero for numeric types, and `null` for references.

Similarly, if you add a serializable field, old versions of the object will not have a value for that field.

The new version of `Person` demonstrates this because it has added an `age` field. When you read an old `Person` stream into a new `Person` class, the `age` value will be zero as shown here:

```
read object Person Julius Drabbih aged 0
```

In the next section, you will see a more advanced use of `readObject` that can help deal with this situation.

Unfortunately, the serialization spec is unclear about what should happen when you make an incompatible change to a class. Based on the term "incompatible," you might expect that an incompatible change would cause deserialization to fail with an exception. In the Java 2 SDK, this is true for some, *but not all,* types of incompatible changes. For example, if you delete a field from the `Person` class, then the stream will have a value for that field, and nowhere to put it. Rather than throw an `InvalidClassException`, `ObjectInputStream` silently drops the field.

Most other incompatible changes will throw exceptions. The exact behavior of the Java 2 SDK version 1.3 for each type of incompatible change is summarized in Table 4–2. Since the spec is not clear in mandating these behaviors, other implementations might be different.

Table 4–2   How Java 2 SDK 1.3 Handles Incompatible Changes

Incompatible Change	Runtime Response
Deleting a field	Silently ignored
Moving classes in inheritance hierarchy	Exception
Adding `static`/`transient`	Silently ignored
Changing primitive type	Exception
Changing use of default field data	Exception
Switching `Serializable` and `Externalizable`	Exception
Removing `Serializable` or `Externalizable`	Exception
Returning incompatible class	Depends on incompatibility

COMPONENT DEVELOPMENT FOR THE JAVA™ PLATFORM

4.5 Explicitly Managing Serializable Fields

With default serialization, the mapping between class fields and stream fields is automatic and transparent. At serialization time, a field's name and type in the class become the field's name and type in the stream. The fields written by default serialization are called the *default field data*. At deserialization, a field's name and type in the stream are used to find the correct field to assign in the new instance.

The serialization API exposes hooks so that you can take control of any of these steps. Two nested classes do most of the work. `ObjectInput-Stream.GetField` allows you to explicitly manage pulling fields out of the stream, and `ObjectOutputStream.PutField` allows you to explicitly manage inserting fields into the stream.

`ObjectOutputStream.GetField` presents all the stream fields as name/value pairs. In order to access the stream in this fashion, you have to implement `readObject`, but instead of calling `defaultReadObject`, you call `read-Fields`. Then, it is up to you to extract each field by name and assign it to the appropriate field in the object. Consider the new version of `Person` in Listing 4–7. This version of `Person` stores both names in the single field `fullName`.

Listing 4–7   Person Using readFields to Handle Different Versions

```java
import java.io.*;
public class Person implements java.io.Serializable {
  private String fullName;
  static final long serialVersionUID=388032154234815834L;
  public Person(String fullName) {
    this.fullName = fullName;
  }
  public String toString() {
    return "Person " + fullName;
  }
  private void readObject(ObjectInputStream ois)
    throws IOException, ClassNotFoundException
  {
    ObjectInputStream.GetField gf = ois.readFields();
    fullName = (String) gf.get("fullName", null);
    if (fullName == null) {
      String lastName = (String) gf.get("lastName", null);
```

```
        String firstName = (String) gf.get("firstName", null);
        if ((lastName == null) || (firstName == null))
          throw new InvalidClassException("invalid Person");
        fullName = firstName + " " + lastName;
      }
    }
  }
```

The `readObject` method has been implemented to correctly read either new- or old-format streams. Instead of calling `defaultReadObject`, the `readObject` implementation begins with a call to `readFields`, which exposes the fields as a collection of name/value pairs. You can then extract the field values using a family of

```
type get(String name, type default)
```

methods, one for each primitive type and one for `Object`. The first call to `get` optimistically assumes that the stream version matches the class, and that `fullName` is available. If it is not, then `readObject` continues and tries to interpret the stream as the original `Person` version, extracting `firstName` and `lastName` fields. You can make your `readObject` implementations as complex as necessary, possibly handling multiple old versions of a class.

4.5.1 ObjectInputStream.GetField Caveats

There are two caveats to remember when you are using `ObjectInput-Stream.GetField` to manage fields. First, it is an all-or-nothing deal. If your class has 70 fields, there is no way to tell `ObjectInputStream` to "use `defaultReadObject` for these 65 fields, and let me handle the rest myself." Once you decide to call `readFields`, you have to assign all the fields yourself.[6]

The second caveat is that the `GetField.get` methods do not like field names that do not appear in *any* version of the class being deserialized. If you attempt to `get` a field that cannot be found in the stream and that field also cannot be found in the local version of the class, the runtime will throw an

---

6. The spec does not appear to mandate this behavior. In fact, the source for `readFields` has this comment: "TBD: Interlock w/ defaultReadObject." Perhaps a future version will allow you to call `defaultReadObject` and `readFields` for the same `Object`.

"`IllegalArgumentException`: no such field."[7] This situation is likely if you are dealing with three or more versions of a class over time. To handle this situation, wrap calls to `get` inside a `try` block.

4.5.2 Writer Makes Right

When you use `readObject` and `GetField` to control deserialization, the writer of an object does not worry about the stream format, instead, it leaves the reader to make things right. This can be more efficient than having the writer try to guess the format; if the writer guesses incorrectly, the result is that both writer *and* reader do extra work. However, the reader-makes-right approach has a disadvantage as well. While new versions of a class can read either old or new versions from the stream, an old version of a class cannot handle a newer version of the stream format.

If your design does not permit you to update all versions of a class everywhere, then you may need to code newer versions of a class to respect the original format. Serialization provides a hook for this with `GetField`'s mirror image, the `PutField` class. You customize serialization output by implementing `readObject`'s counterpart, `writeObject`:

```
private void writeObject(ObjectOutputStream oos)
        throws IOException;
```

The `PutField` class has a set of `put` methods that write field values to the stream. Listing 4–8 shows a version of `Person` that uses `writeObject` to control which fields are serialized. The first line of `writeObject` retrieves the `PutField` instance that is used to write objects to the stream. Then, the `put` method is used to assign name/value pairs, and the `writeFields` method adds all the fields to the stream. By implementing both `readObject` and `writeObject`, this new version of `Person` continues to both read and write the format established by the original version of `Person`.

---

7. This is an unnecessary complication. There are other ways to find out if the field exists in the stream or class; `GetField.get` would be easier to use if it always handled not finding the field by returning the default value passed as its second parameter.

Listing 4–8   Using writeObject for Backward Compatibility

```java
import java.io.*;
public class Person implements java.io.Serializable {
  private String fullName;
  static final long serialVersionUID=388032154234815834L;
  public Person(String lastName, String firstName) {
    this.fullName = firstName + " " + lastName;
  }
  public String toString() {
    return "Person " + fullName;
  }
  private static final ObjectStreamField[]
    serialPersistentFields
    = {new ObjectStreamField("firstName", String.class),
        new ObjectStreamField("lastName", String.class)};
  private void writeObject(ObjectOutputStream oos)
      throws IOException
  {
    ObjectOutputStream.PutField pf = oos.putFields();
    int delim = fullName.indexOf(" ");
    String firstName = fullName.substring(0, delim);
    String lastName = fullName.substring(delim+1);
    pf.put("firstName", firstName);
    pf.put("lastName", lastName);
    oos.writeFields ();
  }
  private void readObject(ObjectInputStream ois)
    throws IOException, ClassNotFoundException
  {
    ObjectInputStream.GetField gf = ois.readFields();
    String lastName = (String) gf.get("lastName", null);
    String firstName = (String) gf.get("firstName", null);
    if ((lastName == null) || (firstName == null))
    throw new InvalidClassException("invalid Person");
    fullName = firstName + " " + lastName;
  }
}
```

4.5.3 Overriding Class Metadata

Using the `writeObject` method introduces one additional complexity not present when using `readObject`. You cannot just write any field name and type that you choose; you can only write fields whose names and types are part of the class metadata. This information cannot be modified at runtime because class metadata is only written to a stream once; later references to the same class simply reference the original metadata. Remember that by default serialization will use reflection to discover the names and types of a class's nonstatic, nontransient fields.

If you want to bypass reflection and specify the class serialization metadata directly, you must specify the class field

```
private static final ObjectStreamField[] serialPersistentFields
```

The runtime will discover the `serialPersistentFields` array by reflection, and it will use them to write the class metadata to the stream.

`ObjectStreamField` is a simple collection class that contains a `String` holding a field name and a `Class` holding a field type. In the `Person` example in Listing 4–8, `writeObject` needs to write `firstName` and `lastName` to the stream, so `serialPersistentFields` is set to contain appropriate `ObjectStreamField` instances. If you change the class metadata by setting `serialPersistentFields`, you must also implement `writeObject` to write instance fields that match your custom metadata, and you must implement `readObject` to read those fields. If you don't, `ObjectOutputStream` will try to reflect against your class, find fields that do not match the metadata, and fail with an `InvalidClassException`.

4.5.4 Performance Problems

The current SDK implementations of `GetField` and `PutField` perform poorly. The class metadata, whether generated by reflection or specified explicitly via `serialPersistentFields`, is stored as an instance of `ObjectStreamClass`. Instead of using an efficient hash table, `ObjectStreamClass` stores the field information in a sorted array and uses a binary search to find fields at runtime. If you make heavy use of `GetField` and `PutField`, these binary searches become the primary bottleneck when serializing an object.

The default serialization mechanism does not pay this penalty because it makes a linear traversal of the sorted array. Unfortunately, this linear traversal is not accessible to user code. This implementation defect may be repaired in a future version of the SDK.

4.5.5 Custom Class Descriptors

In addition to instance-specific metadata hooks, serialization also provides a mechanism for customizing the reading and writing of class metadata. This mechanism is rarely used because it requires matching modifications to both input and output streams, and it makes your streams usable only by stream subclasses that use the modified version. Consult the API documentation for details under `ObjectOutputStream`'s `writeClassDescriptor` and `ObjectInputStream`'s `readClassDescriptor`.

4.6 Abandoning Metadata

In all the scenarios discussed so far, class metadata is part of the serialization format. The first time an instance of a particular class is written, the class metadata is also written, including the class name, SUID, field names, and field types. When default serialization is used, the field names are discovered by reflection, and the SUID is calculated by taking an SHA-1 hash of the class metadata. When you override these behaviors by specifying `serialVersionUID` or `serialPersistentFields`, you are not eliminating metadata. Instead, you are just taking explicit control of what the metadata looks like.

The serialization mechanism also provides several hooks that allow you to skip sending metadata at all. This section will show you various techniques for reducing metadata, and then it will explain why you should avoid these techniques in most cases. There are three techniques for bypassing metadata: adding data after `defaultWriteObject`, making your object `Externalizable`, and replacing `defaultWriteObject` entirely.

4.6.1 Writing Custom Data after defaultWriteObject

The first technique, adding data after `defaultWriteObject`, allows you to make ad hoc extensions to an instance's serialization packet. `ObjectOutputStream` and `ObjectInputStream` implement `DataOutput` and `DataInput`, respectively. These interfaces provide helper methods for reading and writing primitive types. Return to the original `Person` example from Listing 4–1. One of `Person`'s problems was that the `Humanoid` base class data was not written to the stream. You could solve this problem by adding extra lines to `readObject` and `writeObject` like this:

```
//add to Person.java. This is _not_ a great design!
private void writeObject(ObjectOutputStream oos)
  throws IOException
{
  oos.defaultWriteObject();
  oos.writeInt(noOfHeads);
}
private void readObject(ObjectInputStream ois)
  throws IOException, ClassNotFoundException
{
  ois.defaultReadObject();
  noOfHeads = ois.readInt();
  System.out.println("had " + noOfHeads + " heads");
}
```

After calling `defaultWriteObject` to write the standard fields and metadata, the call to `writeInt` simply tacks on an extra piece of data. Similarly, the call to `readInt` extracts that extra data item. Unlike `Person`'s `lastName` and `firstName` fields, this extra data travels naked—without any metadata describing what it is. This means that somebody with a different version of the class (or no version of the class at all) will be unable to determine what the int value in the stream means. In fact, a reader without this exact version of the class probably cannot even tell if the value is an int, as opposed to two shorts or four bytes. A more flexible solution to this problem is to use `serialPersistentFields` and `PutField` as discussed in the previous section. That way, you can explicitly guarantee that the correct metadata is present, which will vastly increase the chances that a reader of your stream will be able to interpret the data.

4.6.2 Externalizable

A more heavy-handed approach to bypassing metadata is to declare that your class implements `java.io.Externalizable`, which extends `Serializable`. When you implement `Externalizable`, you make your class `Serializable`, but you also take full responsibility for transmitting data and metadata for that class and for transmitting data and metadata for any base class data and metadata. You must explicitly manipulate the stream using `Externalizable`'s two methods, shown here:

```
public void writeExternal(ObjectOutput out)
            throws IOException;
public void readExternal(ObjectInput in)
            throws IOException, ClassNotFoundException;
```

For our old friend `Person`, these methods might be implemented as shown in Listing 4–9. There are several important points to notice in this example.

1. The `Person` class deals explicitly with all fields for itself and its base classes.

2. Because the `readExternal` method must be declared public, malicious or ignorant code might invoke the `readExternal` method at any time, blasting some arbitrary state into your object.

3. An `Externalizable` class must have a public constructor.[8]

4. Finally, *no metadata is written*. Only the actual value of the fields is written to the stream.

Listing 4–9   Externalizable Version of Person

```
public class Person extends Humanoid
                    implements java.io.Externalizable
{
  //other fields, methods, as before
  public Person() { /*required! */}
  public void readExternal(ObjectInput oi)
    throws IOException
  {
    lastName = oi.readUTF();
    firstName = oi.readUTF();
    noOfHeads = oi.readInt();
  }
```

---

8. The requirements that methods be public and that `Externalizable` objects have a public constructor are completely out-of-step with the rest of serialization. Most other serialization behaviors and customizations are implemented using reflection and naming conventions. Because serialization can use reflection to bypass language protections, it can hide its details in private methods. The designer of externalization must have momentarily forgotten about these advantages.

```
public void writeExternal(ObjectOutput oo)
  throws IOException, ClassNotFoundException
{
  oo.writeUTF(lastName);
  oo.writeUTF(firstName);
  oo.writeInt(noOfHeads);
}
}
```

Using `Externalizable` introduces three dangers:

1. Other versions of the class may not be able to figure out what is in the stream.

2. Generic tools that analyze serialization streams will have to skip over `Externalizable` data, treating it as an opaque array of bytes.

3. It is easy to introduce bugs when writing `Externalizable` code. If you write the fields out in one order, and then read the fields back in a different order, the best you can hope for is that the stream will break. If the wrong ordering is type-compatible with the correct ordering, you will silently assign data to the wrong fields.

Given all of the dangers of `Externalizable` objects, what purpose do they serve? In some situations, `Externalizable` objects offer better serialization performance. Skipping metadata has three potential performance benefits:

1. The stream is smaller because the metadata is not present.

2. There is no need to reflect over metadata for the class.

3. There is no need to use reflection on a per-instance basis to extract and assign values from fields.

How much actual performance benefit you get from externalizing a class will depend heavily on how that class is used, when it is serialized, and what type of stream `ObjectOutputStream` is wrapping. In many cases, the performance benefit will be negligible. Externalization should never be your first option; only consider it when your application is functioning correctly and you have profiling data to prove that externalization provides an essential speedup. The most likely place for externalization is for simple classes that never change, so for them, metadata is not important.

4.6.3   Using writeObject to Write Raw Data Only: Bad Idea

The third option for bypassing metadata is to implement writeObject to write data directly, without first calling defaultWriteObject or putFields to invoke the normal metadata mechanism. You should *never* use this option. The ability to write data in this way was an unintended loophole in the serialization specification. Unfortunately, this technique is used in a few places in the core API, so the spec is not likely to preclude this tactic anytime soon.

Listing 4–10 shows this technique. This version of Person uses the readObject and writeObject hooks for serialization-with-metadata, but the code looks like it belongs in an Externalizable object instead. You should never write code like this. If you truly want to bypass all metadata, you should (1) reconsider one last time; then (2) implement Externalizable.

Listing 4–10   Bad Style in writeObject

```
public class Person extends Humanoid
                    implements java.io.Serializable
{
  //other fields, methods, as before
  private void readObject(ObjectInputStream ois)
    throws IOException
  {
    lastName = ois.readUTF();
    firstName = ois.readUTF();
    noOfHeads = ois.readInt();
  }
  private void writeObject(ObjectOutputStream oos)
    throws IOException, ClassNotFoundException
  {
    oos.writeUTF(lastName);
    oos.writeUTF(firstName);
    oos.writeInt(noOfHeads);
  }
}
```

To understand the problem with this use of writeObject, you need to look at the details of serialization's binary format. The binary format relies on the following assumptions about objects that implement writeObject.

1. The default field data will occur exactly once, and it will occur first. There is no need for a special marker in the binary format because this data will always be present. The implication for developers is that you should always begin your `writeObject` implementation with a call to `defaultWrite-Object`, or with calls to the `PutField` nested class that do essentially the same thing.

2. If custom data is present, it will follow after the normal serialization data. Because custom serialization data is optional, the byte flag `TC_BLOCKDATA` indicates the beginning of custom data.

If you do violate these assumptions in your own code, either by writing to the `ObjectOutputStream` before writing the normal data, or by never writing the normal data at all, your code will still execute correctly. However, if anyone ever tries to read your stream without having the original class, they stand a 1-in-256 chance of being stymied.

If the first byte of your instance's serialized data happens to be the constant `TC_BLOCKDATA`, readers cannot depend on metadata to tell them what they are looking at, as demonstrated by Figure 4–1. Maybe that first byte is the beginning of some custom data, or maybe it is the beginning of normal data that just happens to start with that value. The benefit of metadata is lost because now readers must have a class file that knows how the original stream was produced. In your own code, you should obey the intent of the specification, and always write normal serialization data first.

I would summarize the options for avoiding metadata as ranging from bad, to worse, to worst.

- Bad: If you implement `writeObject` to first write the normal serialization data, and then use the stream's `DataOutput` capabilities to tack on extra data, your serialization stream will be an odd hybrid. The normal data will include metadata, and the extra data will not.

- Worse: If you implement `Externalizable`, you lose all metadata benefits, you have to handle base classes yourself, and you must write (and debug!) a lot of per-class code. However, both of these options have their uses. Appending extra data to `writeObject` is slightly easier than using `serialPersistentFields` to provide full metadata, and it may be suitable if you value development speed over flexibility. `Externalizable` objects may be enough faster and smaller that you are willing to deal with inflexible, error-prone code.

- Worst: Never violate the spirit of the specification by skipping the normal serialization data in your `writeObject` implementation. If you do, it will be impossible for a generic tool to reliably extract the data from the stream.

Do not throw metadata away. Instead of using the techniques explained here, use the metadata-friendly techniques described in §4.5.

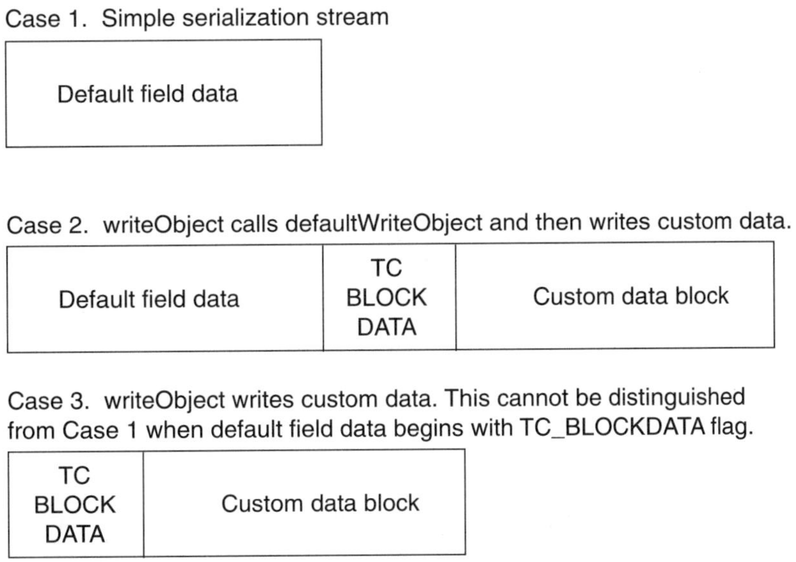

Case 1. Simple serialization stream

Default field data

Case 2. writeObject calls defaultWriteObject and then writes custom data.

Default field data	TC BLOCK DATA	Custom data block

Case 3. writeObject writes custom data. This cannot be distinguished from Case 1 when default field data begins with TC_BLOCKDATA flag.

TC BLOCK DATA	Custom data block

Figure 4–1 Streams generated by WriteObject

4.7 Object Graphs

Serialization is recursive. When you serialize an object, all of its serializable fields are also serialized. Primitives are serialized by the `DataOutput` methods of the stream, and objects are serialized by `writeObject`. This fact is implicit in the `Person` example of this chapter, since `lastName` and `firstName` are themselves object types, not primitives. Recursion to referenced objects is highly desirable because it simplifies serializing complex graphs of objects all in one step. However, the fact that `writeObject` actually serializes an entire *graph* of objects introduces a few wrinkles that you need to be aware of.

The first issue is the danger of serializing far more data than you wanted. Consider a data object that lives inside a hierarchical container:

```java
public class PhotonTorpedo implements Serializable {
  private int range;
  private int power;
  private Starship ship;
  //etc.
}
```

In this design, all `PhotonTorpedo`s are contained by a `Starship`. Perhaps each `Starship` in turn belongs to a `Fleet`. This is a perfectly reasonable model, but when you serialize a `PhotonTorpedo`, you wind up attempting to serialize all the other weapons on the `Starship`, and all the other `Starship`s in the `Fleet`. If a single one of these connected instances is not serializable, serialization will fail with a `NotSerializableException`. More amusingly, if the entire graph *is* serializable, you will wind up scratching your head wondering why a `PhotonTorpedo` takes up 48.7MB on disk, or why it takes four hours to send one over the network!

4.7.1 Pruning Graphs with Transient

If the reader does not care about containers like the `Starship`, you can use the `transient` keyword to block serialization of container references like `ship`. Once `ship` is marked `transient`, you probably will also need to add code to `readObject` or `readExternal` to correctly reinitialize the value of `ship` at deserialization time.

4.7.2 Preserving Identity

Another situation that arises when you are serializing an entire object graph is the possibility that the same instance might be serialized more than once.[9] Consider the following additions to the `Person` class:

```java
public class Person {
  private Person spouse;
  private Person boss;
}
```

---

9. Of course, this can also happen if you simply call `writeObject` twice on the same object.

In this situation, it is very likely that `spouse` and `boss` are the same Java identity. However, serialization only writes the state once, and it uses that state to reinitialize both references when the object is deserialized. To track identity, each object is assigned a numeric token the first time it is written. When the same object needs to be written again, only the token needs to be written to the stream.

There are three reasons why the architecture works this way:

1. Sending the state only once is more efficient.

2. Sending the state only once provides more intuitive semantics. If I deserialize a `Person` and call `p.getSpouse().appease()`, I expect both the `spouse` and the `boss` to be appeased. This will only work if a single instance is deserialized and assigned to both references.

3. Failing to track object identity will lead to an infinite loop if there are circular references. Consider the `Person` example again. When you serialize a `Person`, you recursively serialize the `spouse` instance. But `spouse` is also a `Person`, so you end up serializing `Person.spouse.spouse`, which (hopefully!) is the original `Person` again. Serialization has to recognize that this is a `Person` it has seen before, or else it will run in circles until it blows the stack.

4.7.3 Encouraging the Garbage Collector with reset

Because Java tracks object identities and does not write an instance to the stream more than once, all these problems are solved without any effort on the programmer's part. However, the tracking mechanism must keep a reference to every object ever written to a stream.[10] As a result, no object that is written to an object stream can be garbage collected! In a long running application that uses serialization, this can cause poor performance and may eventually lead to an `OutOfMemoryError`. In order to avoid this problem, `ObjectOutputStream` provides a `reset` method.

```
public void reset() throws IOException
```

---

10. This is not strictly true. The design could have used a `java.lang.ref.WeakReference` to track streamed objects while still allowing them to be garbage collectable. This option was rejected as unnecessarily expensive in the general case.

When you call `reset`, the stream nulls its internal table of already-written objects. If an object is written to the stream before and after the reset point, the object's state will be written twice, and the receiver will see two different object identities. If this identity-destroying behavior is desirable or acceptable in your application, then you can call `reset` regularly to allow streamed objects to be garbage collected. If this behavior is *not* desirable, you will have to carefully coordinate calls to `reset` to preserve the semantics required by the receiver.

The relationship between `reset` and garbage collection is needlessly complex in older versions of Java. For example, in SDK version 1.3, the following rules apply:

1. If an `ObjectOutputStream` is no longer reachable, then its references to streamed objects will no longer prevent them from being garbage collected. This is just vanilla GC behavior.

2. Calling `close` on an object stream does *not* `reset` the stream! If you want to free resources in a timely fashion, you must explicitly call `reset`, in addition to explicitly calling `close`.

3. Calling `reset` does *not* immediately clear the references to objects that have been streamed. This is an unfortunate accident of the `ObjectOutputStream`'s nested `HandleTable` implementation, which marks the table as empty without explicitly setting references to null. As a result, objects that pass through an object stream will only be collectable if a call to `reset` is followed by streaming some additional objects through to overwrite the old references.

These rules are demonstrated by the `YouMustReset` class in the accompanying source code. Note that rules 2 and 3 are inferred from the source code, not mandated by the serialization spec. The memory management problems of `close` and `reset` are fixed in the 1.4 version of Java. In 1.4, calling `close` does clear the object table and null out all old references. So, rules 2 and 3 apply only to versions of Java prior to 1.4.

4.8 Object Replacement

Both object streams and objects themselves have the ability to nominate replacement objects at serialization time. This object replacement feature has many uses. If your object graph contains an object that is not serializable, you can replace it with an object that is serializable. If you are doing distributed programming, you can replace an object's state with an object's stub, causing the receiver to get a reference to the remote object, instead of a local by-value copy of the object. RMI uses object replacement for this purpose. Replacement may also be useful if you want to add additional semantics to serialization that go beyond the capabilities of the `readObject` and `writeObject` methods.

4.8.1 Stream-Controlled Replacement

You can implement stream-controlled object replacement by subclassing `ObjectOutputStream` and/or `ObjectInputStream`. The relevant methods are shown in Listing 4–11. You must call the `enableReplaceObject` and `enableResolveObject` methods to turn replacement on or off; the default is off. These methods also act as a chokepoint for a security check. Because a stream might use object replacement to corrupt an object graph, the `enable` methods require that the caller have the `SerializablePermission` `"enableSubstitution"`.[11]

Listing 4–11   Stream-Level Object Replacement APIs

```
package java.io;
public class ObjectOutputStream {
  //ObjectOutputStream replacement methods
  protected boolean enableReplaceObject(boolean enable);
  protected Object replaceObject(Object obj);
  //rest of class omitted for clarity
}

public classs ObjectInputStream {
  //ObjectInputStream replacement methods
  protected boolean enableResolveObject(boolean enable);
  protected Object resolveObject(Object obj);
  //rest of class omitted for clarity
}
```

---

11. See [Gon99] for a detailed explanation of Java 2 permissions.

To actually perform replacement and resolution, you override `replaceObject` and `resolveObject`, respectively. If replacement is enabled, these methods will be called once for every object serialized to the stream, allowing you to substitute a different object. You may substitute any object you want. However, if you replace an object with an object that is not type-compatible, you will need to resolve it back to a type-compatible reference or the stream will throw an exception.

One use of stream-controlled replacement is to serialize an object that would not otherwise be serializable. Consider the `SimplePerson` class in Listing 4-12. If you tried to serialize a `SimplePerson`, a normal object stream would throw a `NotSerializableException`. If you control the source for `SimplePerson`, you can fix this by declaring that `SimplePerson` implements `Serializable`. If you do not have control of the source code, the next best thing to do is to replace the `SimplePerson` instance with some other class instance that is serializable.

Listing 4–12 Serializing a Nonserializable Instance

```java
public interface PersonItf {
  public String getFullName();
}

public class SimplePerson implements PersonItf {
  String fullName;
  public SimplePerson(String fullName) {
    this.fullName = fullName;
  }
  public String getFullName() {
    return fullName;
  }
}

import java.io.*;
public class WriteSimplePerson {
  private static class Replacer extends ObjectOutputStream {
    public Replacer(OutputStream os) throws IOException {
      super(os);
      enableReplaceObject(true);
    }
```

```java
    protected Object replaceObject(Object obj) {
      if (obj instanceof PersonItf) {
        PersonItf p = (PersonItf) obj;
        return new StreamPerson(p.getFullName());
      }
      return obj;
    }
  }
  public static void main(String[] args)
    throws IOException
  {
    FileOutputStream fos = new FileOutputStream
        (args[0]);
    ObjectOutputStream oos = new Replacer(fos);
    oos.writeObject(new SimplePerson("Fred Wesley"));
  }
}

public class StreamPerson implements java.io.Serializable,
PersonItf {
  String fullName;
  public StreamPerson(String fullName) {
    this.fullName = fullName;
  }
  public String getFullName() {
    return fullName;
  }
  public String toString() {
    return "StreamPerson " + fullName;
  }
}
```

The `WriteSimplePerson` class in Listing 4–12 demonstrates using replacement to cope with an instance that is not serializable. The `Replacer` class checks to see if an object implements `PersonItf`. If it does, then `Replacer` replaces it with the `StreamPerson` class, which is known to be `Serializable`. You could implement a corresponding `Resolver` subclass of `ObjectInputStream` to convert the object back to a `SimplePerson` at deserialization time. However, in this example there is probably no need to do so. If the receiver is expecting only a `PersonItf`, then `StreamPerson` is just as good as `SimplePerson`. The `ReadInstance` class from Listing 4–2 certainly doesn't care since it never casts the result to anything more specific than

`Object`. If you use `WriteSimplePerson` to create a file SimplePerson.ser, `ReadInstance` will happily deserialize a `StreamPerson` as shown here:

```
java -cp classes ReadInstance SimplePerson.ser
read object StreamPerson Fred Wesley
```

As long as type relationships are maintained, replacement is totally transparent for the reader. As far as `ReadInstance` knows, there never was any class other than `StreamPerson` involved. If the receiver did want to cast an object to the original implementation class, or if the object was referenced via its specific subtype in an object graph, then a resolution step would also be necessary to convert the stream type back into the type expected by the reader.

The usage of replacement without resolution opens an interesting possibility. Imagine that there are hundreds of implementations of the `PersonItf` interface, and that some of them are very large and expensive to serialize. One mechanism to trim down the cost of serializing the various classes would be to go through the source code marking fields `transient`. However, `transient` is a property of the field itself, not of any particular instance. If different clients care about different fields, you cannot selectively set the `transient` bit at runtime. Because you cannot use `transient` selectively, you end up having to serialize all the fields, even though any particular client might only care about some subset.

Object replacement allows you to customize serialization on a per-stream basis, unlike the `transient` keyword, which operates on a per-class basis. Look again at the `Replacer` class. It replaces *all* `PersonItf` implementations with `StreamPerson`s. If you know in advance that the receiver of an object stream cares only about the `PersonItf`ness of objects, then the `Replacer` class saves you from worrying about whether a particular `PersonItf` is serializable, and it gives serialization a predictable cost.

4.8.2 Class-Controlled Replacement

Replacement at the class level is syntactically very similar to stream-level replacement. A class that desires replacement implements the methods in Listing 4–13. Like many serialization hooks, these methods are not part of any interface and are discovered by reflection.[12] The type compatibility rules for class-

---

12. This is also why the access modifier does not matter.

level object replacement are the same as for stream-level replacement. If you replace an object, you need to make sure that the replacement is, or later resolves to, a type expected by the receiver.

Listing 4–13   Class-Level Object Replacement Hooks

```
ANY-ACCESS Object writeReplace()
                  throws ObjectStreamException;
ANY-ACCESS Object readResolve()
                  throws ObjectStreamException;
```

Class-level replacement has several important differences from stream-based replacement. Because it operates at the level of the class being serialized, you can use class-level replacement only if you have access to the source code for the class being replaced. On the positive side, no security check is necessary; since all the relevant code is in the same class, it is assumed to be within a single trust boundary.

Classes use the class-level object replacement mechanism to separate their serialized form from their in-memory representation. Explicitly coding a separate serialized form may be useful if a class has complex serialization code, or serialization code that is shared with other classes.

Another place where class-level replacement is useful is in designs that rely on object identity, such as certain implementations of the singleton design pattern. A *singleton* is a unique object in a system, often represented by a single object identity. Deserialization creates new object identities, so if a singleton is deserialized more then once, its unique identity is lost.

Object resolution can be used to patch this situation, as shown in Listing 4–14. The author of the `Planet` class wants to guarantee that there are only two singleton `Planet`s in the entire VM: `earth` and `mars`. To prevent accidental planet creation, `Planet`'s constructor is marked private. For a nonserializable class, this would be good enough, but remember that serialization acts like a public constructor. When a `Planet` is deserialized, the serialization architecture creates a new instance and populates its fields by reflection.

If `earth` were deserialized twice, there would be two different object identities holding the same `earth` state. This could cause program bugs if code relies on reference equality to compare `Planet`s, and at the very least it wastes memory with unnecessary copies of semantically identical `Planet`s. The `re-solve-Object` method sidesteps this problem by looking up the singleton `Planet` and returning it instead. Because of this, the `Planet` reference created by deserialization is never visible to client code and is available for garbage collection.

Listing 4–14   Using Class-Controlled Resolution to Preserve Identity

```
import java.io.*;
public class Planet implements Serializable {
  String name;
  private static final earth = new Planet("Earth");
  private static final mars = new Planet("Mars");
  private Planet(String name) {
    this.name = name;
  }
  public static Planet getEarth() {
    return earth;
  }
  public static Planet getMars() {
    return mars;
  }
  private Object readResolve() throws IOException
  {
    if (name.equals("Earth"))
      return earth;
    if (name.equals("Mars"))
      return mars;
    throw new InvalidObjectException("No planet " + name);
  }
}
```

4.8.3   Ordering Rules for Replacement

Object replacement has a number of ordering rules that you must take into account if you are doing any nontrivial replacements.[13]

1. *Class*-level replacement is invoked prior to *stream*-level replacement. This is the only sensible ordering; letting the stream go first could violate a class's internal assumptions about how it will be serialized. Similarly, class-level resolution occurs prior to stream-level resolution.

---

13. These ordering rules live in a gray area between the specification and a specific implementation's detail. I would expect most vendors to follow the SDK's lead, but if you are relying on these behaviors it wouldn't hurt to test them on each Java implementation you plan to support.

2. Class-level *replacement* is recursive; that is, a replacement can nominate another replacement and so on ad infinitum. Class-level *resolution* is not recursive.[14]

3. Stream-level replacement/resolution is not recursive. Streams get exactly one chance to replace/resolve an object.

4. During serialization, objects are replaced as they are encountered. During deserialization, objects are replaced only after they are fully constructed.

These rules are shown graphically in Figure 4–2 and Figure 4–3.

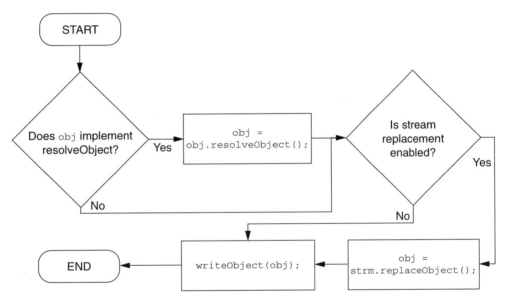

Figure 4–2   Choosing a replacement for obj during serialization

Rules 2 and 4 have asymmetries that are counterintuitive. While class replacement executes recursively, class resolution does not. So, if class A nominates replacement B, and B nominates replacement C, the only way you can force C to resolve to A is in a single step.

---

14. This behavior has an odd history. In SDK version 1.2, neither replacement nor resolution were recursive. This was reported as bug ID 4217737, and subsequently "fixed" in SDK 1.3 Beta. While the bug report asked that both behaviors be made recursive, only replacement was changed.

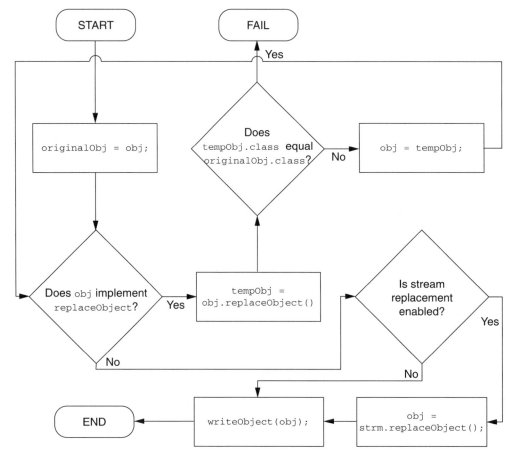

Figure 4–3   Resolving obj

Rule 4 implies that an object graph with both circular references and object replacement may be impossible to deserialize correctly. Consider the `Worker` and `Boss` classes in Listing 4–15.

Listing 4–15   Circular References May Cause Problems During Resolution.

```
import java.io.*;
public class Worker implements PersonItf, Serializable {
  private String name;
  private PersonItf boss;
  public Worker(String name, PersonItf boss) {
    this.name = name;
    this.boss = boss;
```

```java
      }
      public String toString() {
        return "Worker " + name + " (boss " + boss.getFullName()+")";
      }
      private Object writeReplace() {
        System.out.println("Replacing worker");
        return new WireWorker(name, boss);
      }
      public String getFullName() {
        return name;
      }
      public PersonItf getBoss() {
        return boss;
      }
  }

  import java.io.*;
  import java.util.*;
  public class Boss implements PersonItf, Serializable {
    private String name;
    private ArrayList workers = new ArrayList();
    public Boss(String name) {
      this.name = name;
    }
    public String toString() {
      StringBuffer sb = new StringBuffer("Boss " +
                          name + ", workers:");
      for (int n=0; n<workers.size(); n++) {
        sb.append("\n\t").append(workers.get(n));
      }
      return sb.toString();
    }
    public void addWorker(PersonItf worker) {
      workers.add(worker);
    }
    public String getFullName() {
      return name;
    }
  }
```

Serializing an instance of one of these classes is likely to involve a circular reference since `Boss` keeps an `ArrayList` of `Worker`s, and each `Worker` keeps a
reference to its `Boss`. Serialization will also involve replacement, as `Worker`
nominates a replacement class `WireWorker`. To keep the example simple,

`WireWorker` does not actually add any functionality; it simply holds references to the data members of the original `Worker` instance. Consider what happens when a `Worker`/`Boss` tandem is serialized as shown in Listing 4–16.

Listing 4–16 Serializing a Worker

```
import java.io.*;
public class WriteWorker {
  public static void main(String[] args) throws IOException
  {
    FileOutputStream fos = new FileOutputStream(args[0]);
    ObjectOutputStream oos = new ObjectOutputStream(fos);
    Boss b = new Boss("Queen");
    Worker w = new Worker("Drone", b);
    b.addWorker(w);
    System.out.println(w);
    System.out.println(b);
    oos.writeObject(w);
    System.out.println("wrote worker to " + args[0]);
  }
}

import java.io.*;
public class ReadWorker {
  public static void main(String [] args)
    throws Exception
  {
    String fileName = args[0];
    FileInputStream fis = new FileInputStream(fileName);
    ObjectInputStream ois = new ObjectInputStream(fis);
    Worker w = (Worker) ois.readObject();
    System.out.println("read worker from " + args[0]);
    System.out.println(w);
    System.out.println(w.getBoss());
  }
}
```

The stream replaces w with a `WireWorker`, call it w'. While the stream continues to chase references, it writes b, which has *another* reference to w in the `workers` array. Because replacement occurs as references are encountered, this reference to w will also be replaced by w'. The stream's view of the object graph is depicted in the middle portion of Figure 4–4.

At deserialization time, the object graph is read back into memory. When the top-level object w' is reconstructed, it gets a chance to readResolve. At this point, the top-level reference is turned back into a Worker—call it w for symmetry. However, the runtime does not keep a table of previously resolved objects. When the runtime encounters w' again, it sees a handle for a WireWorker instance and returns that instance, as shown in the bottom stripe of Figure 4–4.

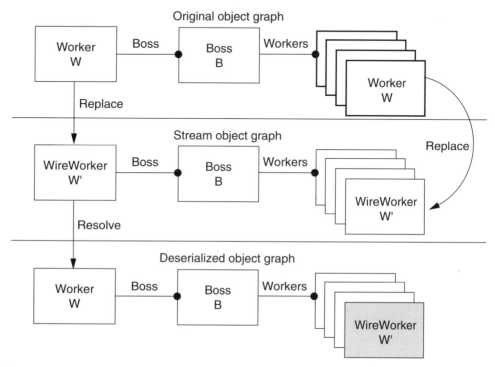

Figure 4–4   The worker object graph in transit

The resulting object hierarchy contains a WireWorker instance in the Boss's workers array, almost certainly counter to the programmer's intent. This behavior can produce bizarre symptoms. Since the workers array is not strongly typed, the fact that the object hierarchy has changed will not be detected as a ClassCastException during deserialization. Later, some method of Boss will fail because it expects the entries in the workers array to be of type PersonItf, not WireWorker.

4.8.4 Taking Control of Graph Ordering

The problem with circular references and object replacement is only the most egregious example of a problem shared by all of the serialization hooks discussed so far. Serialization is designed to transparently handle object graphs, without forcing you to know or worry about the exact order in which objects in the graph are serialized. Custom serialization hooks are also designed to hide the ordering of the object graph. Unfortunately, some hooks are likely to have ordering dependencies, which leads to the need for potentially confusing ordering rules such as the object replacement rules discussed earlier. The situation calls for some way to take explicit control of the order of events during deserialization. The `registerValidation` hook, shown in Listing 4–17, addresses this need.

Listing 4–17   Object Validation APIs

```java
package java.io;
public class ObjectInputStream {
   public void registerValidation(ObjectInputValidation obj,
                                   int prio)
            throws NotActiveException,
            InvalidObjectException;

   //remainder omitted for brevity
}

package java.io;
public interface ObjectInputValidation {
   public void validateObject() throws InvalidObjectException
}
```

The `ObjectInputStream` class implements the method `registerValidation`. You can call this method at any time during deserialization, by passing in an `ObjectInputValidation` implementation that will be called after the entire object graph is reconstructed. The `validateObject` method has two advantages over `resolveObject`. First, because `validateObject` is called after the entire object graph has been reconstituted, the graph is in a reliable, reproducible state. Second, you can exert additional control over multiple `validateObject` calls by setting the `prio` value when registering the callback.

Callbacks with a higher `prio` value are made first, and there are no guarantees for callbacks with the same priority.

The modified version of `Boss` shown in Listing 4–18 registers a callback to fix the nested references that are not handled by object resolution. Rather than attempt to validate an individual object's state in `readObject`, `SafeBoss` calls `registerValidation` so that it can validate the object after the entire object graph has been re-created. Then, `validateObject` verifies that each field is correct and iterates over the `workers` array making sure each worker is, or is convertible to, a `PersonItf`.

Even though the `validateObject` method says nothing about replacement, it is fully capable of replacing nested objects such as those in the `workers` array. However, `validateObject` returns `void`, so it cannot replace the top-level object being validated. You will often use `resolveObject` and `validateObject` in tandem to deal with ordering dependencies caused by circular references.[15]

Listing 4–18   Using ObjectInputValidation to Control Ordering

```
public class SafeBoss implements PersonItf, Serializable,
                        ObjectInputValidation
{
  //only methods that differ from Boss included, for brevity
  private void readObject(ObjectInputStream ois)
    throws IOException, ClassNotFoundException
  {
    System.out.println("registering validation");
    ois.defaultReadObject();
    ois.registerValidation(this, 0);
  }
  public void validateObject()
    throws InvalidObjectException
  {
    System.out.println("running validation");
    if ((name == null) || (workers == null)) {
      throw new InvalidObjectException("unexpected null field");
    }
    for (int n=0; n<workers.size(); n++) {
```

---

15. If the object graph is very simple, it doesn't matter much which approach you use.

```
      Object o = workers.get(n);
      if (o instanceof PersonItf) continue;
      if (o instanceof WireWorker) {
        WireWorker w = (WireWorker) o;
        workers.set(n, new Worker(w.data1, w.data2));
      } else {
      throw new InvalidObjectException(
                  "unexpected worker type " + o.getClass());
      }
    }
  }
}
```

4.9 Finding Class Code

The serialization hooks discussed thus far either customize how instances are serialized or customize what data is written in the standard class metadata format. The serialization specification also includes hooks for extending or replacing the class metadata format. The `annotateClass` and `resolveClass` methods of the object streams allow arbitrary per-class payloads to be added to a stream.

While there are no restrictions on the data included in a class annotation, the primary use for this mechanism is to help the receiver locate the correct class file if it is not available locally. The sender writes a URL string for each class, and the receiver uses the URL to instantiate a `ClassLoader` if it cannot find a local definition for the class. Consider the object streams in Listing 4–19; these serialize and load objects from a location not on the classpath.

Listing 4–19 Annotating Classes with a URL

```
class AnnotatedOutputStream extends ObjectOutputStream {
  private final String url;
  public AnnotatedOutputStream(OutputStream os, String url)
        throws IOException {
    super(os);
    this.url = url;
  }
  protected void annotateClass(Class cl)
                              throws IOException {
    writeObject(url);
  }
```

```
}

class ResolvingInputStream extends ObjectInputStream {
  public ResolvingInputStream(InputStream is)
                              throws IOException
  {
    super(is);
  }
  protected Class resolveClass(ObjectStreamClass v)
          throws IOException, ClassNotFoundException
  {
    String url = (String) readObject();
    URL u = new URL(url);
    URLClassLoader ucl = new URLClassLoader(new URL[]{u});
    String cls = v.getName();
    System.out.println("resolving " + cls + " from " + url);
    return Class.forName(cls, true, ucl);
  }
}
```

The `AnnotatedOutputStream` class marks every class it serializes with a URL string. The `ResolvingInputStream` class reads in the string and uses it to create a `URLClassLoader`, which then loads the class. This simple system allows the sender of an object to tell the receiver how to download the code necessary to deserialize and use the object. To flesh out this idea, you would want to add the ability to annotate different classes with different locations and cache the class loaders created during resolution.

4.9.1   Annotation in RMI

The primary customer of many advanced serialization features is Java RMI. RMI includes a full solution for dynamically downloaded code that is basically an elaborate version of the annotation classes shown in Listing 4–19. Dynamic code download makes it possible for RMI to ship serialized objects around the network without worrying about installing class files; they will be downloaded when and where needed.

As powerful as this mechanism is, it works harder than necessary due to a weakness of the serialization architecture. Reading a serialized graph is an all-or-nothing prospect. If a single class cannot be found, deserialization fails and both the object graph and the stream become unusable. This can be particularly irritating when class files need to be downloaded. Consider the distributed workflow situation depicted in Figure 4–5. A `Message` object is passed from machine to machine, and each machine operates on a fragment of the `Message`'s contents.

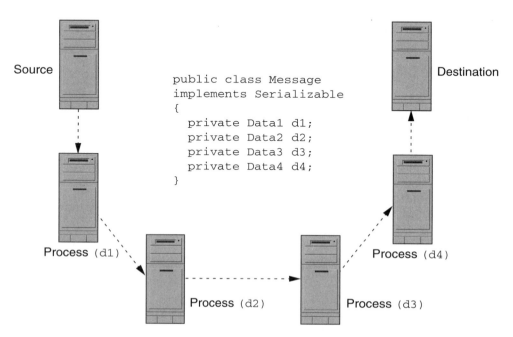

```
public class Message
implements Serializable
{
    private Data1 d1;
    private Data2 d2;
    private Data3 d3;
    private Data4 d4;
}
```

Figure 4–5   Message must be entirely deserialized at each node.

Because the `Message` is transmitted as a serialized Java object, every single class in the graph must be downloaded to every machine. This is overkill since each machine looks at only one of the `Data(N)` classes that make up the overall `Message`. It would be nice if there were some way to mark objects in a stream as "deserialize only when absolutely necessary" and then have each virtual machine deserialize and download code for only the instances actually used.

Serialization does not provide a marker for deserialize-on-demand, but you can achieve the desired effect in a straightforward manner. Simply write a wrapper class that, instead of holding a reference to an object, holds a reference to a byte array that contains the serialized form of the object. The wrapper class can be serialized and deserialized as much as you like without ever having to touch the contents of the byte array. An object wrapped in this fashion can travel through many intermediate steps until it is needed, without there being any need to load the object's class. When you finally do need the object, you build an `ObjectInputStream` around the array and extract the object, downloading its class if necessary. RMI includes an implementation of this technique called a `MarshalledObject`.

4.9.2 RMI MarshalledObjects

The deserialize-on-demand idiom is so useful that RMI provides a complete implementation in the `java.rmi.MarshalledObject` class. The `Marshalled-Object` API is simple and is shown in Listing 4–20. When you pass an object to the `MarshalledObject` constructor, that object is stored in serialized form until you later request it with the `get` method. RMI uses the `MarshalledObject` to store initialization parameters for `Activatable` objects, but you can use a `MarshalledObject` anywhere that you need to maintain the *ability* to instantiate an object at any time without actually holding a reference to the object itself.

Listing 4–20   Key MarshalledObject Methods

```
package java.rmi;
public class MarshalledObject {
  public MarshalledObject(Object o);
  public Object get();
  remainder omitted for clarity
}
```

4.10 Onward

Java metadata makes basic serialization trivial. If you mark a class `Serializable`, an `ObjectOutputStream` can discover your class's fields via reflection, and it can automate the process of writing an instance to a stream or reading it back again. This alone is quite a trick if you come from a language background that does not include metadata.

The interesting parts of Java serialization, though, are the hooks that Java provides to fine-tune how your classes transition to and from object streams. You can use the `readObject` and `writeObject` methods to add custom per-instance data or validation to the default serialization behavior. With class annotation, you can add custom per-class data, typically to support dynamically downloading the code necessary to deserialize an object. The `registerValidation` hook copes with order dependencies by providing control at the level of an entire object graph, instead of on a per-instance basis. You can use the `serialPersistentFields` to change the metadata associated with a class, keeping the serialized form readable by all class versions as the code evolves.

With these powers, however, come some dangers. The `Externalizable` interface is tempting because it is often associated with better performance, but it accomplishes this by eliminating metadata from the stream format, and this can lead to a maintenance nightmare. The serialVersionUID (SUID) provides an efficient way to compare two classes for compatibility, but it gives an all-or-nothing answer. You may have to provide custom `readObject` and `writeObject` code to glue together serialized forms that are *almost* compatible and that the SUID test would have rejected.

You can replace objects during serialization, in order to control the semantics of transmission for higher efficiency or to clearly separate a class's serialization format from its in-memory format—but you have to be careful when you deal with cyclical graphs. Finally, you must be aware that serialized objects cannot be garbage collected until the stream itself is collectable, or until you call `reset`. As of SDK version 1.4, calling `close` has the same GC-friendly effects as calling `reset`.

Serialization is not a general persistence mechanism. It does not provide random access to objects embedded in the graph. For long-term storage, or for query and update operations against data, JDBC or Enterprise JavaBeans (EJB) may be more appropriate. For simple transmission of objects across space or time, serialization is a simple and flexible solution.

4.11 Resources

For more on Java serialization, you should probably begin with [Har99], which covers Java I/O in general. In particular, Chapter 11 is devoted entirely to object serialization, providing coverage that is more basic but also more systematic than the material presented here. [Blo01] is a wide-ranging, excellent book on using Java effectively. It includes a short chapter on serialization that discusses performance and validation in a fashion complementary to this chapter. Finally, the serialization specification [Ser] is clear and concise, although it emphasizes "what" and "how" instead of "why."

COMPONENT DEVELOPMENT FOR THE JAVA™ PLATFORM

Chapter 5

Customizing Class Loading

Chapter 2 described using the class loaders installed by the Java launcher and also using your own instances of `URLClassLoader`. These techniques solve many of the class loader problems you are likely to face. However, there are times when it would be nice to use a custom class loader. For instance, you may want to distribute classes with a protocol other than http, load classes from an object database, or extract classes from a version control system. More interestingly, you may want to modify the semantics of class loading. You might insert additional information, such as instrumentation for debugging, profiling, or auditing, or you might want to process custom metadata that you have added to the binary class format. In these situations, you will want to customize class loading.

This chapter will present two different techniques for customizing class loading. The first, and most obvious, is writing your own subclass of `ClassLoader`. Your own class loader implementation is free to choose any strategy it wants for mapping class names to class bytes, but you must be careful about security. Class loaders tell the security architecture where code came from, and the security manager uses this information to grant permissions. So before I show you how to write a custom class loader, I will take a brief detour through the security architecture. You will see that in most cases, you should subclass `Secure-ClassLoader`, not `ClassLoader`.

The second option for customizing class loading splits the security and resource-resolution tasks into separate classes, leveraging the core API. A standard `URLClassLoader` instance manages the details of Java security, and a

Java class called a *protocol handler* resolves resources by parsing a customized URL protocol string, like

```
objectdb://server/MyClass.class
```

instead of

```
http://server/MyClass.class
```

This separation of concerns provides two benefits over simply extending `SecureClassLoader`. First, the protocol handler can be implemented in relatively untrusted code since the `URLClassLoader` handles security. This is useful because though you might trust a piece of unknown code to go and find other classes that it needs, you certainly would not trust it to tell you what permissions those classes should have! Second, the protocol handler can request any kind of resource, not just binary classes.

§5.4 explains how to create and use class loaders in a secured environment. Most application code in a secured environment does not have permission to create a class loader because of the sensitive role that class loaders play in assigning permissions to classes as they are loaded. However, you will often want the ability to request a specific class loader from application code. There are several ways to work around this issue. Usually application code does not need to *create* a class loader; all it needs is *access* to a class loader pointed at the correct classes. Instead of attempting to instantiate a class loader directly, you call back into more trusted code, requesting a class loader that uses a resource resolution strategy defined by you. You can write code to do this yourself, or you can use `URLClassLoader,` which includes a factory method specifically designed to handle this problem.

§5.5 shows you how to modify the class bytes after you have compiled a class. You can use this technique to insert or remove debugging information, performance instrumentation, or optimization hints. In combination with a custom class loader, you can modify classes as they are loaded, or you can simply change the binary classes offline in the file system or whatever other repository you use. To illustrate the power of this technique, I create a new custom class attribute that tracks version dependencies between packages and then implement a `URLClassLoader` subclass that always finds the correct version of dependent classes.

Writing a custom class loader is an interesting exercise, but you should not reinvent the wheel. The core API already handles the most common class loading scenarios. Before you write a custom loader, you should study the source for `SecureClassLoader` and `URLClassLoader` to ascertain that you cannot accomplish your purpose simply by leveraging these classes.

5.1   Java 2 Security

Brace yourself for some massive simplification;[1] it's time to talk about Java security. In Java 2 security, classes are assigned *permissions* based on their *code source*. A permission is simply a description of some secured operation that you might want to perform. Permissions are defined as subclasses of `java.security.Permission`, and have optional targets and actions. For example, a class might have the `FilePermission` permission with target `<<ALL FILES>>` and action `delete`. This means exactly what you think it means—that the class can delete any or all files.

A code source contains the URL a class came from, plus any certificates used to sign the code. These two data items are stored in an instance of `java.security.CodeSource`. An instance of `java.security.Policy` manages the mapping between code sources and permissions.

The reference implementation of `Policy` is file-based. If you wanted to give your code permission to delete all files, you would create a policy file like the one in Listing 5–1. Both the `signedBy` and `codeBase` attributes are optional. If you omit `signedBy` or `codeBase` then the permissions are granted regardless of signer or location, respectively.

Listing 5–1   A Simple Policy File

```
//file your.policy
grant signedBy "you" codeBase "file:/yourclassdir" {
  permission java.io.FilePermission "<<ALL FILES>>", "delete";
};
```

---

1. See [Gon99] for the full story.

```
//command line to use your.policy
>java -Djava.security.manager \
     -Djava.security.policy=your.policy MainClass
```

A class's permissions come into play at runtime when a security manager is installed and the class attempts to perform an operation that is protected by the security manager. Consider the `SelfDestruct` class, shown in Listing 5–2, which attempts to destroy its own class file on the local file system. If you run this class from the folder where the file is located, it will delete itself and be unavailable for future runs. However, if you turn on Java security with the `-Djava.security.manager` flag but do not specify a policy file, your code will run with a minimal set of permissions[2] and you will see the exception trace shown in Listing 5–3. The security manager rejects the call to `File.delete` because the `SelfDestruct` class does not have the necessary permission. The standard security manager will grant permission only if *all* the classes on the call stack have the requisite permission.[3]

Listing 5–2   The SelfDestruct Class

```
import java.io.*;
public class SelfDestruct {
  public static void main(String[] args) {
    try {
      File f = new File("SelfDestruct.class");
      System.out.println("deleted file? " + f.delete());
    }
    catch (Exception e) {
      e.printStackTrace();
    }
  }
}
```

Listing 5–3   Blocked by the Security Manager

```
$ java -Djava.security.manager SelfDestruct
java.security.AccessControlException: access denied
     (java.io.FilePermission SelfDestruct.class delete)
```

---

2. The default behavior of the security manager can be modified by editing the java.security and java.policy files in your $[JAVA_HOME]/jre/lib/security directory.
3. The default behavior of checking the entire call stack can be modified with privileged scopes.

```
at java.security.AccessControlContext.checkPermission(…)
at java.security.AccessController.checkPermission(…)
at java.lang.SecurityManager.checkPermission(…)
at java.lang.SecurityManager.checkDelete(…)
at java.io.File.delete(…)
at SelfDestruct.main(SelfDestruct.java:6)
```

In the call stack shown in Listing 5–3, the `SelfDestruct` class is the only problem because all the other classes on the call stack were loaded by the bootstrap loader and are exempt from permission checks. In order to give `SelfDestruct` the requisite permission, you could reference a policy file similar to the one in Listing 5–1. You would accomplish this by removing the `signedBy` field and setting the `codeBase` value to a file URL where the `SelfDestruct.class` is located.

The permission granted by the policy file does not have to exactly match the permission listed in the `AccessControlException`. The policy file in Listing 5–1 grants `FilePermission, <<ALL FILES>>, delete`, but the security manager in Listing 5–3 is looking for `FilePermission, SelfDestruct.class, delete`. This difference causes no confusion because the permission architecture supports *implication*. Each permission subclass defines its own notion of implication, so for example, the `FilePermission` class knows that `<<ALL FILES>>` implies any particular file name. The built-in permission classes support implication without any special effort by the developer.

That's Java 2 security in brief. When you deploy an application, you determine the permissions that code will need, and you associate those permissions with code locations and signers in the policy file. The default policy implementation then extracts these permissions when the class is loaded. When the security manager wants to check an operation, it verifies that every class on the call stack has the necessary permission, directly or by implication. The relationships between the players are shown in Figure 5–1. There is only one thing missing: What does all of this have to do with class loaders?

5.1.1 The Role of Class Loaders

Class loaders are the bridge between the policy and the security manager. A class loader takes a code source and permissions pair from the policy and binds

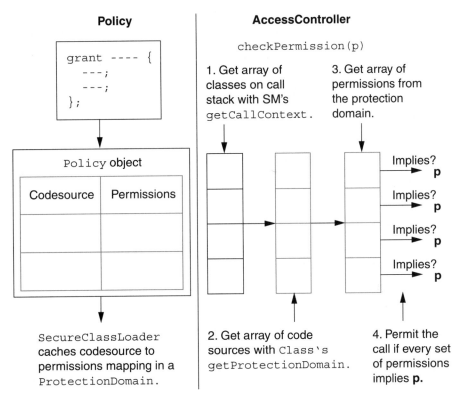

Figure 5–1 The Java 2 security architecture

them into an instance of `java.security.ProtectionDomain`. The class loader then hands the protection domain to the virtual machine via `Class-Loader`'s native method `defineClass`. When the security manager wants to verify a call stack, it extracts all the protection domains for classes on the stack via a native method of `java.security.AccessControlContext`. The Java 2 security architecture depends on honest class loaders telling the truth when they define classes.

The key role that class loaders play in security has two consequences for application developers. First, you should rarely grant the `RuntimePermission` `createClassLoader`. Code with this permission can create a class loader that lies about protection domains in an attempt to compromise security. Second, because you cannot allow untrusted code to create class loaders, you may need to provide some other mechanism to help untrusted code find the classes and resources it needs. §5.2 presents the basics of custom class loaders, and §5.4 shows how to make class loading services available to untrusted code without compromising security.

5.2 Custom Class Loaders

The rules for writing class loaders have changed over time, but the principle has remained basically the same. You implement a subclass of `ClassLoader` that knows, given a class name, how to create or find a byte array that is the class bytes for that class.

5.2.1 Pre-Java 2 Custom Class Loaders

Prior to SDK version 1.2, the relevant methods were `loadClass`, `define-Class`, and `resolveClass`, as shown in Listing 5–4. To implement a custom loader, you override the abstract method `loadClass`. Using the `name` argument, you find or create an array of bytes that has the correct binary class format, and then you pass these bytes to the `defineClass` method. `ClassLoader`'s `defineClass` implementation then calls to native code inside the virtual machine that loads the class. If the `resolve` flag is set, your subclass should also call `resolveClass` after `defineClass` completes. `Class-Loader`'s `resolveClass` makes the class ready for use by verifying, resolving, and initializing the class.[4]

Listing 5–4 Pre-Java 2 Custom Class Loader APIs

```
package java.lang;
public class ClassLoader {
protected abstract Class loadClass(String name,
                                   boolean resolve);
protected final Class defineClass(byte[] data, int offset,
                                  int length);
protected final Class defineClass(String name, byte[] data,
                                  int offset, int length);
protected final void resolveClass(Class c);
//other methods omitted for clarity
}
```

---

4. This process is described in detail in [Ven99].

5.2.2 Class Loading since SDK 1.2

The pre-1.2 method of implementing class loaders worked, but it suffered from two important flaws. First, there was no mechanism for passing security information from the `Policy` implementation into the virtual machine. Second, there was no guarantee that custom class loaders would follow the rules for class loaders laid out in Chapter 2.[5] An overridden `loadClass` method could cheat by either refusing to delegate to its parent loader, or by reloading classes that had already been loaded.

The 1.2 Java SDK introduced several modifications to the `ClassLoader` class to address these problems. The 1.2 `ClassLoader` includes a new overloaded form of `defineClass` that passes security information to the VM via a `ProtectionDomain` argument. 1.2 also provides a concrete implementation of `loadClass` that enforces the basic rules of class loading. Developers should no longer override `loadClass`; instead, they should override a new method, `findClass`. The `findClass` method is called only after `loadClass` fails to find the class from a parent class loader or the current loader's cache. The changes to the 1.2 `ClassLoader` API are summarized in Listing 5–5.

Listing 5–5   SDK 1.2 Enhancements to ClassLoader

```
package java.lang;
public class ClassLoader {
//only new/changed methods shown here
protected final Class defineClass(String name, byte[] b,
          int off, int len, ProtectionDomain pd);

//override this instead of loadClass
protected Class findClass(String name)
          throws ClassNotFoundException
{
   throw new ClassNotFoundException(name);
}
```

---

5. A more historically accurate account would acknowledge that both the `Policy` and the class loader rules did not exist in SDK 1.1 either, so there was no way that `ClassLoader` *could* work with them. In my account, I am following the tradition that winners get to rewrite history so that the outcome appears obvious and inevitable.

```
//do not override this method
protected synchronized Class loadClass(String name,
         boolean resolve) throws ClassNotFoundException
{
  // First, check if the class has already been loaded
  Class c = findLoadedClass(name);
  if (c == null) {
    try {
      if (parent != null) {
        c = parent.loadClass(name, false);
      } else {
        c = findBootstrapClass0(name);
      }
    } catch (ClassNotFoundException e) {
      // If still not found, then call findClass in order
      // to find the class.
      c = findClass(name);
    }
  }
  if (resolve) {
    resolveClass(c);
  }
  return c;
}
```

The 1.2 API represents a big improvement over previous incarnations of `ClassLoader`. The `loadClass` method pulls all the common code into the core API where it belongs, so all you have to worry about is finding or creating the class bytes. Notice, however, that `loadClass` is not marked `final`. You could still override `loadClass` and implement an old-style class loader. This loophole was left in deliberately to preserve binary compatibility with existing code. In a world without legacy software, `loadClass` would be `final`, and you should treat it as such when writing new programs.

The various signatures of `defineClass` are also a concession to legacy code. You should always use the version that takes a `ProtectionDomain` argument so that code loaded by your class loaders can participate fully in the Java 2 security model. An easy way to accomplish this is to always extend the 1.2 class `java.security.SecureClassLoader`. `SecureClassLoader` provides yet another `defineClass` method, as shown in Listing 5–6. This version of `defineClass` takes a `CodeSource` instance, and the `getProtectionDomain` method manages a cache of `ProtectionDomain`s for efficiency. If you are going to write a custom class loader, your best bet is to subclass `SecureClassLoader` and override `findClass` to call the `CodeSource`-aware version of `defineClass`.

Listing 5–6   SecureClassLoader's defineClass Implementation

```
protected final Class defineClass(String name, byte[] b,
                int off, int len, CodeSource cs)
{
  if (cs == null)
    return defineClass(name, b, off, len);
  else
    return defineClass(name, b, off, len,
                        getProtectionDomain(cs));
}
```

5.2.3   A Transforming Class Loader

As an example of a custom class loader, consider a `TransformingClassLoader`. This loader is very similar to a `URLClassLoader`, except that it may perform arbitrary transformations on the bytes of a class before handing them off to the virtual machine. These transformations could modify the class bytes to add logging, profiling, debugging, or other services. Since the transforming loader needs to handle URLs anyway, it will extend `URLClassLoader`, and thereby implicitly extend `SecureClassLoader`.

The transforming loader and related classes are shown in Listing 5–7. The `ResourceTransformer` class defines the various transformations that might be made. For now, the interesting method is `transformClassBytes`, which modifies an array of class bytes after the `URLClassLoader` retrieves the bytes but before they are passed to `defineClass`. The `TransformingClassLoader` repeats all the constructors of `URLClassLoader` but with a `ResourceTransformer` parameter added. The transformer implementation will get a chance to modify the class bytes before they are used to define a class.

Listing 5–7 The TransformingClassLoader and Related Classes

```
//class com.develop.xload.ResourceTransformer
package com.develop.xload;
import java.io.IOException;
import java.net.URL;
import java.util.Enumeration;

public interface ResourceTransformer {
  public byte transformClassBytes(byte[] inout,
                                  int start, int len);
  public URL transformResourceURL(URL resource);
  public Enumeration transformResources(Enumeration resrcs);
}


//class com.develop.xload.TransformingClassLoader
package com.develop.xload;

import java.io.*;
import java.lang.reflect.*;
import java.net.*;
import java.security.*;
import java.util.jar.*;
import java.util.jar.Attributes.*;
import sun.misc.*;

public class TransformingClassLoader extends URLClassLoader {
  private final ResourceTransformer xr;

  public TransformingClassLoader(URL[] urls,
                                 ResourceTransformer xr) {
    super(urls);
    this.xr = xr;
  }

  public TransformingClassLoader(URL[] urls,
                                 ClassLoader parent,
                                 ResourceTransformer xr) {
    super(urls, parent);
    this.xr = xr;
  }

  public TransformingClassLoader(
        URL[] urls, ClassLoader parent,
```

```
            URLStreamHandlerFactory fact,
            ResourceTransformer xr)
{
  super(urls, parent, fact);
  this.xr = xr;
}

private URL getURLBase(URL url) {
  URL[] urls = getURLs();
  int length = urls.length;
  String stringForm = url.toExternalForm();
  for (int n=0; n<length; n++) {
    if (stringForm.startsWith(urls[n].toExternalForm())) {
     return urls[n];
     }
  }
  return null;
}

protected Class findClass(final String name)
  throws ClassNotFoundException
{
  String className = name.replace('.', '/') + ".class";
  URL url = super.getResource(className);
  if (url == null) {
    return null;
  }
  URL urlBase = getURLBase(url);
  if (urlBase == null) {
    throw new Error("url has no base");
  }
  InputStream is = null;
  try {
    is = url.openStream();
    if (is == null) { return null; }
    ByteArrayOutputStream baos =
                    new ByteArrayOutputStream();
    for (int ch=0; -1 != (ch=is.read()); )
    baos.write(ch);
    byte[] classbytes = baos.toByteArray();
    xr.transformClassBytes(classbytes, 0,
        classbytes.length);
    return defineClass(name, classbytes, 0,
          classbytes.length, new CodeSource(urlBase, null));
```

```
    }
    catch (IOException ioe) {
      return null;
    }
  }
}
```

The meat of the example is the `findClass` implementation. First, `findClass` takes the string class name passed into it and turns it into a relative URL string by replacing occurrences of '.' with '/' and then appending '.class'. Then, the superclass's `getResource` method locates the URL for the class. The method then opens a stream to the URL and reads it into an array of bytes. Before these bytes are passed to `defineClass`, the call to `xr.transform` converts the bytes, using whatever algorithm the transformer implements.

The helper method `getURLBase` returns the base URL; for instance,

```
http://server/MyClass.class
```

would have a base URL of

```
http://server/
```

The base URL is used to construct a `CodeSource`, which is then passed to the security-aware version of `defineClass`. The `TransformingClassLoader` has most of the abilities of a `URLClassLoader`,[6] and it adds the ability to plug in arbitrary transformations as code is loaded.

As a simple transformation example, consider a `ClassNotter` that decrypts a binary class that was encrypted by NOTting every bit in the binary class format. Such encryption is not very secure, but it is easy to implement for a quick example. The `ClassNotter` is shown in Listing 5–8. `ClassNotter` extends `NoOpResourceTransformer`, which is an adapter class that provides empty implementations of `ResourceTransformer` methods. This allows the `ClassNotter` to implement only the method(s) of interest, in this

---

6. Notice that this implementation passes `null` as the second argument to the `CodeSource` constructor. This loses any signer information, so this implementation supports location-based security only—not digital certificates. The design of `URLClassLoader` does not encourage inheritance-based reuse because it does not make the certificate information easily available to derived classes. It is tucked away in private members of `URLClassLoader` and requires some classes in the `sun.misc` package. Since you should not use `sun.misc` code, a certificate-aware version of `TransformerClassLoader` would be nontrivial.

case `transformClassBytes`. The `ClassNotter` implementation inverts every bit in the class byte array.

The test harness `test.TestTransformingLoader` creates a `TransformingLoader` that uses the `ClassNotter` to transform bytes after they are loaded from the file system and before they are handed off to the virtual machine. If you encrypted your classes as part of deployment, then anyone trying to use a standard `URLClassLoader` would be unable to interpret the class and would see a `ClassFormatError` (bad magic number).

Of course, this encryption is very simple, and would be defeated by any but the most casual adversary.[7] The point here is that the `TransformingLoader` enables any transformation you can imagine. You focus on the transformation process, and let the built-in capabilities of `URLClassLoader` take care of correctly setting your `ProtectionDomain`.

Listing 5–8   ClassNotter, a Very Simple ResourceTransformer

```
package com.develop.xload;
import java.io.IOException;
import java.net.URL;
import java.util.Enumeration;

public class NoOpResourceTransformer
            implements ResourceTransformer {
  public byte[] transformClassBytes(byte[] inout,
                                    int start,
                                    int length) {
    return inout;
  }
  public URL transformResourceURL(URL resource) {
    return resource;
  }
  public Enumeration transformResources(
                    Enumeration resources) {
    return resources;
  }
}
```

---

7. In fact, even far more complex "unbreakable" encryption schemes are easily defeated unless you have physical control over every box in which the decryption will occur. Otherwise, an adversary can simply use debugging tools to grab the class bytes *after* they are decrypted without troubling to attack the encryption head-on.

```
package test;
import com.develop.xload.NoOpResourceTransformer;

public class ClassNotter extends NoOpResourceTransformer {
  public byte[] transformClassBytes(byte[] inout,
                                    int start,
                                    int len) {
    int end = start+len;
    for (int n=start; n<end; n++) {
      inout[n] = (byte)~inout[n];
    }
    return inout;
  }
}


package test;
import com.develop.xload.*;
import java.io.*;
import java.net.*;

public class TestTransformingLoader {

  public static void main(String [] args) {
    try {
      if (args.length != 4) {
        System.out.println("usage: test.TestTransformingLoader " +
                           " url1 url2 cls1 cls2");
        System.exit(-1);
      }
      URL u1 = new URL(args[0]);
      URL u2 = new URL(args[1]);
      URLClassLoader cl = new TransformingClassLoader(
                       new URL[]{u1,u2}, new ClassNotter());
      System.out.println(cl);
      URL[] urls = cl.getURLs();
      Class cls1 = Class.forName(args[2], true, cl);
      System.out.println(cls1);
      Class cls2 = Class.forName(args[3], true, cl);
      System.out.println(cls2);
    }
    catch (Exception e) {
      e.printStackTrace();
    }
  }
}
```

5.3 Protocol Handlers

In most cases, writing your own custom class loader is overkill, thanks to yet another feature of the ubiquitous `URLClassLoader`—pluggable URL protocols called protocol handlers. If you look at the code for the `java.net.URL` class, you will see that it doesn't actually do very much. `URL` includes code to parse a URL string into its component parts: protocol, host, port, and file. Everything else is delegated to helper classes called protocol handlers, or synonymously, stream handlers. Protocol handlers can be used with any `URL`, so you can use them for other purposes besides just class loading.

The Java 2 platform comes with several protocol handlers built in, including handlers for the all-important `http` and `file` protocols. In addition to these, you can install your own protocol handlers to do any sort of resource lookup that you want. Integration with Java security is automatic. The policy file already understands URL syntax, so you can combine your custom handler with a standard `URLClassLoader` and policy file.

To demonstrate protocol handlers in action, I will rebuild the simple encryption scheme from the previous example, this time using a protocol handler. The first step is to define the custom URL protocol stream to use. The syntax for using the sample protocol `not` is shown in Listing 5–9. Notice that the second example syntax does not include the hostname. This follows the convention for URL syntax, where the host name defaults to localhost, if it is omitted. This behavior is built into the `URL` class parsing logic, and it will be available for free to the `not` stream handler.

Listing 5–9 The 'not' Custom Protocol

```
'not' URL syntax:
  not://host:port/file/
example xform for NOTting every byte:
  not://localhost/d/halloway/src/
  not:/halloway/src
```

5.3.1 Implementing a Handler

To create a protocol handler, you must create at least two classes: a `java.net.URLStreamHandler` subclass that understands your protocol syntax, and a `java.net.URLConnection` subclass that the handler can return to clients. Annotated listings for these base classes appear in Listing 5–10.

Listing 5–10 URLStreamHandler and URLConnection

```
package java.net;
public abstract class URLStreamHandler {
  //always override this method:
  abstract protected URLConnection openConnection(URL u)
                   throws IOException;
  //override these only if your URL syntax differs from
  //standard URLS:
  protected void parseURL(URL u, String spec,
                          int start, int limit);
  protected String toExternalForm(URL u);
  //NOT SHOWN: several other methods you might override
}

package java.net;
//All listed methods can throw IOException
public abstract class URLConnection {
  //probably override these
  abstract public void connect();
  public InputStream getInputStream();
  public OutputStream getOutputStream();
  //remainder omitted for brevity
}
```

The `URLStreamHandler` class does two things. First, it parses the protocol string into a `URL` in the `parseURL` method. Then, it creates a connection for that `URL` in the `openConnection` method. The `URLStreamHandler` class should always be named `Handler`, and its full package name should be

```
{arbitrarypkgs.}protocolname.Handler
```

If your URL protocol has syntax similar to HTTP URLs, then the handler is trivial to implement; all it needs to do is return your custom connection class. The handler for the `not` protocol is shown in Listing 5–11.

Listing 5–11 Handler for the not Protocol

```
package test.not;

import java.io.*;
import java.net.*;

public class Handler extends URLStreamHandler {
  protected URLConnection openConnection(URL u)
          throws IOException
  {
    return new NotConnection(u);
  }
}
```

The `URLConnection` subclass for a protocol handler provides connection semantics. Because the design is inspired by HTTP, the notion of connection semantics feels very much like HTTP. The `URLConnection` class is full of methods that are relevant to setting and extracting common HTTP headers, such as `getContentType`, `getExpiration`, `setExpiration`, and `getDate`. These methods will often be irrelevant in a custom connection.

The three key methods of `URLConnection` were shown previously in Listing 5–10. The `connect` method should actually begin a communication with the resource. If the resource is across the network, this will typically involve opening a socket, speaking the correct wire protocol, and verifying that somebody is listening. If the resource is local, then `connect` may do nothing. The `getInputStream` and `getOutputStream` methods enable two-way communication with the resource. If the resource is across the network, then these calls may return the socket streams directly, or they may preprocess them in some way, such as by reading and interpreting headers first. If the resource is local, then these streams might be file streams or some custom stream class.

The `NotConnection` implementation is straightforward and is shown in Listing 5–12. Because the `not` URL does not access a network resource, the `connect` method does nothing. Also, communication is unidirectional; there is no need to send anything *to* a `not` URL. All the information to locate a class is in the URL itself, so there is no need to implement `getOutputStream`. The interesting method is `getInputStream`, which opens a file stream and then wraps it with a filter stream `NotInputStream` that inverts each byte.

Listing 5–12   The NotConnection Class

```
package test.not;
import java.io.*;
import java.net.*;

public class NotConnection extends URLConnection {
  private InputStream is;
  private Object lock = new Object();
  public NotConnection(URL u) {
    super(u);
  }
  public void connect() throws IOException {
  }
  public InputStream getInputStream() throws IOException {
    synchronized (lock) {
      if (is == null) {
        String file = getURL().getFile();
        FileInputStream fis = new FileInputStream(file);
        is = new NotInputStream(fis);
      }
      return is;
    }
  }
}
```

5.3.2   Installing a Custom Handler

Once you have created a handler and supporting classes, the trick is to get the runtime to recognize them. By default, the Java SDK uses only handlers that have a package prefix sun.net.www.protocol, a package suffix name matching the protocol, and the name Handler. For example, when you use an http URL, the runtime uses reflection to load the class

```
sun.net.www.protocol.http.Handler
```

and create an instance. Then the runtime casts the instance to type URL-StreamHandler and uses it to parse and connect to the URL.

The Java license forbids creating your own classes in the sun.* namespace, so do not bother trying to install your handlers this way. Instead, there are two hooks you can use to install your own custom handler. The URL class has a setURLStreamHandler factory that allows you to install your own mapping from protocols to handlers. It takes as its argument an instance of URL-StreamHandlerFactory, an interface whose one method takes a protocol name and returns a handler.

The URLStreamHandlerFactory code is shown in Listing 5–13. You can install a stream handler factory once per VM, and the factory will be used prior and in addition to consulting the standard handlers.[8] In Listing 5–14, the Not-URLReader class installs a factory that understands the not protocol, and then it outputs a hex dump of the data found at a URL passed on the command line.

Listing 5–13 URLStreamHandlerFactory

```
//from java.net.URLStreamHandlerFactory
public interface URLStreamHandlerFactory {
  public URLStreamHandler createURLStreamHandler(
        String prot);
}

//from java.net.URL
public static void
setURLStreamHandlerFactory(URLStreamHandlerFactory fac);
```

Listing 5–14 The NotURLReader Class

```
package test;

import com.develop.util.*;
import java.io.*;
import java.net.*;
public class NotURLReader implements URLStreamHandlerFactory
{
  public URLStreamHandler createURLStreamHandler(String prot)
  {
    if (prot.equals("not")) {
      return new com.develop.handlers.not.Handler();
    }
    return null;
  }
```

---

8. Because your custom handler is consulted first, you could replace the standard handlers for http et al. if you wanted to.

```
      public static void main(String [] args) throws Exception {
        if (args.length != 1) {
          System.out.println("usage: test.NotURLReader url");
          System.exit(-1);
        }
        URL.setURLStreamHandlerFactory (new NotURLReader());
        URL u = new URL(args[0]);
        InputStream is = u.openStream();
        byte[] buf = new byte[4096];
        int length = 0;
        while (0 < (length = is.read(buf))) {
          System.out.println(HexFormatter.convertBytesToString(
                           buf, 0, length, 16, true));
        }
      }
    }
  }
```

Though it is possible to install new handlers from within Java code as shown above, it is typically more convenient to give control of handlers over to an administrator. To this end, you can set a property that specifies where to look for custom handlers. The `java.protocol.handler.pkgs` property contains a list of "|"- delimited package prefixes. The URL class attempts to create handlers based on custom package prefixes after checking the installed `URLStream-HandlerFactory` but before checking the standard `sun.net.www.proto-col` handlers.

Given a command line as shown in Listing 5–15's Example 1, the URL class would try the following steps until one succeeded:

1. If a `URLStreamHandlerFactory` is installed, see if it supports `not`.

2. Try to use an instance of `foo.not.Handler`.

3. Try to use an instance of `bar.not.Handler`.

4. Try to use an instance of `sun.net.www.protocol.not.Handler`.

5. Report a `MalformedURLException: unknown protocol: not`.

Listing 5–15, Example 2, shows the correct command line to locate the `not` handler from Listing 5–11.

Listing 5–15 Specifying URLStreamHandlers on the Command Line

```
Example 1.
java -Djava.protocol.handler.pkgs=foo|bar MainClass

Example 2.
java -Djava.protocol.handler.pkgs=test.not
MainClass
```

5.3.3 Choosing between Loaders and Handlers

At first glance, writing your own protocol handler may appear to be a lot more work than just writing your own custom class loader. After all, you have to write at least two classes, and probably more. The simple `not` handler required the `Handler`, `NotConnection`, and `NotInputStream` classes. However, these classes are mostly boilerplate code, and they factor the process of locating a resource process into the following distinct pieces:

1. Protocol handlers parse URLs and return connections.
2. Connections manage communication and return streams.
3. Streams read and write data and possibly apply transformations.

Moreover, stream handlers can be used to connect to any resource, whereas custom class loaders can be used only to load classes and other co-located resources. Finally, stream handlers leverage the security features already built into the `URLClassLoader`. And, because they can be installed on the command line, you can make the presence of stream handlers completely transparent to the rest of your code.

The only downside of stream handlers comes when you try to handle a URL whose string format is radically different from `http` syntax. For example, consider the hypothetical URLs shown in Listing 5–16. These URLs do not map to the standard

```
protocol://host:port/file
```

format, and to implement them, you would have to hack around the fact that the `URL` class pretty much assumes this format. Your stream handler would be much more complex, implementing at least the `parseURL` method and possibly several others. Except in cases like these where the semantics of your class loader are very difficult to express as a URL, you should prefer stream handlers to custom class loaders.

Listing 5–16 Some Hypothetical Custom URLs

```
For connecting to a database:
  db://hostname:port/user=stu;pwd=hmph;table=ORDERS
A URL that applies a transform to data from a wrapped URL:
  xform://xformtype/xformargs/http://localhost/file
  xform://xformtype/xformargs/http://localhost/file
```

5.4 Getting Past Security to the Loader You Need

In the situations discussed so far, only two levels of trust are involved in class loading. Trusted code launches the process and chooses security settings, and then it instantiates class loaders to load less trusted code. Less trusted code may have a greater or lesser degree of permissions, but it will almost never have permission to create a `ClassLoader` instance. If it did, it might lie about the `ProtectionDomain` of classes that it loaded, thereby subverting the security model.

To give your less-trusted code the ability to use class loaders, authors of trusted code (such as J2EE containers) need to provide a callback mechanism whereby you can request a specific class loader. The trusted code can then create a class loader that meets your specifications for how class bytes are located. Note that this does not compromise security in the slightest. The security is not in locating the class, but in assigning its `ProtectionDomain`. The trusted code keeps this prerogative for itself.

As an example of where this might be useful, consider a servlet container run by an application hosting company. The container is the process owner. It is highly trusted and will activate Java security to protect itself (and other customers) from damage that your code might cause. Your code is less trusted than the container code, but you still might want to customize class loading. For example, you might write a custom class loader that checks for new versions of classes on your development server and then makes them available to the servlet container based on some criteria you define. You cannot simply create a class loader in your code because the application hosting company will not give you the necessary security permission.

You can see the problem by simply turning on Java security for any program that creates a class loader. If you try this, the program will fail as soon as it attempts to instantiate the `ClassLoader`, as shown in Listing 5–17. Fortunately, the `URLClassLoader` class includes code specifically designed to address this problem. You should rarely instantiate a `URLClassLoader` directly. Instead, use one of the static factory methods named `newInstance`.

Listing 5–17 Instantiating a Class Loader in a Secure Process

```
java -Djava.security.manager  UseAClassLoader
  java.security.AccessControlException: access denied
  (java.lang.RuntimePermission createClassLoader)
  ...
  at java.lang.ClassLoader.<init>(ClassLoader.java:234)
  ...
```

The code for `newInstance` is shown in Listing 5–18. Without delving too deeply into the security model, you can see the basic idea. The field `acc` saves away the protection domains that are current when the call begins. The code inside the `PrivilegedAction` runs with the permissions of the `URLClassLoader` class, ignoring possibly untrusted classes higher on the call stack. This makes it possible to create the class loader, and it is secure because the privileged action has been carefully coded not to do anything that would compromise security.

Listing 5–18 Swapping Access Control Contexts

```
package java.net;
public class URLClassLoader extends SecureClassLoader {
public static URLClassLoader
newInstance(final URL[] urls, final ClassLoader parent)
{
  // Save the caller's context
  AccessControlContext acc = AccessController.getContext();
  // Need a privileged block to create the class loader
  URLClassLoader ucl = (URLClassLoader)
    AccessController.doPrivileged(new PrivilegedAction() {
      public Object run() {
        return new FactoryURLClassLoader(urls, parent);
```

```
    }
  });
  // Now set the context on the loader using the one we saved,
  // not the one inside the privileged block...
  ucl.acc = acc;
  return ucl;
}
//remainder omitted for brevity
}
```

Remember that *using* a class loader does not open a security hole, but *instantiating* one does. Once the class loader has been created, it is assigned the set of protection domains `acc` that were on the stack when `newInstance` was called. When you later attempt to use this class loader, it will have to pass essentially two separate security checks: the one implied by `acc`, plus whatever classes are on the call stack at the time of the call.

The important point here is that you should use the `newInstance` method to create `URLClassLoader`s; otherwise, you are likely to get an `AccessControlException` when somebody attempts to execute your code in a secured environment. If you write your own custom class loader, you will need to add a factory method similar to `newInstance` if you want untrusted code to be able to create an instance of your loader.

5.5 Reading Custom Metadata

The Java binary class format provides a standard set of extensions for adding custom data to binary classes. However, to take advantage of any custom class data at runtime, you must write a custom class loader that is aware of your extensions to the class format. In this section, you will see a custom extension to the class format that includes extra version information, and you will see a custom class loader that uses this information to locate the correct versions of classes that it will load.

Before you jump into the example or apply this technique in your own code, you need to be very careful that your additions to the class do not violate the Java license agreement. You cannot create modified classes that *require* a special class loader or virtual machine because this would violate Java's "Prime

Directive"—code must be able to run on any compliant Java platform. The relevant section of [LY99] begins:

> Compilers are permitted to define and emit class files containing new attributes in the attributes tables of class file structures. Java virtual machine implementations are permitted to recognize and use new attributes found in the attributes tables of class file structures. However, any attribute not defined as part of this Java virtual machine specification must not affect the semantics of class or interface types. Java virtual machine implementations are required to silently ignore attributes they do not recognize.

Any semantics that your custom metadata enables must be *optional* semantics, that is, your classes could function just fine without them. The versioning information I am going to introduce here is a good example of this. If a virtual machine does not recognize the custom version information in the binary class, it will still be able to load and execute the class.

5.5.1   Example: Version Attributes

The versioning problem is a fundamental one. Java's class loading architecture does not attempt to verify the version of a class being loaded. If class A references class B, then A's class loader delegation will attempt to find a definition for B. Standard class loaders such as URLClassLoader will load the *first* matching definition of B. This will cause deployment headaches if different components rely on different versions of B.

JAR sealing (§3.6.3) can help some. If you deploy all of your classes in sealed JAR files, and you are careful with your build process, you can guarantee that all the classes in a package are from the same build. However, this does not help with cross-package dependencies. When JAR files are sealed, the runtime can identify potential version problems by throwing an exception, but it cannot automatically locate the correct version.

Package reflection (§3.6) also helps some, but not enough. After a class B is loaded, you may be able to use package reflection to discover the version of B you have found. Unfortunately, this information arrives too late to be of use. If B turns out to be the wrong version, that's too bad. You have already loaded it, and you cannot now unload it short of creating a new class loader and starting over entirely. As with JAR sealing, package reflection simply identifies the problem, and leaves you to solve it.

Here are design goals for a simple version authority that can automatically locate the correct versions of Java classes:

1. The version authority tracks version information for a loaded class. This includes the version of the class and the versions of any other classes that the class depends on.

2. Before a class is loaded, the version authority checks the candidate class's version against the requirements of all the classes already loaded by this loader. If the version does not match, the candidate is rejected and the class loader can continue to search for additional matches.

3. The binary format of the version information and the definition of a version "match" can be customized.

4. The presence of version information is transparent at runtime. Code that uses version information does not look any different from code that does not.

Java's custom metadata is suitable for implementing such a design. The version information is stored in a custom class attribute, which can be accessed via command-line tools during development. At runtime, a special class loader reads and caches the version information and then uses it to rule out classes that do not match.

5.5.2 Serializable Classes as Attributes

The version information needs to take two different forms. The binary class format stores version information as a byte array, but other Java code accesses the version information as a Java object. The obvious approach to writing a Java object that can be converted to and from a byte array is to simply use a `Serializable` object. The `SerializableAttribute` class shown in Listing 5–19 represents a class attribute that is also a Java object.

Listing 5–19   The SerializableAttribute Class

```java
package com.develop.classfile;

import com.develop.util.*;
import java.io.*;

public class SerializableAttribute extends Attribute
{
  private final Object info;
  private final byte [] packet;

  public SerializableAttribute(Object info)
                                  throws IOException {
    super("ser." + info.getClass().getName());
    this.info = info;
    packet = writePacket();
  }
  private SerializableAttribute(String name, short index,
                                  Object info, byte[] packet) {
    super(name, index);
    this.info = info;
    this.packet = packet;
  }

  public static Attribute read(String name, ClassFile cf,
                                  short name_index, int length)
                                  throws IOException
  {
    DataInputStream dis = cf.getStream();
    byte[] packet = new byte[length];
    dis.readFully(packet);
    ObjectInputStream ois = new ObjectInputStream(new
                          ByteArrayInputStream(packet));
    Object info = null;
    try {
      info = ois.readObject();
    }
    catch (ClassNotFoundException cnfe) {
      return new CustomAttribute(name, packet);
    }
    return new SerializableAttribute(name, name_index,
                                     info, packet);
  }
```

```
      private byte[] writePacket() throws IOException {
        ByteArrayOutputStream baos = new ByteArrayOutputStream();
        ObjectOutputStream oos = new ObjectOutputStream(baos);
        oos.writeObject(info);
        return baos.toByteArray();
      }
      public Object getObject() {
        return info;
      }
      public int getLength() {
        return packet.length;
      }
      public void writeToStream(DataOutputStream ds)
                throws IOException {
        super.writeToStream(ds);
        ds.write(packet);
      }
      public String toString() {
        return "Attribute " + getName() + "\n" + info;
      }
    }
```

The `SerializableAttribute` class simply holds two different representations of the same information: `info` holds a Java object, and `packet` holds the serialized form of that same object.

`SerializableAttribute`, and the rest of the code in this section, comes from the Java Class File Editor, an open source project developed by the author (see [JCFE] for details). Classes that are not listed in full here, such as `SerializableAttribute`'s base class `Attribute`, are JCFE classes that deal generically with the binary class format, and they are not specific to the current discussion.

The `SerializableAttribute` class, though originally written for this example, is entirely generic and can store any `Serializable` Java object as a custom class attribute. To construct a `SerializableAttribute` that stores version information, you will pass in an instance of `VersionInfo`, shown in Listing 5–20. The `version` field contains the version of a particular class, in whatever format you find meaningful. The `requiredVersions` field records the versions of other packages that this class depends on. The keys are package names, and the values are version objects in some format that you choose.

Listing 5–20   The VersionInfo Class

```java
package com.develop.version;

import java.io.*;
import java.util.*;

public class VersionInfo implements Serializable {
  private final Object version;
  private final Map requiredVersions;

  public VersionInfo(Object version, HashMap requiredVersions)
  {
    this.version = version;
    this.requiredVersions = requiredVersions;
  }
  public VersionInfo(Object version, String pkgRequired,
                     Object versionRequired) {
    this.version = version;
    requiredVersions = new HashMap();
    requiredVersions.put(pkgRequired, versionRequired);
  }
  public Object getVersion() {
    return version;
  }
  public Map getRequiredVersions() {
    return Collections.unmodifiableMap(requiredVersions);
  }
  public String toString() {
    StringBuffer result = new
                StringBuffer("VersionInfo: ").append(version);
    Set s = requiredVersions.entrySet();
    for (Iterator it = s.iterator(); it.hasNext(); ) {
      Map.Entry e = (Map.Entry) it.next();
      result.append("\t").append(e.getKey())
            .append(": ").append(e.getValue());
    }
    return result.toString();
  }
}
```

5.5.3 Reading Attributes during Class Loading

To take advantage of this version information at runtime, you need a class loader that reads the version attribute *before* loading a class and then compares that version with the `requiredVersions` of all previously loaded classes. Figure 5–2 demonstrates the idea. A `VersioningLoader` searches multiple code sources, and it rejects class versions that do not match the version required by the client.

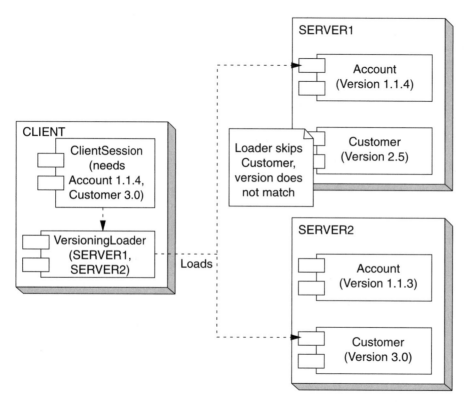

Figure 5–2   Applying a versioning policy

Listing 5–21 shows the `VersioningLoader` class. The meat of the class is the `findClass` method. Rather than loading a class from a single URL that matches the desired class name, the `VersioningLoader` uses `URLClassLoader`'s `findResources` method to return an enumeration of all potential matches, possibly one for each URL searched by the loader. Then, the loader compares each of these classes with the version requirements of previously loaded classes.

Listing 5–21   The VersioningLoader Class

```
package com.develop.version;

import com.develop.classfile.*;
import java.io.*;
import java.net.*;
import java.security.CodeSource;
import java.util.*;

public class VersioningLoader extends URLClassLoader {
  private static boolean auditHit;
  private static boolean auditMiss;
  private static boolean auditFail;
  static {
    String audit =
            System.getProperty("com.develop.version.audit");
    if (audit != null) {
      if (-1 != audit.indexOf("hit")) auditHit = true;
      if (-1 != audit.indexOf("miss")) auditMiss = true;
      if (-1 != audit.indexOf("fail")) auditFail = true;
    }
  }
  private final VersionMatcher vm;
  private static class RequiredVersions {
    HashMap pkgToVersion = new HashMap();
    public List getPackageRequirements(String pkgName,
                                       boolean create) {
      List l = (List) pkgToVersion.get(pkgName);
      if (l == null && create == true) {
       l = new ArrayList();
       pkgToVersion.put(pkgName, l);
      }
      return l;
    }
  }
  RequiredVersions rv = new RequiredVersions();
  public VersioningLoader(URL[] urls, VersionMatcher vm)
  {
    super(urls);
    this.vm = vm;
```

```java
  }
  public VersioningLoader(URL[] urls, ClassLoader parent,
                          VersionMatcher vm) {
    super(urls, parent);
    this.vm = vm;
  }

  public VersioningLoader(URL[] urls, ClassLoader parent,
         URLStreamHandlerFactory fact, VersionMatcher vm)
  {
    super(urls, parent, fact);
    this.vm = vm;
  }
  private URL getURLBase(URL url) {
    URL[] urls = getURLs();
    int length = urls.length;
    String stringForm = url.toExternalForm();
    for (int n=0; n<length; n++) {
      if (stringForm.startsWith(urls[n].toExternalForm())) {
        return urls[n];
      }
    }
    return null;
  }
  private byte[] getClassBytes(URL url) throws IOException {
    InputStream is = url.openStream();
    if (is == null)
      return null;
    ByteArrayOutputStream baos = new ByteArrayOutputStream();
    for (int ch=0; -1 != (ch=is.read()); )
      baos.write(ch);
    return baos.toByteArray();
  }
  private Class defineClass(String name, URL url,
                            byte[] bytes) {
    URL urlBase = getURLBase(url);
    if (urlBase == null) {
      throw new Error("url has no base");
    }
    return defineClass(name, bytes, 0, bytes.length,
                   new CodeSource(urlBase, null));
  }
  private static VersionInfo getVersionInfo(ClassFile cf) {
    SerializableAttribute sa = (SerializableAttribute)cf
```

```
    getAttribute("ser.com.develop.version.VersionInfo");
    if (sa == null) return null;
    return (VersionInfo)sa.getObject();
}
private boolean versionMatches(String name, VersionInfo vi)
{
    int lastDot = name.lastIndexOf('.');
    String pkgName = (lastDot == -1) ? "" :
                        name.substring(0,lastDot);
    List l  = rv.getPackageRequirements(pkgName, false);
    Object version = vi.getVersion();
    if (l == null) return true;
    for (Iterator it = l.iterator(); it.hasNext(); ) {
      if (!vm.verify(it.next(), version)) {
        return false;
      }
    }
    return true;
}
private void updateVersionInfo(VersionInfo newInfo) {
    if (newInfo == null) return;
    Set newEntries = newInfo.getRequiredVersions()
          .entrySet();
    for (Iterator it = newEntries.iterator(); it.hasNext(); )
    {
      Map.Entry entry= (Map.Entry) it.next();
      List l=rv.getPackageRequirements(
          (String)entry.getKey(),
          true);
      l.add(entry.getValue());
    }
}
protected Class findClass(final String name)
    throws ClassNotFoundException
{
    String className = name.replace('.', '/') + ".class";
    try {
      for (Enumeration e = findResources(className);
          e.hasMoreElements() ; ) {
      URL url = (URL) e.nextElement();
      byte[] bytes = getClassBytes(url);
      ClassFile cf = new ClassFile(bytes);
      VersionInfo vi = getVersionInfo(cf);
      if (versionMatches(name, vi)) {
```

```
      //must update version info before resolving class
      updateVersionInfo(vi);
      Class cls = defineClass(name, url, bytes);
      if (auditHit) {
        String vers = (vi == null) ? "" :
                          vi.getVersion().toString();
        System.out.println("VL: Loading " + name + " "
                            + vers + " from " + url);
      }
      return cls;
    }
    if (auditMiss) {
      System.out.println("VL: Missed match " + name
                        + " at URL " + url);
    }
    }
  }
  catch (IOException ioe) {}
  if (auditFail) {
    System.out.println("VL: could not load " + name);
  }
  return null;
  }
}
```

For each candidate class, the loader uses the helper method `getVersion-Info` to extract the class's custom version attribute. Next, the `version-Matches` method compares the candidate's version information with the requirements of previously loaded classes. The `RequiredVersions` nested class manages the cache of requirements. Note that there can be more than one requirement and that the candidate class must match all requirements. If the candidate is satisfactory, then its requirements are added to the cache via a call to `updateVersionInfo`. Finally, the class is loaded into the VM by `define-Class`. The ordering of these last two steps is very important. The version information must be cached before the new class is loaded because loading the class will probably trigger requests for other classes.

The `VersioningLoader` supports a flexible notion of "matching" versions. The actual work of matching version metadata is performed by an implementation of the `VersionMatcher` interface. The interface, plus a trivial implementation that requires an exact match, is shown in Listing 5–22. You can write your own `VersionMatcher` implementations for other common versioning strategies. For example, you can store a standard dotted version number and always insist upon the highest-numbered version, or you can require a specific major version but accept any minor version. The JCFE functions for adding version attributes to a binary class could easily be integrated into a build process, which would make the use of version metadata transparent to application developers.

Listing 5–22   The VersionMatcher Interface

```
package com.develop.version;
public interface VersionMatcher {
  public boolean verify(Object requiredVersion,
                        Object matchVersion);
}

package com.develop.version;
public class ExactMatcher implements VersionMatcher {
  public boolean verify(Object requiredVersion,
                        Object matchVersion) {
    return requiredVersion.equals(matchVersion);
  }}
```

5.5.4   Debugging Support

One final aspect of the `VersioningLoader` deserves mention. During its static initializer, the loader inspects the system property `com.develop.version.audit` looking for the strings `hit`, `miss`, and/or `fail`. If the property includes any of these strings, debugging output is sent to `System.out`. The `hit` output logs classes that are loaded, and the `miss` output logs classes that are skipped because their version data does not match. The `fail` output logs a complete failure to load a class, which means that either no classes were found, or that none of them were of the correct version. This debugging information is very helpful to application developers because the only time they are likely to encounter this infrastructure code is when something goes wrong. The idiom of using a system property to turn on various logging options is borrowed from other infrastructure projects in the Java platform itself, including both security and RMI.

Listing 5–23 shows audit output from the `VersioningLoader`. In this example, the loader is searching five URLs. First, the loader finds the `Caller` class with version information "Version1" at `loc1`. Then, the loader begins to seek for a matching version of a class named `Callee`. Each of the five URLs has a `Callee` class, but only the final URL at `loc5` has the correct version. So, the loader considers and rejects the other `Callee` binaries, finally accepting the correct one at `loc5`.

Listing 5–23   Audit Output from VersioningLoader

```
VL: Loading test.version.Caller Version0 from
file:/E:/jcfe/testout/loc0/test/version/Caller.class
VL: Missed match test.version.Callee at URL
file:/E:/jcfe/testout/loc0/test/version/Callee.class
VL: Missed match test.version.Callee at URL
file:/E:/jcfe/testout/loc1/test/version/Callee.class
VL: Missed match test.version.Callee at URL
file:/E:/jcfe/testout/loc2/test/version/Callee.class
VL: Missed match test.version.Callee at URL
file:/E:/jcfe/testout/loc3/test/version/Callee.class
VL: Loading test.version.Callee Version0 from
file:/E:/jcfe/testout/loc4/test/version/Callee.class
```

While the `VersioningLoader` is valuable in itself, it is intended to be illustrative rather than definitive. There are many other ways to approach versioning on the Java platform. You might want to use JAR metadata in addition to or instead of class metadata. You would almost certainly want to consider versioning relationships across multiple class loaders. The important point of this example is that *custom class metadata provides a way to extend the platform itself.* Rather than working around problems in the Java platform, you may be able to augment the Java platform to fit the way you work.

5.6   Onward

Custom class loaders allow you to define your own strategy for locating code and resources. You can make your own rules, as long as you can take a Java class name and turn it into a byte array in the binary class format. With custom class loaders you might load classes from an object database, from source control, or over a custom network protocol.

Protocol handlers split the responsibility of class loading into two distinct tasks. A `URLClassLoader` instance performs security work, assigning the `CodeSource` that will be used to associate the class with its runtime permissions. A protocol handler defines a URL protocol for locating resources that you can plug in anywhere the Java platform uses URLs. For many custom class loading tasks, you could use either a custom loader or a protocol handler, but protocol handlers have the advantage of being used to locate other resources besides classes.

Custom class loaders have advantages as well. A custom loader can process custom attributes added to a binary class. You can use custom attributes to extend the behavior of the Java classes in arbitrary ways, which are not directly correlated to the Java language itself. The `VersioningLoader` of this chapter is a powerful example; it shows that you can add valuable customizations to the process of Java class loading without changing the appearance of the platform to application developers.

5.7 Resources

There are several resources that cover different aspects of custom class loading. For a thorough treatment of the Java 2 security model, see [Gon99]. If you are writing custom class loaders, [New00] has some interesting examples. If you are writing a custom protocol handler, look at [Mas01], which describes a protocol handler for the Win32 registry.

If you are interested in custom attributes, and the loaders that read them, download the source code at [JCFE], which is a generic architecture for extending class loading and reflection to handle custom attributes.

Chapter 6

Interop 1: JNI

This chapter introduces you to the essentials of using the Java Native Interface (JNI) to integrate Java code with platform-specific code. For further coverage of how to use JNI to build a more intuitive, robust communication layer between Java and Win32/COM components, see Appendix A.

6.1 Why Interoperate?

A key goal of Java is to provide a consistent platform and API over the specific hardware and software of a particular machine. To the extent that this platform functions correctly and delivers services needed by programmers, Java achieves its objective of being write-once, run-anywhere (WORA). Developers write a single code base, which functions correctly across multiple processors and operating systems, saving the cost of redeveloping the same basic logic over and over again for different platforms. Organizations that adopt Java often value cross-platform code so highly that they insist that *all* new development be done in Java. In this brave new world, there is no need to interoperate with other languages or environments because Java replaces everything else.

Now, back to the real world. While 100 percent pure Java is a laudable objective on some kinds of projects, it is usually unrealistic. No single tool, even Java, is perfect for every task. Single-tool aficionados should heed Mark Twain's warning: "When all you have is a hammer, all problems start to look like nails." Here are several tasks for which Java is ill-suited:

- Direct access to system memory. Java deliberately prevents direct access to system memory, which in most situations is a great benefit in reducing bugs. However, some hardware devices are queried and controlled through direct access to memory.

- Accessing platform-specific resources. Java provides a standard API for services that most operating systems provide, such as file and network access. However, by definition, Java cannot provide a cross-platform API to a platform-specific service, such as the Windows Registry.

- Accessing code libraries not written in Java. Many organizations already have a large base of well-understood, field-tested code. Even if they wanted to port all this code to Java, the development time and cost would likely be prohibitive.

- Hand-tuned, peak performance code. Java's performance is sufficient for many types of applications being written today. However, there always have been, and probably always will be, certain code paths that need to be hand-tuned in a systems programming language, such as C++, or even in an assembly language.

All of these examples share a common theme, which is the occasional need to escape the confines of the virtual machine. A well-designed hybrid system gets the best of both worlds: 90 percent of the code lives inside a virtual machine, where it enjoys the comforts of runtime type safety, memory protections, and discretionary access control. The remaining 10 percent visits the hostile space outside of the virtual machine, but only long enough to provide some specialized service.

A poorly designed hybrid system, on the other hand, experiences all the problems of both Java and native code: the overhead of the virtual machine plus the mysterious failures endemic to systems programming. Managing the boundary between Java and native code requires careful attention to preserving the benefits of each environment.

JNI allows a Java virtual machine to share a process space with platform native code, typically written in C or C++. From Java, you can find, load, and invoke a native language method, free of the rules of the virtual machine. The converse is also true; from a native language, you can start a virtual machine and then find, load, and invoke methods on Java classes.

JNI itself is a cross-platform standard that is provided by any compliant Java virtual machine. However, the things that you *do* with JNI are usually platform-specific. For purposes of this chapter, I am going to use C++ and the Microsoft Windows platform for JNI examples. This choice of language and OS probably represents the most common use of JNI, but the examples should be representative of issues you encounter with other languages or platforms as well.

Because C++ and Java are radically different development environments, there are several subtleties to consider when crossing the border between the virtual machine and native code. This chapter will cover the most important of these: the dangers of native code, loading native code, method invocation, error handling, and resource management.

6.2 The Dangers of Native Code

The dangers are the easiest part to understand. When you leave the virtual machine, you leave behind all its built-in protections. Java's memory protections do not apply in native code, so native methods can corrupt memory or the VM itself. Java's security checks do not apply in native code, so your native methods operate with essentially "all permissions." Type safety is a fiction in native code, so feel free to treat a `CArm` like a `CLeg` if you like.[1]

Once you internalize the fact that the virtual machine has no control over the behavior of native code, other JNI design decisions make more sense. For example, JNI allows native code to bypass language protection modifiers and to invoke methods nonvirtually. This would seem horribly dangerous if you had not accepted that JNI is *innately* a dangerous environment when compared to pure Java.

Since JNI is so dangerous, why use it at all? In general, you should avoid it. If Java provides a service, there is typically no reason to reimplement that service in native code. Most of the services you will need are already in the Java APIs: files, sockets, databases, user interfaces, security, and so on. But when

---

1. In a type-safe world, your `CHand` would get tired and callused. In native code, such a type gaffe will cause a memory fault—if you are lucky.

you do need JNI, you *really* need it. Simply make sure that you enter a relationship with JNI with your eyes open. JNI will make your Java projects more expensive to develop and maintain. Poorly written native code can make an otherwise excellent Java system totally unreliable. JNI puts the entire native platform under your control; use that power sparingly and wisely.

6.3   Finding and Loading Native Code

Bridging between Java and native code is both a logical and a physical problem. The logical problem is one of disparate naming and typing systems. To solve this problem, JNI defines a complete, unambiguous mapping from Java names and types to C++ names and types.[2] The physical problem is finding and loading the appropriate native binary. The process of finding and loading native code is very similar to the process of loading Java classes. Both processes are well defined, but they tend to produce cryptic errors and be poorly understood by developers. This section covers the logical and physical mapping between Java and native code, and it shows how to troubleshoot the most common problems.

JNI is normally used to provide native implementations of methods declared in Java. The `native` keyword indicates that a particular method has a native implementation, as shown in the `getAnswer` method of Listing 6–1.

Listing 6–1   The native Keyword

```
package com.develop;
public class UltimateQuestion {
  public static native int getAnswer();
}
```

When the virtual machine encounters a call to `getAnswer`, it will expect that the method has already been successfully coded, compiled, linked, located, and loaded. JNI does not provide an implicit mechanism such as the class loader architecture, so you must manually execute each of these steps.

---

2. JNI does *not* define a complete mapping from C/C++ names and types back into Java.

6.3.1 Name Mappings

JNI defines a specific name mapping from Java method names to C++ library entry points. For a simple method call, the C++ name should be

```
Java_packagename_classname_methodname
```

So, a C++ implementation of `getNative` would have the name

```
Java_com_develop_UltimateQuestion_getNative
```

Return and parameter types pose a more complex problem. In Java, the size of every type is well defined, but in C++ type sizes can vary from platform to platform. JNI introduces a layer of indirection to deal with this. For every Java primitive type `foo`, JNI declares a C++ type `jfoo` in a platform-specific header file. The platform header uses a `typedef` to map `jfoo` to the matching sized C++ type on that platform. For example, Listing 6–2 shows how JNI handles `int` on a Win32 platform.

Listing 6–2   Platform-Specific Native Mapping of Java int Type

```
//from jni.h, located in ${JAVA_HOME}/include
#include "jni_md.h"

//jni_md.h is a platform-specific header file
//this is from the version in ${JAVA_HOME}/include/win32
typedef long jint;
```

On all platforms, the JNI representation of `int` will be called `jint`. As you can see here, the Win32 implementation of `jint` is simply a `long`. Other platforms might define `jint` differently.

6.3.2 Type Mappings

JNI disposes of language differences in the primitive types with ease. It is when you look at passing object references between Java and C++ that you begin to see how different the languages really are. C++ allows arbitrary pointer indirection, distinguishes between structures and classes,[3] permits

---

3. The distinction between the `struct` and `class` keywords is minimal: Structures default to public access while classes default to private. However, structs and classes tend to be used in different ways, and there is no obvious way to capture this in Java.

multiple inheritance, and supports passing parameters by reference or by value. Java has no pointers, has no notion of a structure as distinct from a class, allows only single implementation inheritance, and always passes parameters by value. These differences cause major problems for any generic mapping between Java and C++ objects:

- Since Java does not permit multiple inheritance, there is no easy way to represent an arbitrary C++ class hierarchy in Java.

- Although Java always passes parameters by value, the value that is copied onto a method stack is a reference to the object. Methods have their own copy of the reference, but they share access to the referenced object. As a result, changes made through the reference are visible outside the method. This is usually desirable for C++ "classes" that encapsulate complex behavior and state, but it may be inappropriate for simple C++ "structs" that are simply typed collections of data.[4]

- If a C++ parameter contains multiple levels of indirection, or if it is used to return information to the caller, it is often unclear what the corresponding Java method declaration should look like.

Many of these difficulties stem from the ambiguities permitted by the C++ type system. Consider the following C++ method declarations:

```
void foo(char** arg);
void bar(void* arg);
```

Each of these methods has many possible interpretations. The argument to foo might be a two-dimensional array of characters, an array of null-terminated strings, or an address that the method will assign to point to a single null-terminated string. The argument to bar could be anything at all. From a Java perspective, the problem is a lack of metadata.

There are many possible solutions to the problem of mapping types between different languages such as Java and C++. The most complete solutions

---

4. Remember that the C++ keywords class and struct do not mandate this distinction in intended usage.

supplement the metadata available at the language level with additional metadata to resolve ambiguities between language-level type systems. CORBA and DCOM are examples of this approach; both use an interface definition language (IDL) to completely describe method types and provide a suite of tools to generate the appropriate language mappings.

For better or worse, JNI takes a much simpler approach. JNI does not define *any mapping at all* from C++ types to Java types. JNI defines a complete but minimalist mapping from Java types to C++ types. Instead of representing Java objects as C++ classes or structures, JNI maps Java objects to opaque handles, which are declared as type `jobject` and subclasses. From C++, you can pass these handles to helper functions implemented by a VM-provided object called the JNI environment pointer. The JNI environment pointer, typed as `JNIEnv*`, is a C++ vtable of callback functions that allow reflective manipulation of Java objects.

The `jobject` and `JNIEnv` types are covered in §6.4. For now, the important detail is that every Java native method translates to a C++ method with two extra arguments: the `JNIEnv*` for calling back into the VM, and the `jobject` `this` reference for the method. For example, the declaration for the native implementation of the `getAnswer` method from Listing 6–1 is

```
JNIEXPORT jint JNICALL
Java_com_develop_UltimateQuestion_getAnswer(JNIEnv*,jclass);
```

The `int` return type in Java has been converted to a C++ `jint`, as expected. The Java method declared no arguments, so the C++ implementation has only the two "extra" arguments mandated by JNI. Note that since the method was declared static, there is no `this` and the second argument is a `jclass` subtype of `jobject`, which references the `UltimateQuestion` class. Additional arguments, if there had been any, would have followed these two. The `JNIEXPORT` and `JNICALL` macros are platform-specific and are used to hide the platform-specific details of correctly exporting an entry point that the VM can link dynamically.

6.3.3 Overloaded Names

The naming and type-mapping convention described thus far is fine for most methods, but it breaks down for overloaded methods with the same name. For such methods, JNI defines an additional name-mangling scheme, whereby the method parameters are encoded as valid C++ name characters and tacked onto the end of the method name. For example, consider the following overloaded Java methods:

```
public native void causeConfusion(String arg);
public native void causeConfusion(int[] arg);
```

For overloaded methods, arguments are encoded in a multistep process:

1. Append a double underbar (__) to the nonoverloaded version of the type name.

2. Select the type name used internally by the VM, as shown in Table 6–1.

3. Escape any characters that would be illegal in C++ names, using the escape codes shown in Table 6–2.

Table 6–1   Virtual Machine Type Names

Java Type	VM Name
int	I
float	F
long	J
double	D
byte	B
boolean	Z
short	S
char	C
anytype[]	[*anytype*
somepkg.SomeClass	L*somepkg.SomeClass*;

Table 6–2   JNI Name Mangling of non-C++ Type Names

Character	Mangled Form
_	_1
;	_2
[	_3
Unicode with hex value XXXX	_0XXXX

The correct JNI method declarations for the `causeConfusion` methods look like this when wrapped to fit the printed page:

```
JNIEXPORT void JNICALL
Java_com_develop_UltimateQuestion_causeConfusion__Ljava_lang_Stri
ng_2(JNIEnv *, jobject, jstring);

JNIEXPORT void JNICALL
Java_com_develop_UltimateQuestion_causeConfusion___3I(
JNIEnv *, jobject, jintArray);
```

This gets ugly fast—they don't call it name mangling for nothing. Fortunately, you do not need to generate these method declarations by hand. The Java SDK includes a command-line tool, `javah`, that extracts the metadata for the native methods in a list of classes and generates an appropriate header file. For example, the `javah` command

```
javah -d ../cpp com.develop.UltimateQuestion
```

uses the metadata in the `UltimateQuestion` class to generate the header file `../cpp/UltimateQuestion.h`. To avoid errors when you are linking to native code, you should always use `javah` to generate the correct method names.

6.3.4   Loading Native Libraries

The naming conventions, plus the mappings for primitive and object types, solve the logical problem. The remaining problem is a physical one; that is, where does the virtual machine look to find implementations of native methods? The first important point is that there is no association between the native library name and the methods it contains. It is reasonable and common to implement `Foo`'s native methods in a library named Foo. However, it is equally reasonable to group all native methods for an entire application in a library named App. It is perverse, but still legal, to place the implementation of `Foo`'s native methods in a library named Bar, or to spread them across several libraries. No matter, the virtual machine will automatically match C++ entry points to Java methods using the naming conventions described above. The only thing you have to do is call a JNI load API that loads the requisite native library before a particular native method is actually invoked.

The lowest-level load API is `Runtime.load`, which takes a full path to the shared library. Assuming that you have compiled a C++ implementation of the `UltimateQuestion` methods into a `d:\shared` directory on a Win32 machine, the Java code in Listing 6–3 would cause the library to be loaded:

Listing 6–3   Linking with Full Paths

```
//EXAMPLE ONLY. DO NOT USE HARD-CODED PATH NAMES!
public class HardPathClient {
  public static void main(String [] args) {
    UltimateQuestion uq = new UltimateQuestion();
    Runtime.getRuntime.load(
          "d:/shared/UltimateQuestion.dll");
    System.out.println(uq.causeConfusion("babble"));
  }
}
```

Notice that the call to `load` occurs after an `UltimateQuestion` instance has already been created. Native methods can be loaded at any time: before loading the associated Java class, while loading the class, or after creating instances of a class. Native methods can even be loaded after a prior attempt to invoke them throws an error.

Despite its simplicity, the code above is unmaintainable and should be avoided. The placement of a hard-coded path in the Java source code ties method loading to a compile-time decision, which is contrary to the spirit of Java. Avoid `Runtime.load`.

The preferred approach to loading native code is the `System.loadLibrary` method. Although `loadLibrary` takes a string argument, just as `Runtime.load` does, the argument is interpreted very differently. The string passed to `loadLibrary` is a library name, not a full path. In fact, path names and extensions are illegal in strings passed to `loadLibrary`. With `loadLibrary`, you specify only the short name of the library, and the path to search is controlled through virtual machine options. In order to make library dependencies more clear, and to guarantee that native libraries are loaded in time to service native method calls, you typically place the call to `loadLibrary` in a static initializer for the class that declares the native methods, as shown here:

```
public class UltimateQuestion {
  static { System.loadLibrary("UltimateQuestion"); }
  //as before…
}
```

This style has several advantages over the approach that used `Runtime.load`. Because the native library is loaded in a static initializer of the declaring class, clients of `UltimateQuestion` do not have to worry about loading the native methods. The use of the short form name of the library allows the virtual machine to apply an appropriate name translation for the current platform, for example, UltimateQuestion.dll for Win32, libUltimateQuestion.so for UNIX, and so on. Most importantly, the short form name leaves the exact load path as a runtime configuration issue.

The native library load path is specified by the `java.library.path` system property. You can specify this property yourself on the command line for the Java launcher, like this:

```
java -Djava.library.path=../UltimateQuestion/ \
UltimateQuestionClient
```

If you do not specify a library path, the virtual machine will establish a search path in a platform-dependent fashion. Currently, on Solaris the Sun virtual machine uses the value of the environment variable `LD_LIBRARY_PATH`, and on Win32 it uses the value of `PATH`. Do not rely on these environment settings in a production system. Environment variables are subject to deliberate or accidental modification by users and other programs; so far, the history of Java has seen a constant shift away from environment variables and toward explicit arguments to the command-line tools. In Java, environment variables are a useful crutch for beginners, but nothing more. Minimize the potential for confusion by always specifying the load path on the command line or from a shell script.

6.3.5   Class Loaders and JNI

Native code has a complex relationship with the class loader delegation model. `System.loadLibrary` delegates to the current class loader to actually load the library; the code that analyzes `java.library.path` actually lives in the `ClassLoader` class. Class loaders add three wrinkles to the basic native loading story: the `findLibrary` method, the `sun.boot.library.path` option, and the handling of multiple libraries.

First, a class loader can override the `findLibrary` method, shown in Listing 6–4, to augment the normal library search algorithm.

Listing 6–4   The find Library Method

```
package java.lang;
public class ClassLoader {
  protected String findLibrary(String libname) {
    return null;
  }
  //remainder omitted for clarity
}
```

If a class loader implementation overrides this method and returns a full path, then that path is passed to `Runtime.load` to load the library.

Second, `ClassLoader` checks another path before consulting `java.library.path`. Class loaders first check `findLibrary`, then the paths listed on `sun.boot.library.path`, and only after these checks fail does it resort to checking `java.library.path`. Neither `findLibrary` nor the boot path are widely used. Most class loaders do not override `findLibrary`, and `sun.boot.library.path` is intended not for loading application libraries, but for customizing native code used by the virtual machine itself. Use `sun.boot.library.path` to specify alternate locations for VM code such as JIT compilers, and use `java.library.path` to locate application native code.

The third, and most important, wrinkle introduced by class loaders is the treatment of multiple versions of native code. Remember that class loader delegations define namespaces (§2.4.4). Classes loaded by a more senior class loader are visible to all subordinate class loaders, allowing code to be shared. Classes loaded by junior class loaders are not visible to each other, thus allowing multiple implementations of the same class to coexist.

Unfortunately, JNI makes a brutal simplification of these delegation rules. In early versions of Java, native libraries ignore the delegation model and are visible across all class loaders. This causes problems since two different versions of a class will get the same native implementations whether they want to or not, as shown in Figure 6–1.

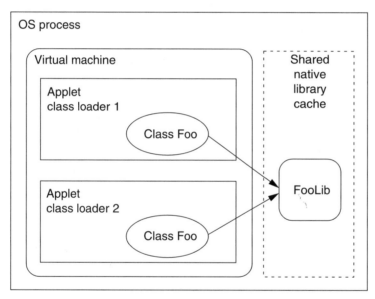

Figure 6–1 Prior to Java 2, multiple class loaders shared the native cache.

Versions of the Java SDK from 1.2 onward partially fix this problem by making native code visible only to a class loader delegation. This prevents unrelated classes from accidentally or maliciously linking with the wrong native methods. However, the specification now says that the same JNI library cannot be loaded into more than one class loader at any given time (see Figure 6–2). This makes it difficult to dynamically update classes with native methods. If the class loads its

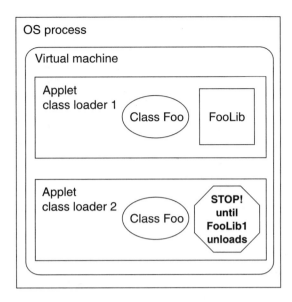

Figure 6–2 Post Java 2, each delegation has its own native libraries.

own native methods, then no other class loader can load the same library, at least not until the first class is garbage collected.

There are three workarounds for JNI's weak handling of multiple native library versions:

1. Load native code via a senior class loader (such as the application loader) that is not involved in hot deployment. The downside is that while the classes can be updated on-the-fly, the native methods can never change.

2. Always make sure that an old version of a native library gets unloaded. This requires careful discipline so that a class loader can be garbage collected, plus a virtual machine with an aggressive, reliable implementation of `System.gc` and `System.runFinalization` functionality.

3. Build your own scheme that avoids collisions by incrementing the library name each time a native library is redeployed.

All of these are gross hacks when compared to the elegance of Java class loading. The unfortunate truth is that interoperability is a fairly low priority, and JNI has evolved just enough to (partially) deflect criticism from developers.

6.3.6 Common Errors Loading Native Libraries

There are several errors associated with loading and linking to native code. The most basic problem is failing to call `loadLibrary` before executing a native method, which leads to a fairly obvious `UnsatisfiedLinkError` at the point where you attempt to invoke the method. In Listing 6–5, the `ForgetToLoadLibrary` class demonstrates this problem:

Listing 6–5 Forgetting to Call loadLibrary

```
public class ForgetToLoadLibrary {
  public static native void neverLoaded();
  public static void main(String [] args) {
    neverLoaded();
  }
}
>java ForgetToLoadLibrary
>java.lang.UnsatisfiedLinkError: neverLoaded
    at ForgetToLoadLibrary.neverLoaded(Native Method)
```

If `loadLibrary` fails to find a library file matching the name specified, a different error is thrown at the point of the `loadLibrary` call, as shown by the `LoadNonExistentLibrary` example in Listing 6–6:

Listing 6–6 Loading a Non Existent Library

```
public class LoadNonExistentLibrary {
  public static native void neverLoaded();
  public static void main(String [] args) {
    System.loadLibrary("DoesNotExist");
    neverLoaded();
  }
}
>java LoadNonExistentLibrary
>java.lang.UnsatisfiedLinkError: no DoesNotExist in
java.library.path
at java.lang.ClassLoader.loadLibrary(ClassLoader.java:1312)
```

Both of the problems generate an `UnsatisfiedLinkError`, which is an unchecked subclass of `Error`. The javadoc documentation for `Error` states that an `Error` "indicates serious problems that a reasonable application should not try to catch." `UnsatisfiedLinkError` is an obvious exception to this rule. It is entirely reasonable to write an application that checks to see if some native-based service is available and then continues down a different path if the service cannot be loaded.

A subtler problem occurs if you make one or more successful calls to `loadLibrary`, but none of them loads an entry point that matches the signature of the native method you are calling. This causes the same `UnsatisfiedLinkError` that you saw in Listing 6–5, as shown by the `LoadTheWrongLibrary` example in Listing 6–7:

Listing 6–7   Loading the Wrong Library

```
public class LoadTheWrongLibrary {
  public static native void neverLoaded();
  public static void main(String [] args) {
    //load some unrelated library
    System.loadLibrary("UltimateQuestion");
    neverLoaded();
  }
}
>java -Djava.library.path=UltimateQPath LoadTheWrongLibrary
>java.lang.UnsatisfiedLinkError: neverLoaded
    at LoadTheWrongLibrary.neverLoaded(Native Method)
```

Old symptom, but new problem. The error does not occur until the native method invocation; this indicates that `loadLibrary` found a library but not one that contained the `neverLoaded` method. There are three likely ways that this problem can occur, all involving abuse of the `javah` tool:

1. If you misspell method or type names in the native method declaration, the JNI naming algorithm will not be able to locate the method. Avoid this problem by obtaining the declaration from the `.h` file that `javah` generates.

2. If you are using a C++ compiler, the compiler may do its own name mangling, changing the names to a form that is unrecognizable by the VM. Wrapping your method declarations or implementations in an `extern "C"` block prevents this, and `#include`ing the `javah`-generated `.h` file does this for you automatically.

3. There is a bug in `javah`'s handling of packages. The native declaration for a method should include a prefix based on the package name, as shown in

Listing 6–8. However, `javah` infers the package structure from the current directory instead of from the package name. Inexperienced Java programmers tend to navigate all the way to a class's directory before running `javah`. Instead of generating an error, `javah` produces a corrupt `.h` file that does not include the package names, as shown in Listing 6–9 below. Listing 6–8 shows the correct usage.

Listing 6–8   Correct Handling of Package Names

```
package com.develop;
public class PackageDweller {
  public native void nativeMethod();
}

>cd classes
>javah com.develop.PackageDweller

//excerpt from com_develop_PackageDweller.h
//with correct package names
JNIEXPORT void JNICALL
Java_com_develop_PackageDweller_nativeMethod
(JNIEnv *, jobject);
```

Listing 6–9   Incorrect Handling of Package Names

```
>cd classes/com/develop
>javah PackageDweller

//excerpt from PackageDweller.h.
//Note package names missing from method
JNIEXPORT void JNICALL Java_PackageDweller_nativeMethod
(JNIEnv *, jobject);
```

6.3.7   Troubleshooting Native Loading

There are some tools that can help to diagnose JNI-related bugs. Just as with class loading, Java provides a debugging flag specific for JNI. The `verbose:jni` flag tells the runtime to generate (among other things) console output for every native method loaded. Unfortunately, it does not tell where the method was loaded from or what files were attempted when a native load fails. It would be straightforward to write a custom version of `java.lang.ClassLoader` that produces a more complete log of native activity and then install the custom version by setting the bootclasspath as described in Chapter 2. Finally, most operating systems have debugging tools that allow you to monitor both file access and loading of shared libraries.

Resorting to any of these techniques is probably overkill because native loading is not nearly as complex as class loading. Now that you are armed with the short list of problem cases above, you should be able to troubleshoot most JNI loading problems by inspection.

The process of loading native code is the source of many beginner headaches, but it is not terribly complex once you know the basics. The naming and search process are important, but arbitrary, details. The one place where the loading process intersects with more significant issues is in the type mappings between Java objects and `jobject` handles. This design decision greatly curtails how JNI can be used, and it is covered more thoroughly in §6.4.

6.4 Calling Java from C++

Once you have crossed the boundary into a native method implementation, you can stay there and do whatever the underlying platform will allow. However, to do anything significant, you will probably need to call back into the virtual machine. Any Java object that is passed into native code appears as an opaque `jobject` handle, not as a C++ structure or vtable. Therefore, the only way to access fields or methods on a `jobject` is to call back into the virtual machine through the provided `JNIEnv` pointer. Also, because the `jobject` type is opaque at compile time, there is no direct invocation of Java methods or direct access of Java fields. Instead, the `JNIEnv*` provides a set of functions similar to the `Field`, `Method`, and `Constructor` objects in Java reflection.

All JNI access to the virtual machine is reflective. This makes calling back into the virtual machine both tedious to code and slow to execute. The essence of good JNI design is to understand the expense of the boundary crossings between native code and the virtual machine and to minimize them.

As a simple example of the problems at the Java/native boundary, consider the `NativePoint` class as shown in Listing 6–10.

Listing 6–10 The NativePoint Class

```
public class NativePoint {
  private int x;
  private int y;
  public String toString() {
    return "x= " + x + " y= " + y;
  }
  public void move(int xinc, int yinc) {
    x += xinc;
    y += yinc;
  }
  public native void nativeMove(int xinc, int yinc);
}
```

In order to implement the `nativeMove` method, you must access the `NativePoint` class, use reflection to discover fields `x` and `y`, then use reflective access to extract the old value of each field, and then use reflective access to set the new value of each field. In total, this requires seven trips from native code back into the virtual machine, as shown here in Listing 6–11.

Listing 6–11 A Simple Native Method Implementation

```
//error handling omitted for brevity
JNIEXPORT void JNICALL Java_NativePoint_nativeMove
  (JNIEnv *pEnv, jobject obj, jint xinc, jint yinc)
{
  jclass cls = pEnv->GetObjectClass(obj);
  jfieldID fldX = pEnv->GetFieldID(cls, "x", "I");
  jfieldID fldY = pEnv->GetFieldID(cls, "y", "I");
  int x = pEnv->GetIntField(obj, fldX);
  int y = pEnv->GetIntField(obj, fldY);
  pEnv->SetIntField(obj, fldX, x + xinc);
  pEnv->SetIntField(obj, fldY, y + yinc);
}
```

If you allow for the omnipresent `JNIEnv*` and for stylistic differences between C++ and Java, this code looks very similar to reflective access code written in Java. This example shows manipulation of integer fields; all the other primitive types have similar methods as summarized in Listing 6–12.

For field access, there are only three substantive differences between JNI and Java reflection:

1. The `GetFieldID` method takes an extra parameter that specifies the type of field. The type must be specified using the virtual machine's internal naming scheme, as shown in Table 6–1 earlier in this chapter.

2. All the handle types in the `jobject` family have special lifetime constraints dictated by the needs of the garbage collector. Unless otherwise noted, JNI references to Java objects are method local and thread local. The reasons for this are discussed in more detail under §6.6.

3. JNI does not make the distinction between public and nonpublic fields implied by reflection's `getField` and `getDeclaredField` methods. JNI-style reflection ignores language-level protections at all times.

Listing 6–12   JNI APIs for Field Access

```
struct JNIEnv {
//introspection:
jfieldID GetFieldID(jclass clazz, const char *name,
                    const char *sig);
jfieldID GetStaticFieldID(jclass clazz, const char *name,
                          const char *sig);

//access: in the following declarations, replace type with
//object, int, float, long, double, boolean, short, byte, char
jtype GetTypeField(jobject obj, jfieldID fieldID);
void SetTypeField(jobject obj, jfieldID fieldID, jtype val);
jtype GetStaticTypeField(jclass clazz, jfieldID fieldID);
void
SetStaticTypeField(jclass clazz, jfieldID fieldID,jtype val);
//remainder omitted for clarity
};
```

The C++ implementation of `nativeMove` is much more tedious and error-prone to write than the Java implementation of `move`, which does essentially the same task. However, C++ programmers are expert in using macros to hide such tedium, so in the long run, this might not be a significant issue.

More important is the performance penalty for making so many crossings back into the virtual machine. In a simple test, the `move` method took approximately 40 nsec, while the `nativeMove` method took 5,000 nsec, which is over

100 times slower. For comparison, you can run the same test on your own configuration using the `TimePoint` and `TimeNativePoint` classes included on the website for this book [Hal01]. The relative numbers can vary widely depending on your virtual machine and hardware, but the native method should always be slower.

There are two conclusions to be drawn from this result. First, you should *not* use JNI to try to speed up small-grained methods. Even if your C++ implementation of an algorithm runs faster than the same algorithm in Java, the overhead of crossing the JNI boundary will overwhelm any language difference for small methods. Second, you should write your code to minimize the number of round trips from Java to native code.

6.4.1 Minimizing Round Trips

Look back at the implementation of `nativeMove` from Listing 6–11, and you will see that the last four method calls are unavoidable. However, the `jfieldID` values are valid for the lifetime of a class, so these values can and should be precalculated. As of SDK 1.2, JNI provides the perfect hook for this, via the `JNI_OnLoad` method. Listing 6–13 demonstrates an improved `nativeMove` implementation that precalculates the `jfieldID`s when the library is loaded.

Listing 6–13   Improving JNI Performance by Precalculating jfieldIDs

```
JNIEXPORT jint JNICALL JNI_OnLoad(JavaVM* vm, void* reserved) {
  JNIEnv* pEnv;
  if (JNI_OK != vm->GetEnv((void **)&pEnv, JNI_VERSION_1_2))
  {
    return JNI_EVERSION;
  }
  jclass cls = pEnv->FindClass("NativePoint");
  s_fldX = pEnv->GetFieldID(cls, "x", "I");
  s_fldY = pEnv->GetFieldID(cls, "y", "I");
  return JNI_VERSION_1_2;
}
JNIEXPORT void JNICALL Java_NativePoint_nativeMove
  (JNIEnv *pEnv, jobject obj, jint xinc, jint yinc)
{ //use the fieldIDs precalculated in JNI_OnLoad
  int x = pEnv->GetIntField(obj, s_fldX);
  int y = pEnv->GetIntField(obj, s_fldY);
```

```
pEnv->SetIntField(obj, s_fldX, x + xinc);
pEnv->SetIntField(obj, s_fldY, y + yinc);
}
```

The documented purpose of JNI_OnLoad is to return the version of JNI that the library expects, in this case JNI_VERSION_1_2. The method also provides a perfect place to cache values that will be useful for the lifetime of the library, such as jfieldIDs. On my test machine, this new version of nativeMove is five times faster than the original (but still twenty times slower than the all-Java move method).

Given this performance disparity, you will probably only use JNI for tasks that are simply impossible to perform in Java. For example, imagine that the NativePoint class actually controls the location of a robot on a grid. The custom software for controlling the object is only exposed as a C-style API, so you cannot move the robot directly from Java. Listing 6–14 shows a version of nativeMove that could be used to move the robot.

Listing 6–14 Using JNI to Call a C-Style API

```
static jmethodID s_methMove;
//stubbed-out robot API
void moveRobot(int xinc, int yinc) {
}
JNIEXPORT void JNICALL Java_NativePoint_nativeMove
  (JNIEnv *pEnv, jobject obj, jint xinc, jint yinc)
{
  moveRobot(xinc, yinc);
  pEnv->CallVoidMethod(obj, s_methMove, xinc, yinc);
}
JNIEXPORT jint JNICALL JNI_OnLoad(JavaVM* vm, void* reserved) {
  JNIEnv* pEnv;
  if (JNI_OK != vm->GetEnv((void **)&pEnv, JNI_VERSION_1_2)) {
    return JNI_EVERSION;
  }
  jclass cls = pEnv->FindClass("NativePoint");
  s_methMove = pEnv->GetMethodID(cls, "move", "(II)V");
  return JNI_VERSION_1_2;
}
```

There are several new things transpiring here. Notice that instead of calling back into the virtual machine four times to get and set `x` and `y`, the `native-Point` implementation is simply leveraging the Java implementation of `move`. Just as with field access, JNI method access looks very similar to reflection. The `GetMethodID` method returns a `jmethodID`, which should be cached just as `jfieldID`s are. The `CallVoidMethod` callback is used to invoke the method, and it is one of a large family of similarly named methods that vary by the return type and by the C++ notation for passing an unknown number of arguments (see Listing 6–15).

Listing 6–15   JNI APIs for Method Access

```
struct JNIEnv {
//introspection:
jmethodID GetMethodID
        (jclass clazz, const char *name, const char *sig);
jmethodID GetStaticMethodID
        (jclass clazz, const char *name, const char *sig);

//access: Replace type with one of object, int, short, long,
//float, double, boolean, char, int, or void
//(exception to the rule: there is no jvoid, just void)
//three types of each method, for different C/C++ styles
//of passing multiple arguments.
jtype CallTypeMethod(jobject obj, jmethodID methodID, ...);
jtype CallTypeMethodV
     (jobject obj, jmethodID methodID, va_list args);
jtype CallTypeMethodA
     (jobject obj, jmethodID methodID, jvalue * args);
jtype CallStaticTypeMethod(jclass c, jmethodID mid, ...);
jtype CallStaticTypeMethodV
     (jclass c, jmethodID mid, va_list args);
jtype CallStaticTypeMethodA
     (jclass c, jmethodID mid, jvalue * args);
jtype CallNonvirtualTypeMethod(jclass c, jmethodID mid, ...);
jtype CallNonvirtualTypeMethodV
     (jclass c, jmethodID mid, va_list args);
jtype CallNonvirtualTypeMethodA
     (jclass c, jmethodID mid, jvalue *args);
```

6.4.2 Performance Comparisons

Table 6–3 summarizes the performance of the various examples shown previously in this chapter. The tests were run on a 1.3 HotSpot VM. Beware that different VMs will have radically different characteristics. If you are using JNI in a performance-sensitive application, you will need to profile your code separately for each target VM.

Table 6–3   Performance of NativePoint Implementation Strategies

Implementation	Time (nsec)
Java move implementation	40
nativeMove, no caching	5000
nativeMove, cached jfieldIDs	1000
nativeMove, cached jmethodIDs	7000

These numbers contain a surprise: Using the `move` method turns out to be slower (7000 nsec) than crossing the JNI boundary four times and manipulating the fields directly (1000 nsec). So, in this particular test case, calling a method back in the virtual machine was more expensive than accomplishing the same thing by four reflective field accesses. You might still choose the callback method since it is cleaner and requires less native code.

In many cases the performance variations may not matter at all. For example, if it takes a millisecond to move the robot, then moving the robot will dwarf all the JNI implementation differences. Even if you *do* care about performance differences in the microsecond range, you should take these results with a large cube of salt. The performance of various JNI services will vary dramatically across virtual machines.

6.4.3   Differences between JNI and Reflective Invocation

Although JNI method invocation and reflective method invocation are similar, there are a few differences. First, JNI invocation never needs special permission to access private or protected class members; there is no JNI equivalent to reflection's `AccessibleObject` class. JNI code has complete access to all class members, regardless of Java access modifiers.

JNI's lax rules for reflection are reasonable when you remember that the virtual machine has no real control over native code anyway. If you introduce native code into your process space, that code can do anything. Once allowed inside the native boundary, a determined hacker can bypass any defense the virtual machine might mount, so respecting access modifiers within JNI would provide only a false sense of security.

A second difference between JNI invocation and reflective invocation is that JNI does not have to respect virtual methods. In Java code, a method is either virtual or it is not. Private, static, and some final methods are not virtual; all other methods are virtual.[5] This is true both of direct invocation and reflection. There is no way in the Java language to bypass these rules, although you can chain back up to the immediate base class implementation with the `super` keyword. In JNI, you can choose to ignore the virtualness of a method. For every normal JNI invocation API, there is a corresponding nonvirtual invocation call that resolves to the exact class used to get the `jmethodID`, as shown in Listing 6–16.

Listing 6–16   Virtual and Nonvirtual Invocation

```
jclass cls = pEnv->FindClass("NativePoint");
jmethodID mid = pEnv->GetMethodID(cls, "move", "(II)V");
//normal virtual call
pEnv->CallVoidMethod(obj, s_methMove, xinc, yinc);
//this will always call NativePoint's method, even on a
//subclass instance that overrides the method
pEnv->CallNonvirtualVoidMethod(obj, s_methMove, xinc, yinc);
```

It is difficult to imagine a use of this feature that is not a hack, in the disparaging sense of the term. Bypassing Java's notion of virtual methods could violate the expectations of a derived class, leading to arcane bugs. Because of this, you should avoid the `Nonvirtual` forms wherever possible.

---

5. Of course, a clever virtual machine implementation such as HotSpot can treat a virtual method as nonvirtual if there is only one implementation of the method currently visible. However, this is a performance optimization that would have to be undone if another class's implementation of that virtual method ever did get loaded.

Most JNI code manipulates the fields and methods of existing instances. JNI also provides functions to manipulate class loaders and create new instances, similar to the services of the `java.lang.ClassLoader` and `java.lang.reflect.Constructor` classes. The most important class loader and construction functions are summarized in Listing 6–17.

Listing 6–17   JNI Class Loader and Construction Functions

```
struct JNIEnv {
jclass DefineClass(const char *name, jobject loader,
                   const jbyte *buf, jsize len);
jclass FindClass(const char *name);
//plug in primitive type names to generate array API decls:
jtypeArray NewTypeArray(jsize len);
jobject NewObject(jclass clazz, jmethodID methodID, ...);
jobject AllocObject(jclass clazz);
//remainder omitted for clarity
}
```

`DefineClass` is equivalent to `ClassLoader.defineClass`. `FindClass` is similar to `Class.forName`, and it will find any class visible to the system class loader. The array constructor methods are straightforward, taking the form `NewTypeArray`, where `Type` is replaced by the name of a primitive or by `object`. `NewObject` is similar to `Constructor.newInstance`.

Notice that `NewObject` borrows the `jmethodID` from JNI method invocation; there is no distinct `jconstructorID` type. In order to find the correct `jmethodID` for a constructor, use the JNI method APIs plus the virtual machine's internal name for a constructor, which is `<init>`, and a phony return type of `void`. For example, to call a constructor for `NativePoint` that takes two `int` arguments you would use the syntax shown in Listing 6–18.

Listing 6–18   Calling a Java Constructor from Native Code

```
jmethodID cons = pEnv->GetMethodID(clsNativePoint,
                "<init>", "(II)V");
pEnv->NewObject(clsNativePoint, cons, 10, 10);
```

The only JNI object construction method with no counterpart in the Java world is `AllocObject`. `AllocObject` creates a Java instance without invoking *any* constructor. This is a very dangerous trick, and it is impossible to do in pure Java code. Most objects rely on constructors to reach an initial valid state. By bypassing the constructor, you risk causing malformed objects that will cause bizarre bugs later on. However, this trick has its uses. If you are re-creating an object from a serialization stream or from some other persistence format, it can be more efficient to skip constructors entirely. The object's state is known to be safe because the object was in a valid state when it was serialized.[6] The Java serialization architecture uses constructorless instantiation to avoid the onerous requirement that all serializable objects have a default constructor. See §4.2.2 for details.

6.5 Error Handling in JNI

When two programming platforms meet, you have to deal with all the idiosyncrasies of both. In JNI, this is most obvious when you are dealing with errors and failures. There are at least four distinct issues to consider:

1. What happens to the virtual machine when native code fails?
2. How should JNI code deal with C++ exceptions?
3. How should JNI code deal with Java exceptions?
4. How should JNI code communicate errors back to the VM?

The answer to each of these questions stems from a single principle: Well-written JNI code should preserve the appearance of Java, even when native code fails. In other words, problems should only reach the virtual machine in the form of Java exceptions.

6.5.1 Failures in Native Code

The first issue, failures in native code, is important because C and C++ introduce many risks not present in Java code. Most of these risks are caused by using pointers incorrectly. If native code inadvertently addresses the wrong memory locations, there are several possible outcomes. The process may fault and immediately be destroyed by the operating system or the hardware. Or,

---

6. Of course, this assumes that the stream format was not accidentally or maliciously corrupted. See Chapter 4 for details on dealing with this problem.

data may be silently corrupted, causing the virtual machine or operating system to fail mysteriously later. Worse, data may be silently corrupted while everything appears to be normal. JNI cannot protect you from any of these problems; all you can do is write and test native code with extra caution.

One surprising aspect of this danger is that the virtual machine itself is exposed to you as native code, through the `JavaVM` and `JNIEnv` pointers. Normally you access the virtual machine's services through Java, with well-defined guarantees that code will either succeed or throw a well-known exception. Not so with the `JNIEnv` and `JavaVM` pointers. With these, if you pass incorrect arguments to any JNI functions, the results are *not defined* and are likely to be catastrophic. For example, an invalid `jobject` handle might cause the following output from the HotSpot VM:

```
# HotSpot Virtual Machine Error, EXCEPTION_ACCESS_VIOLATION
# Please report this error at
# http://java.sun.com/cgi-bin/bugreport.cgi
#
# Error ID: 4F533F57494E13120E43505002D4
```

If you are doing JNI work, do not rush to report messages like this one as bugs against HotSpot—the bugs are almost certainly yours.

6.5.2 Handling C++ Exceptions

The second issue is how to handle C++ exceptions in JNI code. From a programmer's perspective, it would be nice if C++ exceptions were automatically converted into Java exceptions. However, the JNI architecture makes no attempt to derive Java representations for arbitrary C++ objects, so there is no obvious mapping from a C++ exception to a Java exception. Even if there were, there is another problem. While Java is a language and a binary standard, C++ is only a language standard. This means that different C++ compilers can (and do) implement exceptions in slightly different ways.

The lack of a binary standard for C++ exceptions makes it impossible for the Java language to have a one-size-fits-all C++ exception catcher. If Java wanted to catch all C++ exceptions at the native boundary, then JNI would have to include exception-handling code that was rebuilt for each compiler. Rather than face this complexity, JNI simply disallows throwing C++ exceptions across the C++/Java boundary. Disregard this warning at your peril; the behavior of a C++ exception inside the virtual machine is undefined. If a JNI method might encounter a C++ exception, you should catch that exception in native code to prevent it from destroying the virtual machine. In practice, this means you need a top-level catch block for every JNI method.

6.5.3 Handling Java Exceptions from Native Code

The third issue is dealing with Java exceptions that occur while you are in native code. Unless documented otherwise, any JNIEnv function can trigger a Java exception. Of course, you will not see the exception directly because there is no mapping from Java exceptions into C++ exceptions. There are two ways to detect that an exception has occurred. With some JNIEnv functions, you can infer an error from the return value. For example, FindClass will return zero if the class cannot be found. Other methods, such as CallVoidMethod, do not have a return value that can be used to indicate an exception. For these, you must call ExceptionOccurred or ExceptionCheck to detect an exception, as shown in Listing 6–19.

Listing 6–19 Detecting a Pending Exception in JNI

```
pEnv->CallVoidMethod(obj, s_methMove, xinc, yinc);

//option 1. get the jobject that represents the exception
jthrowable exc;
if (NULL != (exc = pEnv->ExceptionOccurred())) {
  //run about, scream, and shout…
}

//option 2. peek to see if the exception is pending
if (JNI_TRUE == pEnv->ExceptionCheck()) {
  //more running about…
}
```

The ExceptionOccurred call returns a jthrowable if an exception is pending, or zero if it is not. Because jthrowable is a subtype of jobject, you can manipulate it from JNI just as you would any other Java object; for example, you can reflectively discover and use its fields and methods.

When an exception occurs in JNI you have two choices: Either handle the exception from native code, or clean up and get out. If you choose to handle the exception, it is just as if you used a catch block in Java code. The exception is vanquished and execution on the thread can continue. Since JNI provides no C++ mapping of a Java catch block, you must handle exceptions using another API call, ExceptionClear:

```
if (0 != (exc = pEnv->ExceptionOccurred())) {
  pEnv->ExceptionClear();
}
```

If you do not handle an exception with ExceptionClear, you cannot continue to use the virtual machine from that thread. You must free any resources you need to free, and then exit the native method.

If you do not intend to handle an exception anyway, there is no need to get a local reference to it. If this is the case, the ExceptionCheck method is an inexpensive shortcut for ExceptionOccurred that does not return the exception itself. When a native method ends with a Java exception pending, the virtual machine discovers the exception and propagates it to the caller of the native method.

If you attempt to continue calling into the virtual machine while an exception is pending, the behavior is undefined.[7] Unfortunately, this leads to very cluttered code, with every JNIEnv call immediately followed by a check that no exception is pending, plus associated cleanup and recovery code if necessary, as seen in Listing 6–20.

Listing 6–20   Error-Safe Version of JNI_OnLoad

```
//Every JNIEnv* call is checked before continuing.
JNIEXPORT jint JNICALL JNI_OnLoad(JavaVM* vm, void* reserved)
{
  JNIEnv* pEnv;
  if (JNI_OK != vm->GetEnv((void **)&pEnv, JNI_VERSION_1_2))
  {
```

---

7. If "undefined behavior" is starting to sound like a mantra, that is because it is one. A great achievement of Java is how many of its behaviors are well defined, even when problems occur. Because JNI is native code, it cannot guarantee well-defined behavior.

```
      return JNI_EVERSION;
   }
   jclass cls;
   if (NULL == (cls = pEnv->FindClass("NativePoint")))
     return JNI_EVERSION;
   if (NULL == (s_fldX = pEnv->GetFieldID(cls, "x", "I")))
     return JNI_EVERSION;
   if (NULL == (s_fldY = pEnv->GetFieldID(cls, "y", "I")))
     return JNI_EVERSION;
   return JNI_VERSION_1_2;
}
```

This is substantially more cluttered than the previous version, and frankly, this example still understates the general problem. All of the method calls above indicate failure by their return value, which is a little easier than calling `ExceptionOccurred` or `ExceptionCheck`. Also, this particular method required no cleanup in case of partial failure. A more complex JNI method would be even more cluttered with cleanup code.

The irony here is that this is the exact problem exceptions were designed to solve. JNI does not use C++ exceptions for simplicity and for backward compatibility with C. However, there is nothing preventing you from using C++ exceptions yourself, so long as you never let them propagate back into the virtual machine. The website for this book [Hal01] includes the `JNIEnvUtil` class, which is a plug-compatible subclass of `JNIEnv` that automates the process of converting a Java error into a C++ exception. For every JNI call that might fail, the `JNIEnvUtil` class calls back to `ExceptionOccurred` and then throws a C++ exception. For example, `CallVoidMethodA` looks like Listing 6–21.

Listing 6-21   JNIEnvUtil

```
struct JNIEnvUtil : public JNIEnv {
  void CallVoidMethodA(jobject obj, jmethodID methodID,
                       jvalue * args) {
    JNIEnv::CallVoidMethodA(obj,methodID,args);
    if (ExceptionOccurred()) {
      throw JNIException();
    }
  }
  //remainder omitted for clarity
}
```

The use of C++ exceptions allows you to structure your JNI code without worrying about virtual machine exceptions. If you were using JNIEnvUtil, the JNI_OnLoad method would look like Listing 6–22.

Listing 6–22   Using JNIEnvUtil

```
//JNIEnv replaced by JNIEnvUtil
JNIEXPORT jint JNICALL JNI_OnLoad(JavaVM* vm, void* reserved)
{
  JNIEnvUtil* pEnv;
  if (JNI_OK != vm->GetEnv((void**)&pEnv, JNI_VERSION_1_2)){
    return JNI_EVERSION;
  }
  try {
    jclass cls = pEnv->FindClass("NativePoint");
    s_fldX = pEnv->GetFieldID(cls, "x", "I");
    s_fldY = pEnv->GetFieldID(cls, "y", "I");
    return JNI_VERSION_1_2;
  }
  catch(const JNIException& exc) {
    //no need to "throw" anything, Java exception is pending
    return JNI_EVERSION;
  }
}
```

The code structure inside the `try` block is linear and easy to understand. Of course, this example assumes that the only reaction to a Java exception is to immediately return, allowing the exception to propagate back to the caller of the native method. More sophisticated use of C++ exceptions is possible; the JNIEnvUtil class simply provides a starting point. Regardless of what helper classes or macros you use to simplify JNI programming, there are two critical things to remember: Always handle Java exceptions before continuing to call through the JNIEnv pointer, and never allow C++ exceptions back into the virtual machine.

6.5.4   Throwing Java Exceptions from Native Code
The last and smallest piece of the error-handling story is throwing your own exceptions back into the virtual machine. This is a simple matter. The JNIEnv

class includes helper functions that allow you to manually set the pending exception for the current virtual machine thread (as seen in Listing 6–23).

Listing 6–23 Throwing Java exceptions from Native Code Struct JNIEnv

```
struct JNIEnv {
  jint Throw(jthrowable obj);
  jint ThrowNew(jclass clazz, const char* msg);
}; //remainder omitted for clarity
```

The `Throw` method sets a pending exception object, which you either caught earlier or created from scratch using the JNI construction APIs. The `ThrowNew` method is a shortcut that instantiates a pending exception and calls its single argument String constructor. You should use these methods in the same situations that you would choose a `throw` statement in ordinary Java code. Just remember that after you set a pending exception, you should do no more work with the `JNIEnv` before returning, unless you first handle the exception by calling `ExceptionClear`.

6.6 Resource Management

One of the most obvious differences between Java and C++ is the model for managing resources. In Java, you simply drop references to unused objects and trust the garbage collector to reclaim memory when necessary. In C++, you typically take explicit control of resource deallocation. The JNI boundary must provide a sensible mapping between these two programming styles. There are four interesting cases to consider:

1. How does native code communicate with the garbage collector to manage the lifetime of Java objects?
2. How does Java code manage the lifetime of native objects?
3. How does JNI handle arrays?
4. How does JNI handle strings?

Arrays are a special case because Java accesses and stores arrays in a way that is not necessarily compatible with the pointer-based access used in C++. Strings are a special case because Java usually uses the two-byte Unicode format for strings, while much existing C/C++ code uses one-byte ASCII or ANSI format.

6.6.1 Interacting with the Garbage Collector

The first problem has to do with the management of Java objects from native code. In Java, the virtual machine keeps track of all object references for you. When you compile an assignment statement in Java, it translates to a bytecode that the virtual machine recognizes as an assignment statement. However, the virtual machine has no way to recognize assignment statements that execute in native code. If you assign a `jobject` reference to another variable, the garbage collector will not know about the new reference, and it may relocate or reclaim the object. Listing 6–24 shows a dangerous assignment.

Listing 6–24   A Dangerous Assignment

```
static jobject rememberedPoint;
JNIEXPORT void JNICALL Java_NativePoint_nativeMove
  (JNIEnv *pEnv, jobject obj, jint xinc, jint yinc)
{
  rememberedPoint = obj;   //BAD:  GC MAY MOVE OR RECLAIM obj
}
```

You cannot simply store a `jobject` reference for use later. Unless specifically documented otherwise, `jobject` references in JNI are *local references*. Local references are only valid until a JNI method returns back to Java, and then only on the thread they rode in on.

The limited lifetime of local references is convenient for the garbage collector. When the virtual machine creates the argument stack for a JNI method, it marks each `jobject` as "currently in a native method," preventing garbage collection from touching the object until the native method returns. After the method returns, the garbage collector is free to treat the object by its normal rules, reclaiming it if it is not referenced elsewhere.

Local reference lifetime is also convenient for JNI programmers because there is nothing for them to do. As long as you are content to use only the `jobjects` passed into the current method, you do not have to worry about explicit resource management. If you want to hold onto `jobject` references for longer periods of time, you must use the global reference APIs.

Global references give native code the ability to mark an object reference as "in use until further notice," thus disabling the garbage collector's ability to reclaim the object. To create a global reference, you call `NewGlobalRef`; to delete a global reference, you call `DeleteGlobalRef`. Use global references to cache objects that you need to use later, in a different method invocation and/or on a different thread. Listing 6–25 demonstrates using a global reference to cache a class object that will be used to throw an exception.

Listing 6–25 Using Global References

```
static jfieldID s_fldX;
static jfieldID s_fldY;
static jclass clsIllegalArgExc;
JNIEXPORT void JNICALL Java_NativePoint_nativeMove
  (JNIEnv *pEnv, jobject obj, jint xinc, jint yinc)
{
  if ((xinc < 0) || (yinc < 0)) {
    pEnv->ThrowNew(clsIllegalArgExc, "increment less than zero");
  }
  int x = pEnv->GetIntField(obj, s_fldX);
  int y = pEnv->GetIntField(obj, s_fldY);
  pEnv->SetIntField(obj, s_fldX, x + xinc);
  pEnv->SetIntField(obj, s_fldY, y + yinc);
}
JNIEXPORT jint JNICALL JNI_OnLoad(JavaVM* vm, void* reserved)
{
  JNIEnv* pEnv;
  if (JNI_OK != vm->GetEnv((void **)&pEnv, JNI_VERSION_1_2))
  {
    return JNI_EVERSION;
  }
  jclass cls = pEnv->FindClass("NativePoint");
  s_fldX = pEnv->GetFieldID(cls, "x", "I");
  s_fldY = pEnv->GetFieldID(cls, "y", "I");
  jclass temp = pEnv->FindClass(
                  "java/lang/IllegalArgumentException");
  clsIllegalArgExc = (jclass) pEnv->NewGlobalRef(temp);
  pEnv->DeleteLocalRef(temp);
  return JNI_VERSION_1_2;
}
JNIEXPORT void JNICALL JNI_OnUnload(JavaVM* vm, void* reserved) {
  JNIEnv* pEnv;
  if (JNI_OK != vm->GetEnv((void **)&pEnv, JNI_VERSION_1_2))
  {
    return;
  }
  pEnv->DeleteGlobalRef(clsIllegalArgExc);
}
```

Listing 6–25 is similar to previous versions of `NativePoint`, except that this time around only positive movements are allowed; negative movements trigger an `IllegalArgumentException`. The `JNI_OnLoad` function calls `FindClass` to get the `jclass` reference for the `java.lang.IllegalArgumentException` class. However, the return value of `FindClass` is a local reference (remember that all JNI references are local unless explicitly documented otherwise). In order to safely cache the `jclass` reference for use later, you must call `NewGlobalRef` and cache the resulting global reference instead. When and if the native library is about to be unloaded, the `JNI_OnUnload` method will call `DeleteGlobalRef` to renounce its hold on the class object.

Managing global references is tricky because they add the complexities of C++ explicit memory management to Java references. In larger projects, it can be very difficult to identify where and when global references should be released. In fact, it can even be difficult to distinguish global from local references! Notice that global and local references both have the same static types, such as `jobject`, `jclass`, and so on. This means that the compiler cannot distinguish reference types. If you call `DeleteGlobalRef` on a local reference, the results are undefined. There is no silver bullet for these problems. However, they are standard fare for C++ developers, so at least writing JNI code is not substantially more difficult than any other kind of C++ programming.

Note that Listing 6–25 also includes a call to `DeleteLocalRef`. Local references expire at the end of the native method anyway, so `DeleteLocalRef` is not mandatory. However, there are two reasons that you might want to consider calling `DeleteLocalRef` as soon as you know that a reference is no longer needed by native code. First, the virtual machine may allocate only a limited number of local reference slots; by default only 16 are guaranteed to be available. By calling `DeleteLocalRef`, you give yourself the ability to do things such as iterating over large object arrays without exceeding the local capacity at any given time.

The second reason to call `DeleteLocalRef` is to guarantee that resources are reclaimed in a timely manner. While the JNI specification claims that local references are invalidated at the end of a native method, the virtual machine is not always aggressive in reclaiming these references. Some virtual machines may not reclaim any local references until there are *no* native methods active on a thread, as shown in Figure 6–3.

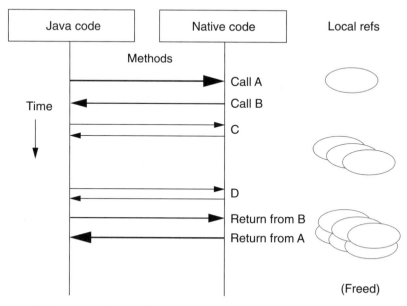

Refs may not be freed until outermost native method A returns.

Figure 6–3   Local references freed after native outermost call returns

It is very important to call `DeleteLocalRef` when you are writing helper functions that may be called from other native methods because you have no idea how many reference slots will be available when the function executes. Expeditiously calling `DeleteLocalRef` can cause dramatic performance improvements in some situations. Of course, this advice depends on JNI implementation details, which can vary from one virtual machine to another. Always profile your code to be sure.

If you need more than the default 16 local references, the SDK 1.2 version of JNI provides APIs for reserving additional capacity and for allocating additional references, as shown in Listing 6–26.

Listing 6–26   JNI Local Reference APIs

```
struct JNIEnv {
  jint EnsureLocalCapacity(jint capacity);
  jobject NewLocalRef(jobject ref);
  //remainder omitted for clarity
};
```

You can call `EnsureLocalCapacity` at any time to set aside storage for a number of local references, which you can later use with any API that returns a new local reference, such as `NewLocalRef`. `EnsureLocalCapacity` returns zero to indicate success; otherwise, it returns a negative number and sets a pending `OutOfMemoryError`. Listing 6–27 shows how you can use `EnsureLocalCapacity` to set aside enough local reference slots to process an entire array.

Listing 6–27   Using EnsureLocalCapacity

```
JNIEXPORT jobject JNICALL Java_NativePoint_findBestMatch
  (JNIEnv* pEnv, jobject pt, jobjectArray ptArray)
{
  jsize size = pEnv->GetArrayLength(ptArray);
  pEnv->EnsureLocalCapacity(size);
  jobject* pts = new jobject[size];
  int n;
  for (n=0; n<size; n++) {
   pts[n] = pEnv->GetObjectArrayElement(ptArray, n);
  }
  int xSearch = pEnv->GetIntField(pt, s_fldX);
  jobject result;
  for (n=0; n<size; n++) {
   jobject objCur = pts[n];
    int xCur = pEnv->GetIntField(objCur, s_fldX);
    if (xCur == xSearch) {
     result = pEnv->NewLocalRef(objCur);
     break;
    }
  }
  for (n=0; n<size; n++) {
   pEnv->DeleteLocalRef(pts[n]);
  }
  delete [] pts;
  return result;
}
```

The `findBestMatch` method first guarantees that is has enough local references with `EnsureLocalCapacity`, then it extracts all the `jobject`s into an array, and then it scans that array looking for the `NativePoint` with the exact same x coordinate as the `pt` reference, a.k.a. `this`. To reclaim references as quickly as possible, the method loops over the array again, calling `Delete-LocalRef`. Note that this example did not strictly require `EnsureLocalCapacity`. This particular array traversal could have been done one local reference at a time, but more complex traversals might require simultaneous access to several elements.

If you are working with a block of references that will all go out of scope together, it is more convenient to use the `PushLocalFrame` and `PopLocal-Frame` APIs shown in Listing 6–28.

Listing 6–28 Managing Reference Frames

```
struct JNIEnv {
  jint PushLocalFrame(jint capacity);
  jobject PopLocalFrame(jobject result);
  //remainder omitted for clarity
};
```

`PushLocalFrame` creates a new frame, and the next `capacity` references will belong to it. Similar to `EnsureLocalCapacity`, `PushLocalFrame` either returns zero on success, or it returns a negative number and sets a pending `OutOfMemory` error on failure. These references can then all be released in one motion with `PopLocalFrame`, which also allows one reference to be kept alive as a logical return value for the frame. These APIs make the `findBest-Match` method much cleaner, as shown in Listing 6–29.

Listing 6–29 Using Reference Frames

```
JNIEXPORT jobject JNICALL Java_NativePoint_findBestMatch
  (JNIEnv* pEnv, jobject pt, jobjectArray ptArray)
{
  jsize size = pEnv->GetArrayLength(ptArray);
  pEnv->PushLocalFrame(size);
  jobject* pts = new jobject[size];
  int n;
  for (n=0; n<size; n++) {
```

```
    pts[n] = pEnv->GetObjectArrayElement(ptArray, n);
  }
  int xSearch = pEnv->GetIntField(pt, s_fldX);
  jobject result;
  for (n=size-1; n>=0; n--) {
    jobject objCur = pts[n];
    int xCur = pEnv->GetIntField(objCur, s_fldX);
    if (xCur == xSearch) {
      result = pEnv->PopLocalFrame(objCur);
      break;
    }
  }
  delete [] pts;
  return result;
}
```

Even if you never call `EnsureLocalCapacity` or `PushLocalFrame`, you may be able to create all the local references you want. The JNI documentation states that "For backward compatibility, the VM allocates local references beyond the ensured capacity."[8] In my tests of the 1.2 Classic and 1.3 HotSpot implementations of the virtual machine on Windows NT 4.0, I found that it is possible to create tens of thousands of local references without any complaint from the virtual machine. The `-verbose:jni` command-line option for the `java` launcher is supposed to provide warning messages if you exceed your local reference capacity, but this works only sometimes. On the classic VM, the warnings appear to work correctly when you reserve small numbers of local references, up to about a thousand. However, if you `Ensure` space for a large number of objects, the call returns successfully, but erroneous warning messages begin to appear claiming that you have exceeded the 16 reference limit. Furthermore, the warning flags appear to have been dropped entirely from the HotSpot VM.

The point of this digression is *not* to encourage you to rely on these idiosyncrasies of the Windows VM implementation, but quite the opposite. Instead, you should be aware that the virtual machine does not reliably warn you if you misuse the local reference APIs. Be careful to follow the local reference rules and

---

8. See the JNI specification [Lia99] section on `EnsureLocalCapacity`.

program to the specification, not to the current behavior of a particular virtual machine. This will give your code the best chance of being portable to a wide variety of virtual machines and operating systems.

6.6.2 Managing Native Resources

There is not much to say about managing native resources from Java because JNI does not define any Java mapping for native objects. You must handroll any resource management scheme you wish to use. Fortunately, the core API has several examples of how to do this. Sockets, files, and database connections are all native resources that are hidden behind Java objects. With each of these native resources, the idiom is the same: At the native API level, there are function calls you can use to allocate the resource and return it to the pool. These function calls must be mapped to appropriate methods on a Java object. For resource allocation, the Java constructor is an obvious match, as shown here:

```
public class NativeResource {
  private int handle;
  private native int allocHandle();
  public NativeResource() {
    handle = allocHandle();
  }
}
```

You cannot use the OS call directly because it does not match the signature expected by JNI, so `allocHandle` maps the JNI signature to the OS function call instead:

```
JNIEXPORT jobject JNICALL NativeResource_allocHandle
  (JNIEnv* pEnv, jobject pt)
{
  return OSAllocResource();  //placeholder for some OS call
}
```

Deallocating the resource is a bit more of a challenge. If you were wrapping an API in C++, you could place the call to `OSDeallocResource` in the class destructor. However, Java does not have destructors. Instead, most Java classes take a two-pronged approach to freeing native resources: Define a `close` method that deallocates any native resources, and then back that up with a `finalize` method that calls `close` automatically, as shown in Listing 6–30.

Listing 6–30   Managing Native Resources

```
//continuing class NativeResource
private native deallocHandle(int handle);
public void close() {
  if (handle != 0) {
    deallocHandle(handle);
    handle = 0;
  }
}
protected void finalize() {
  close();
}
public useResource(String someArg) {
  if (handle == 0) {
    throw new IllegalStateException("object is closed");
  }
  //do work...
}
```

This solution introduces a fair amount of complexity. Since the class is not safe for use once the native resource is closed, all the actual functionality of the class must be guarded by `if (handle == 0)` blocks, as the `useResource` method demonstrates. Clients of the class must be encouraged to call `close` as soon as they know they are finished with the resource so that the resource can be reclaimed as quickly as possible. Clients may even want to call `close` within a `finally` block to guarantee that the object is closed even in exceptional situations.

If a client forgets to call `close`, you can only hope that the `finalize` method will be called soon. However, `finalize` is neither reliable nor efficient in helping reclaim native resources. The simple fact is this: Garbage collection is often a great solution for memory management, but it does not help you with non-memory resource management. Native resources need to be explicitly deallocated, just as they would be in a systems programming language such as C++. If you write a Java class that wraps a native resource, use the `close/finalize` tandem to quickly reclaim resources that are no longer needed.

6.6.3 Managing Arrays

The third problem area that JNI faces is passing arrays. In C++, an array is a contiguous block of memory that can be addressed by a pointer. So, assuming that an int is four bytes long, an array of 10,000 ints would be stored as 40,000 contiguous bytes somewhere in memory. Using pointer math, it is trivial to address any particular element in the array. If the array begins at `0x55551000`, then the fourth element of the array is at `0x55551010`.

The Java definition of an array is looser. Java does not expose pointers to the programmer, and array accesses in Java are actual bytecode instructions processed by the virtual machine. Since the VM is queried for each item in the array, it does not need to store the array contiguously in memory. As long as the VM is willing to do the bookkeeping, it can choose to store the array as several smaller pieces. This is entirely transparent to the Java programmer, of course. Figure 6–4 demonstrates possible C++ and Java storage of the same array.

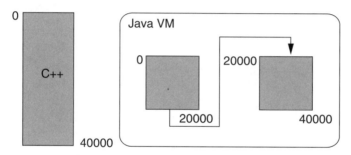

Figure 6–4   Contiguous versus fragmented storage for a byte array

This difference in storing arrays becomes a problem when you are passing an array between Java and native code. A C++ programmer cannot simply take the raw pointer address of a Java array and then index to a particular element because that part of the array might be elsewhere in memory. JNI provides three related API sets to address this problem. All of the APIs do basically the same thing: They take a Java array and convert it into the format expected by a C++ programmer, and vice versa.

The simplest array API functions have the word `Region` in their names, and they simply copy pieces of arrays between C++ and Java formats. The `Region` APIs are shown in Listing 6–31.

Listing 6–31   JNI Array Region API

```
struct JNIEnv {
  // Only the int version is shown; there are similar calls
  //for boolean, byte, char, short, long, float, and double
  void GetIntArrayRegion(jintArray arr, jsize start,
                         jsize len, jint* buf);
  void SetIntArrayRegion(jintArray arr, jsize start,
                         jsize len, jint* buf);
//remainder omitted for clarity
}j
```

Because the `Region` API functions always create a new copy of the data they manipulate, you do not have to worry about how the source or destination arrays are stored in memory. As a result, these functions are the easiest to understand. Listing 6–32 shows how to use the `Region` API to increment each element in a Java array.

Listing 6–32   Using the Region API

```
JNIEXPORT void JNICALL Java_TestNativeArray_incByRegionAPI
  (JNIEnv *pEnv, jclass cls, jintArray arr, jint inc)
{
  jint size = pEnv->GetArrayLength(arr);
  jint* carray = new jint[size];
  //copy initial Java array into contiguous C array
  pEnv->GetIntArrayRegion(arr, 0, size, carray);
  for (jint n=0; n<size; n++) {
    carray[n] += inc;
  }
  //copy result elements back into Java array
  pEnv->SetIntArrayRegion(arr, 0, size, carray);
  delete [] carray;
}
```

Because the array is copied into a C-style array, you must allocate an array to receive the contents, as was done here with C++ `new` and `delete`. The logic is simple but potentially very wasteful. The entire array is copied twice, once into

C++ contiguous memory, and again back into whatever storage the virtual machine is using. For large arrays, this copying overhead can easily dwarf the work being done. If it does, you should consider using one of the two other array APIs, which do not mandate a copy every time.

The second array API is the `Element` API (see Listing 6–33). Again, there are API functions for each primitive type, and for simplicity, the text will always refer to the `int` version. Unlike the `Region` APIs, the `Element` APIs will attempt to give native code a direct pointer to the array elements; however, this may not always be possible. If the virtual machine keeps the array in contiguous memory, it may give a direct pointer to native code. If the Java array is not contiguous, then the virtual machine will have to copy the array to a contiguous block for use from native code.

Listing 6–33 JNI Array Element API

```
struct JNIEnv {
//element APIs. Only the int version is shown; there are
//calls for boolean, byte, char, short, long, float, double
jint* GetIntArrayElements(jintArray arr, jboolean* isCopy);
void ReleaseIntArrayElements(jintArray arr, jint* elems,
                             jint mode);
};
```

The Java Language Specification does not provide any technique to guarantee how an array is stored, or to query whether an array is stored contiguously. Even if the array *is* stored contiguously, the virtual machine could still choose to copy the array when it was making it accessible to native code. When you use the `Element` APIs, you must write code that functions correctly regardless of whether the array is being copied or modified in place.

This complicates the programming model in several ways. Since you do not know whether the array will be copied, you cannot allocate native memory in advance. If the `Element` API decides to copy the array, it will allocate the memory internally, and you must use the corresponding `Release`*Type*`ArrayElements` function to deallocate the memory. This contrasts with the `Region` APIs discussed above, where it is perfectly acceptable to call `GetIntArrayRegion` without ever making a corresponding call to `SetIntArrayRegion`. Listing 6–34 reimplements the prior example, shown in Listing 6–32, this time using the `Element` APIs.

Listing 6–34   Using the Array Element API

```
JNIEXPORT void JNICALL Java_TestNativeArray_incByPinning
  (JNIEnv *pEnv, jclass cls, jintArray arr, jint inc)
{
  jint size = pEnv->GetArrayLength(arr);
  //pass zero because code does not depend on whether array
  //       is copied
  jint* carray = pEnv->GetIntArrayElements(arr, 0);
  for (jint n=0; n<size; n++) {
   carray[n] += inc;
  }
  pEnv->ReleaseIntArrayElements(arr, carray, 0);
}
```

When you call `GetIntArrayElements`, you pass in a `jboolean*` that will record whether you actually have direct access to the array. If the array is copied, then you must call `ReleaseIntArrayElements` to copy your changes back to the master version of the array and to deallocate the temporary copy of the array. Even if you are directly manipulating the master copy of the array, you still need to call `ReleaseIntArrayElements`, because of array *pinning*.

Pinning prevents the garbage collector from moving the array to another location while you are using it. Moving memory out from under a native pointer would cause undefined behaviors that are very difficult to debug, so the virtual machine marks the array as unmoveable, preventing it from moving until you call `ReleaseIntArrayElements`. In order for `ReleaseIntArrayElements` to give precise control over the pinning process, it takes a `mode` flag that controls unpinning the array. The modes work differently for copied versus pinned arrays, as shown in Table 6–4.

The good news is that you rarely need to write special case code based on whether an array was copied or pinned. The excitingly named 0 flag is generally appropriate for read/write traversal of an array. If the array was copied, it copies the temporary array back into the master copy, and if the array was pinned, it unpins it.

The `JNI_ABORT` flag supports read-only traversal. If the array was copied, `JNI_ABORT` does not bother to copy the array back, which improves performance. Note that the `JNI_ABORT` flag does not function as a transactional roll-

Table 6–4   Array Unpin Modes

Mode Flag	Meaning	Effect on Copied Array	Effect on Pinned Array	Usage
0	Done, post changes	Copies back to master, frees temp array	Unpins	Read/write traversal
JNI_ABORT	Done, drop changes	Frees temp array	Unpins, *changes kept anyway!*	Read-only traversal
JNI_COMMIT	Not done, post changes	Copies back to master	No effect	Rarely used

back. If the changes were made directly to the pinned array, JNI_ABORT will not unmake the changes. JNI_NOCOPY would probably be a better name for the JNI_ABORT flag.

The JNI_COMMIT flag allows you to copy changes back without releasing the temporary array. This is useful in rare circumstances in which you are making many changes to an array and want those changes to be quickly visible to another thread.[9]

Some virtual machines do not support pinning and always return a copy of the array to the GetIntArrayElements call. In order to give such virtual machines another performance option with large arrays, SDK 1.2 introduced a third array access API called the Critical API, which is shown in Listing 6–35.

Listing 6–35   JNI Array Critical API

```
struct JNIEnv {
//Unlike the other APIs, there are no
//typed versions for each primitive type, just void*.
void* GetPrimitiveArrayCritical(jarray array,
                                jboolean* isCopy);
void ReleasePrimitiveArrayCritical(jarray array,
                                   void* carr,
                                   int mode);
//remainder omitted for clarity
};
```

---

9. To make this work, you must also correctly use synchronized blocks in Java and the MonitorEnter and MonitorExit functions in JNI. Interesting topics in themselves, but outside the scope of this book.

The `Critical` API is very similar to the `Elements` API discussed previously. `GetPrimitiveArrayCritical` may choose to copy or pin, and `ReleasePrimitiveArrayCritical` uses the same control flags that were described earlier. The key difference is that the `Critical` APIs are more likely to provide direct access because they do not require pinning. However, the better odds come at a price. After calling `GetPrimitiveArrayCritical`, you enter a *critical region*. Until you call `Release`, you must not call other JNI functions, block the thread at the native or Java level, or take very much time. These restrictions allow a virtual machine to employ simple, draconian means for protecting the array while you access it (for example, it may *stop all other VM threads*). Listing 6–36 shows the `Critical` array APIs being used.

Listing 6–36 Using the Critical Array APIs

```
JNIEXPORT void JNICALL Java_TestNativeArray_incCritical
  (JNIEnv *pEnv, jclass cls, jintArray arr, jint inc)
{
  jint size = pEnv->GetArrayLength(arr);
  //pass zero because code does not depend on whether array
  //        is copied
  jint* carray = (jint*)
                pEnv->GetPrimitiveArrayCritical(arr, 0);
  //BEGIN CRITICAL SECTION
  for (jint n=0; n<size; n++) {
    carray[n] += inc;
  }
  //END CRITICAL SECTION
  pEnv->ReleasePrimitiveArrayCritical(arr, carray, 0);
}
```

After taking the extra care required to use the `Critical` APIs, you may discover that their impacts on overall performance are positive, negative, or indifferent. If the speed gain from direct access to the array outweighs the cost of stopping other threads, then the `Critical` API is a better choice than the `Elements` API, but the reverse can also be true. If the virtual machine supports pinning arrays, or if all of the APIs are forced to copy arrays, you may discover no performance effects at all.

If you reach a point where the performance of the JNI array APIs is significant to your application, you will need to profile so that you can choose between the `Region`, `Elements`, and `Critical` APIs. Moreover, you will need to profile on the variety of operating systems, virtual machines, and hardware you intend to support. This is true throughout Java, but it is especially true with JNI, which may vary widely from one operating system to another. Write once, run anywhere, profile everywhere.

6.6.4 Managing Strings

Strings create many of the same problems that arrays do, which is not surprising since strings are basically arrays with some additional semantics attached. As you can see in Listing 6–37, JNI provides the same three API families for strings that it does for arrays. As with arrays, the `Region` functions always copy the string into a preallocated buffer. The `Chars` API for strings corresponds to the `Element` array API, and it will try to pin the string in memory, otherwise copying it. The `Critical` string API attempts to provide direct access to the string without pinning it. The `Critical` API functions by basically shutting down the rest of the virtual machine, and its use is governed by the same rules listed for the `Critical` array API: no JNI callbacks, no thread blocking, and quick execution.

Listing 6–37 JNI String API

```
struct JNIEnv {
  //basics, available since 1.1
  jstring NewString(const jchar *unicode, jsize len);
  jsize GetStringLength(jstring str);
  jstring NewStringUTF(const char *utf);
  jsize GetStringUTFLength(jstring str);

  //region API, available since 1.2
  void GetStringRegion(jstring str, jsize start,
                       jsize len, jchar *buf);
  void GetStringUTFRegion(jstring str, jsize start,
                          jsize len, char *buf);

  //pinning strings, available since 1.1
  const jchar* GetStringChars(jstring str, jboolean *isCopy);
```

```
void ReleaseStringChars(jstring str, const jchar *chars);
const char* GetStringUTFChars(jstring str,
                                      jboolean *isCopy);
void ReleaseStringUTFChars(jstring str, const char* chars);

//critical API, available since 1.2
const jchar * GetStringCritical(jstring string,
                                      jboolean *isCopy);
void ReleaseStringCritical(jstring string,
                                const jchar *cstring);
//remainder omitted for clarity
}
```

There are two special characteristics of Java `Strings` that deserve attention. First, Java `Strings` are immutable—that is, they cannot be changed once they are instantiated. This greatly simplifies the various APIs. `Strings` have `GetRegion` but no `SetRegion` because it would be illegal to copy changed characters into a `String`. Similarly, the `Chars` and `Critical` APIs do not have a flag to control unpinning behavior. There is no behavior to control because changes can never be copied back.

Second, Java strings are likely stored internally as Unicode. The JNI string API comes in two flavors. The flavor that uses the UTF acronym in its name and takes `char*` parameters converts Java strings into UTF-8 format,[10] which is a single-byte format that is compatible with ASCII in the lower seven bits. The other flavor takes `jchar` arguments and works with two-byte Unicode strings. Since virtual machines tend to use Unicode internally, it is a good bet that the UTF functions will always return copies, while the Unicode functions have some chance of providing direct access. Unfortunately, most legacy C++ code uses single-byte string encoding, so you will likely find yourself using the UTF APIs.

6.7 Onward

Very few software systems build on only one technology, so interoperability is key to the success of large projects. JNI provides a low-level, in-process model for interoperation between Java and systems code written in C or C++. Studying

---

10. Java's UTF-8 format is slightly different from the standard UTF-8 format. The Java format is documented in [LY99].

JNI is a valuable way to learn about both C++ and Java because JNI has to deal with how the language worlds differ. JNI provides a mapping from Java types to a dynamic, metadata-driven, handle-based, C-callable API.

JNI provides a dynamic loading architecture for native code that is a stripped-down version of Java's powerful class loader architecture. JNI provides APIs to make Java exceptions, arrays, and strings usable from native code, and it copes with the fact that these constructs do not naturally map to their C++ counterparts. JNI provides an API for explicitly managing Java object lifetime, which is necessary when you need long-lived "global" references that are safe from garbage collection.

Unfortunately, JNI is too low-level to be the perfect solution. Frankly, it is the assembly language of interop. JNI makes no attempt to map C/C++ objects into Java. Nor does it provide tools to automate wrapping existing native code libraries; instead, you have to manually write wrapper functions that translate from JNI signatures to your existing native code APIs. If anything, this chapter should convince you to avoid JNI wherever possible.

The Java world needs a higher-level approach for interoperating with other component platforms. Many attempts have been made and some have become commercially viable, but none have become part of Java. Appendix A describes an open-source library for interoperation with Win32 and COM components, and [JavaWin32] lists the various interop products.

6.8 Resources

[Lia99] is a well-written guide from a designer of JNI; you will find that Chapters 9 and 10 of this guide are particularly valuable. [Lia99] also includes the JNI specification, which is clear and concise. The only real complaint you may have is that the Java 2 SDK enhancements are in a separate add-on document, so you have to guess when a feature was implemented in order to find its documentation.

As mentioned previously, [JavaWin32] lists interop products that provide enhancements over raw JNI for calling between Java and native code on Windows operating systems.

Chapter 7

Generative Programming

Generative programming (GP) is code reuse via the automation of code development. Instead of writing Java code directly, you describe a problem in a specification language tailored to the problem space, and then you employ a tool to generate the necessary Java source code or bytecode. Java is widely hailed as a language suitable for object-oriented development, but it is equally suited for GP. In fact, object-oriented programming and GP are complementary, and many of the most exciting technologies in the Java world today combine the two. This chapter has four purposes:

1. Present the motivations for using GP.

2. Develop a taxonomy of the binding times and modes that are possible in Java and the tools that each employs.

3. Demonstrate how GP is already in wide use in the Java world, especially J2EE.

4. Present examples of GP that will jump-start your thinking on how to use GP in your own projects.

7.1 Why Generate Code?

The reason to generate code is simple: to efficiently capture and reuse knowledge of a problem domain. [Cle01] provides several useful terms to describe *domain analysis*, the design process that often leads to a GP implementation. Domain analysis identifies the *commonalities* and *variabilities* of a family of related software systems. Commonalities are standard features that are coded into the system and shared by all permutations of the system. Variabilities are features that can differ in various products, or in different invocations of the same product. At some point in the lifecycle of a system, you must make a choice, or *specification,* for each variability. The point in time that a choice is made is the *binding time.*

For example, consider the simple online bidding system depicted in Figure 7–1. The commonalities shown in the figure are the relationships between auctioneers, bidders, sellers, and items to be sold. You can imagine some of the variabilities: legal bid increments, number of bidding rounds, and the types of information available about each item. Choices can be binary (Does the item have a picture?), numeric (How many bidding rounds will there be?) or something much more complex. The binding time for each choice depends on the implementation, as you will see.

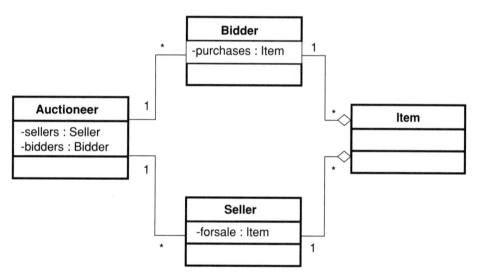

Figure 7–1   A simple online bidding system

7.1.1   Object-Oriented Approaches to Modeling Variabilities

In a traditional object-oriented design, variabilities are modeled with a combination of inheritance and parameterization. The code in Listing 7–1 shows fragments of two different approaches to implementing an Auctioneer interface, which is responsible for enforcing the number of bidding rounds and the legal bid increments. The ThreeRoundFiveDollar implementation uses inheritance to model each choice. With this approach, each combination of the number of rounds and the minimum bid increment would result in a distinct concrete implementation.

The second example, `AuctioneerImpl`, models all possible `Auctioneer`s with a single implementation class. The specification of rounds and minimum bid increment are made explicitly at runtime by passing in parameters.

Listing 7–1   Modeling Auctioneer with Inheritance and Parameterization

```
//using inheritance to model every variability
public class ThreeRoundFiveDollar implements Auctioneer {
  public void runAuction(Item i) {
    for (int n=0; n<3; n++) {
      runBidRound(i, 5);
    }
  }
  //etc.
}

//using parameters to model every variability
public class AuctioneerImpl extends Auctioneer {
  public AuctioneerImpl(int rounds, int minIncrement) {
    this.rounds = rounds;
    this.minIncrement = minIncrement;
  }
  public void runAuction(Item i) {
    for (int n=0; n<rounds; n++) {
      runBidRound(i, bid);
    }
  }
  //etc.
}
```

In this example, the `AuctioneerImpl` is obviously the better design; because the choices are across a range of values, the first approach might require an unlimited number of subclasses. Since the choices do not imply different logic or storage requirements, the `AuctioneerImpl` class can trivially encode the choices as parameter values.

One can just as easily concoct a scenario that favors inheritance over parameterization. Imagine that the `Item`s being sold can have text information, a picture, or a movie. This situation favors inheritance, as Listing 7–2 demonstrates. Each choice in Listing 7–2 is binary—either the media is present or it is not. The number of possible classes in an inheritance-based solution is therefore bounded. Because each choice implies different storage and logic, the parameterized implementation is inefficient. The `ItemImpl` must keep fields for each possible data type, and it must execute branching logic each time through its display method. Real problems and real designs tend to fall between the two extremes and employ parameterization and inheritance in tandem.

Listing 7–2 Modeling Items with Inheritance and Parameterization

```
//using inheritance to model every variability
public class ItemWithText implements Item {
  Text t;
  public void display() {
    t.print();
  }
}

//using parameterization to model every variability
public class ItemImpl implements Item {
  Text t;
  Image i;
  Movie m;
  public void display() {
    if (t) t.print();
    else if (i) i.draw();
    else if (m) m.play();
  }

}
```

7.1.2 Thinking in Terms of Bind Time

Now consider the bind times implied by each approach. With the inheritance-based solution, each different specification is instantiated as a different concrete class. Therefore, the specification is bound during development, which is often called compile-time binding.

This has important consequences. The *developer* must choose the specification since the choice is made during development. Of course, the developer could be acting on detailed instructions from an end user, but the important point is that the end user cannot change the specification later, after the developer is gone.

For the parameterized solution, the specification is bound at runtime by passing in parameters. This implies that an end user can choose the specification at runtime if the program yields control of the parameters. In general, later binding gives more flexibility to the user, but earlier binding may offer better performance. The compiler can optimize code based on your specifications only if the specifications are available before the compiler runs.

The Java development world has four obvious bind times.

1. Compile-time binding happens when the compiler runs.

2. Design-time binding happens when a designer configures the initial state of an already compiled component. JavaBeans are designed specifically with design-time binding in mind; designers often use a visual tool to examine and modify bean properties.

3. Deployment-time binding occurs when components are installed onto the network where they will be used. Deployment-time binding is distinct because even though the developer may no longer be present, a system administrator will be.

4. Runtime binding occurs after an application starts to execute.

To the generative programmer, bind time is a very important issue that needs to be treated separately from the actual specification that is bound.

7.1.3 Separating Specification from Bind Time

The online bidding examples discussed earlier suffer from a basic flaw. The pure Java approach hopelessly tangles the binding time with the specification chosen. A single object design cannot elegantly handle both issues simultaneously, as the examples demonstrate. Changing the specification requires only small edits, but switching from inheritance to parameterization requires a wholesale rewrite of the code.

To take a generative approach to the auction simulation, you need to separate these two concerns into distinct artifacts: a specification document that enumerates the choices for each variability, and a set of *generators* that process the specification document and produce the application code. An example specification document for the auction simulation is shown in Listing 7–3. This specification describes an entire bidding system, and it will be processed by one or more generators, as shown in Figure 7–2. The generators manufacture the program that will actually run the simulation. The specification document encodes the choices, and the generators select the binding times.

Listing 7–3   Specification Document for the Auction Simulation

```
auction.rounds=3
auction.minIncrement=5
item.1=text
item.2=movie
```

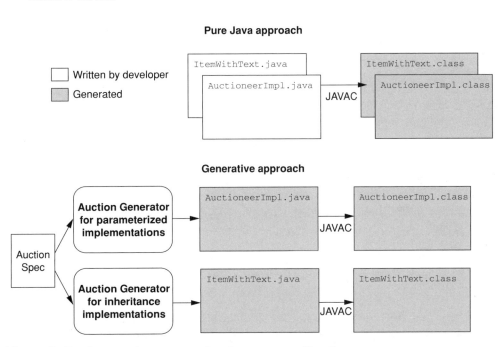

Figure 7–2   Generating an auction from a specification

The separation of specification data into a separate layer lets you experiment with different binding strategies. From the same specification, you could generate any number of different implementations, including the examples above. You could have separate generators that prioritized readability of the generated code, fast performance, small code size, or any other measure that you value. If your bind-time priorities change, the critical domain knowledge of your specification is not lost. You simply reuse it with a new generator.

Object designs have other issues besides binding time that tend to *cross-cut* object hierarchies. A cross-cutting issue does not fit neatly into a single class. Synchronization, transactions, security, and auditing are notorious cross-cutters. Dealing with them tends to litter small amounts of code across many of the classes in your design. With a separate specification, you can hoist these concerns out of your code into a single place, and then you can generate the code that interleaves them.

7.1.4 Choosing a Specification Language

The generative approach has a number of other desirable properties as well. While the configuration document in Listing 7–3 is in the format of a Java properties file, you can choose the format most convenient to your problem domain (just remember that your generators will have to read this format). You do not have to use the same language for the generators and for the generated code, so everything you have seen so far applies equally well to any programming language. Nor are generators limited to creating application code. You could also generate documentation, test scripts, and deployment instructions. Generating all these project artifacts from a shared configuration document makes it much easier to keep various elements of your project in sync.

7.1.5 Reuse Requires More Than One Use

The primary disadvantage to a generative approach, as with other reuse approaches, is that you must build more than one system for the initial effort to pay off. If you only plan to build one application within a problem domain, then analyzing commonalities and variabilities will be valuable, but the effort to develop a suite of generators will not. Fortunately, many development projects do belong to a large family of similar tasks. The online auction in Figure 7–1 is a good example, as is an online shopping cart, and several other kinds of online transactions.

7.1.6 A Little Domain Analysis Is a Dangerous Thing

This has been a lightning introduction to generative programming. In the interest of space, I have been economical with the truth. Domain analysis can be far more intricate than it is when you use it to simply identify variabilities, and it often leads to implementation strategies other than GP. If you want to know more, [Cle01] provides a gentle introduction to GP using Java and XML, and [CE00] stands to be the bible of this emerging field. The purpose of the remainder of this chapter is not to rehash these books in capsule form; instead, the objective is to look at the possible relationships between GP and the component services described earlier in this book. Class loading, type information, and metadata explode the simplistic notion of binding time presented thus far, and they greatly enhance the utility of GP on the Java platform.

7.2 Why Generate Code with Java?

Since the principles of generative programming apply to other languages as well, why use Java? One could argue that Java is not particularly well suited to code generation. After all, C++ has built-in support for code generation with macros and templates. Scripting languages like Perl are very good with string operations and might be better suited for writing generators. Despite these valid objections, Java is particularly suited to GP for five reasons:

1. High quality type information acts as a valuable implicit specification document.

2. Flexible class loading supports any combination of binding times and binding modes.

3. Java source files are simple to read and generate.

4. Java bytecode files are simple to read and generate.

5. Generated code can provide dramatic performance improvements which can obviate the overhead of the VM.

7.2.1 Type Information Acts as a Free Specification Document

High quality type information and reflection can act as a specification document for GP. Best of all, you do not even have to write the document since it is implicit in all Java classes. Many services can be generated from type information alone.

As a very small example, consider your Java IDE. Most IDEs have an "implement interface" wizard that creates a new class to implement some interface. The wizard uses reflection to build a Java file with all the method signatures already in place and just waits for you to fill them in. This is a tiny but useful example of GP.

7.2.2   Class Loading Supports Flexible Binding Modes

The class loading architecture makes it easy to load new classes on-the-fly at runtime. This shatters the simplistic assumptions made about bind time in the previous section. In order to capture the possibilities opened by dynamic class loading, you need to augment bind time with the notion of *bind mode*. Bind time is *when* a decision is encoded, while bind mode is *how* that decision is encoded. At one extreme, static bind mode means that decisions are frozen into the code. At the other extreme are dynamic bindings, which are encoded as runtime branches, perhaps via a parameter or virtual method invocation. With dynamic class loading, you can bind specifications at runtime and still have excellent performance by generating a class that statically binds the specification.

Because class loading is so flexible, generators can create classes that efficiently encode binding decisions at runtime. Dynamic proxies are one example; they use type information to generate an implementation of a batch of interfaces specified at runtime. Another example is JavaServer Pages (JSP). JavaServer Pages have their own, presentation-oriented configuration document. You write your code as a JSP page and then drop it into a JSP container. The container acts as a generator and converts this format into a normal Java source file, which it then compiles and loads dynamically.

7.2.3   Java Source Is Easy to Generate

The simplicity of Java syntax encourages code generation projects. It is easy to write a program that will emit a valid Java source file. Because Java source files do not have macros or templates, it is also easy to use a Java file as input to a generator or even to write a generator that modifies a file in-place. On the minus side, since macros and templates are not supported, you are forced to build your own generation schemes to mimic these capabilities.

7.2.4 Java Binary Classes Are Easy to Generate

The class file format is also straightforward, so you can write a generator that emits valid Java class files, and omits the source code step entirely. This feature is crucial if your generator will execute at runtime in an environment where a compiler may not be available. The portability of the class file format also guarantees that your generated code will work on any compliant Java platform.

7.2.5 Code Generation Boosts Performance

Perhaps the most important motivation for GP in Java is the potential for performance gains. These performance gains come from two sources. First, your code generators are free to generate efficient code regardless of readability.[1] Your domain knowledge is stored in the specification file and in the generators, so these are the artifacts that need to be readable and maintainable. Second, you can get late binding semantics with early binding performance.

In general, early binding makes for better performance. For example, if you could hard-code *all* your choices during development, your code would not need conditional statements or virtual methods at all, and it would be blazingly fast. Of course, many choices must be made at runtime. Generative techniques allow you to use runtime binding with a static binding mode, which enables you to generate the code once and reuse it for future iterations. For example, Java serialization uses reflection every time you read or write a Java instance. You could write a generator that uses reflection only once during development to generate a helper class that binds statically to the field values.[2]

7.2.6 Levels of Commitment to Code Generation

It is useful to divide code generation schemes by scale. Code generation in-the-large is a complete commitment to code generation for an application. Here, the

---

1. This is true only up to a point since you may need to read the generated code when you are debugging. Ideally debugging tools can relate the generated code back to the specification, but this will not always be the case.
2. This would also require that the fields be at least package-protected instead of private, and it is an argument in favor of small packages with shared access to class fields. With some additional effort you could even optimize access to private fields by modifying classes as they were being loaded.

entire architecture assumes that generation is being used, and in fact, it may only accept specification files as inputs. Helper components are provided to service the generated code, and they may not even be documented or accessible for direct programmer consumption. This style of code generation is widely used in the J2EE architecture. For example, JavaServer Pages (JSPs) and Enterprise JavaBeans (EJBs) are worthless without a code generation step that creates the code that the client will actually invoke.

Code generation in-the-small suggests techniques that can be used within part of a project, at the class, method, or field level. Code generation in-the-small can enhance your development process in a more encapsulated way, without binding you to a particular architecture such as J2EE. This chapter will leverage J2EE for examples of generation in-the-large, and it will introduce some custom examples for generation in-the-small.

7.3   A Taxonomy of Bind Times and Modes

The flexibility of Java class loading means that you can bind your specifications at any time and in any mode. Table 7–1 categorizes some generative programming techniques by bind time and mode. Notice that the divisions are somewhat arbitrary. Because Java preserves full type information in its compiled class file format, most of these techniques *could* be used at any time. Deployment time and runtime have been combined in the table because dynamic class loading makes it straightforward to redeploy at runtime. I have listed each technique where it is most likely to be used today. Some of these divisions will change in the future; for example, future versions of `rmic` might generate stubs at runtime.

Table 7–1   Generative Programming in Java by Bind Time and Mode

	Static Bind Mode	Dynamic Bind Mode
Development time	IDE wizards, `rmic`, JavaBeans	Default serialization
Design time		JavaBeans
Deployment/runtime	JSP, EJB	EJB, dynamic proxies

In general, as you move up in the table, you have more services available, both human and software. At development time you have access to developers, high-end developer machines, and end users. At runtime you have only end users and whatever software they install. As you move left in the table, you *need* more services because there is more code to generate, but the resulting code can be faster if the overhead of generating the code is affordable.

Start from the top of the table and work down. IDE wizards run at development time and produce code that is compiled into the application. The RMI stub compiler (`rmic`) also runs during development and produces implementations that are specific to a particular remote object, while default serialization is more dynamic. Although field types are bound during development, they are traversed reflectively at runtime. JavaBean property types and names are chosen during development, but their values can be dynamically modified at design time. Java-Server Pages are translated into servlets, which are then statically compiled at runtime.

Table 7–1 lists EJB under both static and dynamic bind mode. The Enterprise JavaBeans specification is flexible; EJB functionality can be produced by generating static code or by passing parameters through dynamic code. Dynamic proxies are, of course, dynamic. The dynamic proxy architecture generates an in-memory class file that forwards all of its interfaces to an `InvocationHandler`, which almost always uses dynamic invocation to forward the call to another object.

Another way to characterize various styles of generative programming is by inputs and outputs. In the Java world, inputs might be any combination of Java source code, Java class files, and non-Java vocabularies suited to the problem domain. Outputs are typically Java source or class files. Table 7–2 organizes some common Java technologies by inputs and outputs. Generators that work only with Java class files use Java type information to build connectors. RMI stubs connect objects in different virtual machines, and dynamic proxies connect objects through an intermediary handler. JSP defines its own file format that includes embedded Java code, and EJB includes both Java code and XML-based deployment descriptors. SOAP is an XML specification for describing request and response methods in a language-neutral way. SOAP generators take the XML description of types and generate language-specific mappings.

Table 7–2 Generative Programming in Java by Inputs and Outputs

Inputs/Outputs	Source Files	Class Binaries
Java class binaries	RMI stubs, IDE wizards	RMI stubs, dynamic proxies
Non-Java data	SOAP	
Mixed data	JSP, EJB	EJB

Note that source files are easier to generate than class files. In fact, most of the technologies that output class files "cheat" by emitting and compiling a source code file. The only example listed in Table 7–2 that goes directly to byte-code is dynamic proxies, which can run on client-side machines that do not have access to a compiler.

Subsequent sections of this chapter describe RMI, JSP, and EJB in more detail. Dynamic proxies are described earlier in the book in §3.4.

7.4 Code Generation in RMI

Java Remote Method Invocation (RMI) uses code generation to build *stubs* and *skeletons*. A stub implements a remote interface by serializing method calls into a stream and forwarding that stream to the actual implementation class, often on a different physical machine. RMI clients never hold a direct reference to an implementation class; instead they use a local stub class, which forwards the call to the implementation. A skeleton receives stream-encoded method calls from a stub, converts them back into call stacks, and invokes the corresponding methods. Figure 7–3 shows an RMI call passing through a stub and skeleton to the implementation class.

To create RMI stubs and skeletons, you run the Java RMI stub compiler `rmic`, passing in the name of a remotable class—one that implements the `Remote` marker interface. This ties stub generation to development time, or deployment time at the latest, since you cannot expect clients to have (or correctly

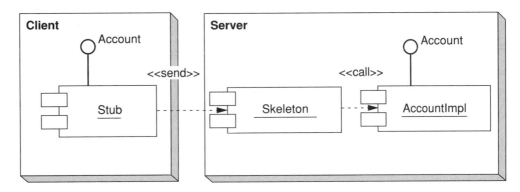

Figure 7–3 RMI calls pass through stubs.

use) `rmic`. The `rmic` tool reads the remote class's type information to discover method signatures, which it then uses to generate the stubs and skeletons.

The RMI stub compiler does not generate class files directly (although this is certainly possible in theory). Instead, it first generates a Java source code file, and then it invokes the compiler on it. Unlike the situation with dynamic proxies, generating a source file first is a reasonable approach because `rmic` is installed along with the compiler. Normally, `rmic` deletes the source file so that you never see it, but the `-keep` option allows you to see the Java code for the stubs if you like.

If you refer back to Table 7–1, you will see that `rmic` is listed as a compile-time use of code generation. However, the RMI stubs and skeletons are driven entirely by type information and require no additional semantic knowledge of the interfaces being implemented. This sounds like a situation tailor-made for reflection, and indeed it is. Skeletons can be replaced entirely by a single generic skeleton that uses the `Method` class's dynamic invocation capabilities to invoke the correct method at runtime. Similarly, dynamic proxies can be generated at runtime to take the place of specific stubs, requiring only a single generic stub that knows how to serialize arguments and communicate over the network. This would move RMI stub generation down two rows in the table, into the "runtime" category.

In fact, RMI is moving toward this more dynamic approach to stubs and skeletons. In SDK 1.2, RMI added the ability to use generic skeletons, as discussed above. A future version of RMI will probably allow dynamic proxies to be used in place of stubs, and [Öbe00] demonstrates how to trick the SDK 1.3 implementation of RMI into using dynamic proxies.

Automating the generation of stubs at runtime is a big win for developers. Because stubs are generated at runtime, there is no need to figure out how to make stub classes available to clients—an exercise in class loading gymnastics that often stymies rookie RMI developers. The potential disadvantage of runtime stub generation via dynamic proxies is that dynamic proxies use reflection, which imposes a performance penalty on every method call. In the case of RMI, this performance issue is a red herring. Dynamic proxies are hundreds of times faster than the simplest RMI calls across machines, especially when network latency and likely file operations are taken into account.

7.5   Code Generation in JSP

JSP represents an entirely different use of code generation. JSP provides a web-content-oriented language that can include escapes to blocks of Java code. The idea is that web developers experienced with HTML and XML can design pages that have a substantial amount of static content, and then they can occasionally use escape sequences to introduce blocks of Java code. These blocks of Java code execute when the page is accessed and can add dynamic content to the page.

A JSP engine converts JSP syntax into a normal Java source file containing the code for a Java servlet, which it then compiles and executes. Listing 7–4 shows a simple Hello.jsp servlet that displays a greeting. Normal text in the page is sent directly to the client as HTML by default. The text bracketed by `<% %>` represents special instructions to be evaluated by the JSP engine.

Listing 7–5 shows the servlet generated by this simple JSP page; it has been edited for space and for readability on the printed page.[3] The generated servlet is simply normal Java code. When a page request arrives at the servlet container, it locates an instance of the appropriate servlet and invokes its `doGet`

---

3. I used Tomcat to generate this servlet. Tomcat is open source and is the reference implementation for servlets. See http://jakarta.apache.org for more details. If you want to see the servlets generated by your JSPs, they are the Java files with funky names in the tomcat/work directory.

method. The servlet `doGet` method is forwarded to the generated servlet's `_jspService` method, which then writes back to the client through the `out` variable. If you look through the generated servlet, you can find Java code corresponding to each line in the JSP. The `page import` directive becomes a simple import statement. Normal text blocks are simply written through the `out` variable. Code in an expression, delimited by `<%= expr %>`, is evaluated, and the result is written back through the `out` variable.

Listing 7–4 A Simple Hello.jsp

```
<%@ page import = "java.util.*" %>

<h1>Hello</h1>
Hello, you have reached this page at
<%= new Date().toString() %>. Have a nice day.
```

Listing 7–5 Servlet Generated from Hello.jsp

```
import javax.servlet.*;import javax.servlet.http.*;
import javax.servlet.jsp.*;
import javax.servlet.jsp.tagext.*;
import java.io.PrintWriter;
import java.io.IOException;
import java.io.FileInputStream;
import java.io.ObjectInputStream;
import java.util.Vector;
import org.apache.jasper.runtime.*;
import java.beans.*;
import org.apache.jasper.JasperException;
import java.util.*;
public class _0002fhello_0002ejsphello_jsp_2
extends HttpJspBase {
public void _jspService(HttpServletRequest request,
                        HttpServletResponse  response)
          throws IOException, ServletException {
   JspFactory _jspxFactory = null;
   PageContext pageContext = null;
   HttpSession session = null;
   ServletContext application = null;
   ServletConfig config = null;
   JspWriter out = null;
   Object page = this;
   String _value = null;
```

```
try {
    _jspxFactory = JspFactory.getDefaultFactory();
    response.setContentType("text/html;charset=8859_1");
    pageContext = _jspxFactory.getPageContext(this, request,
                response, "", true, 8192, true);
    application = pageContext.getServletContext();
    config = pageContext.getServletConfig();
    session = pageContext.getSession();
    out = pageContext.getOut();
    // HTML // begin [file="E:\\gj\\jakarta-tomcat-\
    //3.2.1\\webapps\\ROOT\\hello.jsp";from=(0,34);to=(4,0)]
    out.write("\r\n\r\n<h1>Hello</h1>\r\nHello, you have reached
            this page at \r\n");
    // end
    // begin [file="E:\\gj\\jakarta-tomcat-\
    //3.2.1\\webapps\\ROOT\\hello.jsp";from=(4,3);to=(4,26)]
    out.print( new Date().toString() );
    // end
    // HTML // begin [file="E:\\gj\\jakarta-tomcat-\
    //3.2.1\\webapps\\ROOT\\hello.jsp";from=(4,28);to=(6,0)]
    out.write(". Have a nice day.\r\n\r\n\r\n");
    // end
} catch (Exception ex) {
    if (out.getBufferSize() != 0) out.clearBuffer();
    pageContext.handlePageException(ex);
} finally {
    out.flush();
    _jspxFactory.releasePageContext(pageContext);
}
}
}
```

The JSP in Listing 7–4 and the servlet in Listing 7–5 are functionally equivalent. However, Listing 7–4 is much easier to read. In this example, code generation enables a syntax that is more suited to a specific problem domain than Java. For web content that is mostly text, the JSP syntax is simpler than a servlet with hundreds of calls to `out.write`.

JSP code generation is different from dynamic proxies or RMI stubs in that type information is not needed to generate the code. The transformations are based mostly on the JSP text. In fact, programming syntax errors in the JSP will pass undetected through the servlet generation stage, only to be detected when the servlet is compiled.

The JSP conversion is also more performance sensitive than dynamic proxy invocation. Fortunately, there is no need to convert the JSP every time a request comes in. The conversion and compilation can take several seconds. However, the conversion needs to be done only once. The JSP engine only translates the page and compiles the resulting servlet once when the page is first accessed,[4] and then it caches the class to service future requests. If you direct your browser to a JSP that has not yet been compiled, you will see a substantial pause before the page is returned. Subsequent requests for the same page will return instantaneously.[5]

7.6 Code Generation in EJB

The most interesting use of code generation in the J2EE environment is Enterprise JavaBeans. Despite the similar names, EJBs are completely unrelated to JavaBeans.[6] An EJB represents data and logic that executes in a server environment. There are two primary kinds of EJBs. Session beans represent short-lived conversational state between a client and server, and entity beans represent long-lived data, often in a back end database.

For our purpose here, the interesting thing about EJBs is that they leverage generated code to add semantics beyond the semantics specifically encoded in Java classes. Most importantly, EJBs can acquire transactional semantics at deployment time. Developers write their Java code as normal, and application deployers describe the transactional requirements of the beans in an XML-based deployment descriptor.

To build an Enterprise JavaBean, you specify the following four things:

1. The *home interface* specifies how clients find or create the bean.

2. The *remote interface* defines business methods that clients call.

---

4. The JSP page could also be compiled on application startup, or it could be recompiled when the source on the disk changes, but the basic point remains the same.

5. Well, maybe not instantaneously, but any delays you experience will not be related to converting the page.

6. There are only so many coffee metaphors, so the coolest ones have to be reused.

3. The *bean* object contains implementation code.

4. The *deployment descriptor* describes services the deployer wants to make available to the bean.

Listing 7–6 shows fragments from each of these text files. The home interface and remote interface delineate separate interfaces for creating, finding, and using an object. The bean object executes a simple `transfer` operation by withdrawing from one account and adding to another.

Listing 7–6   Relevant Fragments of an EJB

```
//home interface
public interface TellerSessionHome extends EJBHome {
  public TellerSession create() throws CreateException,
    java.rmi.RemoteException;
}

//remote interface
public interface TellerSession extends EJBObject {
  public boolean deposit(Money m, Account a)
    throws java.rmi.RemoteException, TellerException;
  public boolean transfer(Money m, Account a1, Account a2)
    throws java.rmi.RemoteException, TellerException;
}

//bean
public class TellerSessionBean implements SessionBean {
  //several other methods omitted
  public boolean transfer(Money m,Account a1, Account a2) {
    a1.withdraw(m);
    a2.deposit(m);
  }
}

<!-- deployment descriptor -->
<ejb-jar>
  <enterprise-beans><session>
    <ejb-name>Teller</ejb-name>
    <transaction-type>Container</transaction-type>
  </session></enterprise-beans>
  <assembly-descriptor>
    <container-transaction>
      <method>
```

```
      <ejb-name>Teller</ejb-name>
      <method-intf>Remote</method-intf>
      <method-name>*</method-name>
    </method>
    <trans-attribute>Required</trans-attribute>
  </container-transaction>
 </assembly-descriptor>
</ejb-jar>
```

What happens if `transfer` fails halfway, for instance, `withdraw` succeeds but `deposit` fails? Ideally, the entire operation should rollback, and the client should receive an exception indicating that the operation failed. Of course, this could be accomplished by explicit transaction programming, but the code would be much more complex, as Listing 7–7 shows (additions to the original code are in bold). The `transfer` method must begin by looking up a transaction object via the Java Naming and Directory Interface (JNDI). Then, all data access in the rest of the method should *enlist* on this transaction, specifying that if the transaction fails, any changes should be rolled back.

Listing 7–7   EJB-Like Code, but with Manual Transaction Programming

```
public class TellerSessionBean implements SessionBean {
  //several other methods omitted
  public boolean transfer(Money m,Account a1, Account a2) {
    Context ctx = new InitialContext();
    UserTransaction tx = (UserTransaction)
      ctx.lookup("java:comp/UserTransaction");
    tx.setTransactionTimeout(30);
    tx.begin();
    try {
      a1.withdraw(m, tx);
      a2.deposit(m, tx);
    catch (Throwable t) {
      tx.rollback();
      throw t;
    }
    tx.commit();
  }
}
```

Ironically, an encapsulated design makes it difficult to know where data access might be occurring. To be safe, you must recode all the methods on the `Money` and `Account` objects to take a transaction object as a parameter. This changes interfaces as well as implementations, as the extra parameter to `withdraw` and `deposit` demonstrates. There are other concerns as well. If a method throws an uncaught exception, then the transaction should abort quickly so that any resources associated with the transaction are released as soon as possible.

Transaction programming is a concern that cross-cuts traditional object designs. As Listing 7–7 shows, the transactional code is interleaved with the code that executes the business logic. All of the other classes, such as `Money` and `Account`, would need similar interleaving. This spreads transactional code throughout an application, making it difficult to extend and maintain.

7.6.1 The Deployment Descriptor

EJB attacks the cross-cutting problem by separating the transactional aspect of the system into a separate XML file called a deployment descriptor. In Listing 7–6, the `container-transaction` element specifies that the remote methods of `Teller` should always be protected by a transaction. This causes the container to generate or otherwise simulate the bolded code from Listing 7–7. Whenever a client calls a method on `Teller`'s remote interface, the container will create a transaction object. If `Teller` then calls out to other objects such as `Money` and `Account`, the container will propagate the transaction to these components as well. As a result, all of the work done on behalf of a `Teller` remote method can be bound to the same transaction, even if dozens of other objects are involved.

Thanks to the deployment descriptor, control of the transaction is situated in a single location that is easy to maintain. There are other transaction settings, not shown here, that allow components to block the flow of a transaction, or to start a different transaction even if one transaction is already in process. The deployment descriptor also supports other cross-cutting aspects, such as security roles, and more aspects may be added in the future.

In order to create transactions and to guarantee that transactions flow from one component to another as specified by the descriptor, the EJB container needs to intercept all calls into an EJB. Containers typically do this by generating additional classes, either at deployment time or possibly even on-the-fly at run-time. Figure 7–4 shows the classes typically generated by an EJB container and their relationship to classes that you author.

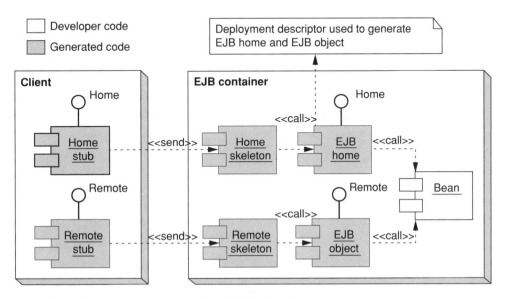

Figure 7–4   Classes generated by an EJB container

EJB generates stubs and skeletons that are similar to RMI stubs and skeletons. These classes are generated from type information and handle forwarding method calls around the network. EJB containers use the information in the deployment descriptor to generate the EJB home and EJB object, which handle aspects such as transactions and security before invoking the business logic of the bean itself. Clients make RMI connections to the EJB home and EJB object, *never* to the bean itself.

Relate Figure 7–4 back to the definition of a component given at the beginning of the book: "an independent unit of production and deployment that is combined with other components to assemble an application." An EJB is a single component that contains the following nine classes:

1. Home interface*
2. Remote interface*
3. Home stub
4. Remote stub
5. Home skeleton
6. Remote skeleton
7. EJB home
8. EJB object
9. The bean itself*

Of these nine classes, you only need to write the three labeled with asterisks—the interfaces and the bean. The other classes are generated from type information and from the data in the deployment descriptor. In other words, much of the work of authoring an EJB component is not writing Java code at all. Instead, you write some Java code, write some XML, and the container builds most of the Java code that eventually executes on both the client and the server.

7.6.2 Alternate Implementations

Not all EJB containers function exactly as described above. Many of the services provided by generated classes could also be provided in other ways. Figure 7–5 shows an EJB container that makes minimal use of code generation. The client-side stubs must be generated, but they could be generated at runtime using dynamic proxies. All of the generated classes on the server side have been replaced with generic classes that perform the same operations.

This is very different from the previous figure because the generic classes are not specific to any bean. Instead, they use reflection's `Method.invoke` to call any EJB in a generic fashion. From a generative programming perspective, the difference is one of bind mode. The container architectures in Figure 7–4 and Figure 7–5 both bind the deployment descriptor during deployment (hence

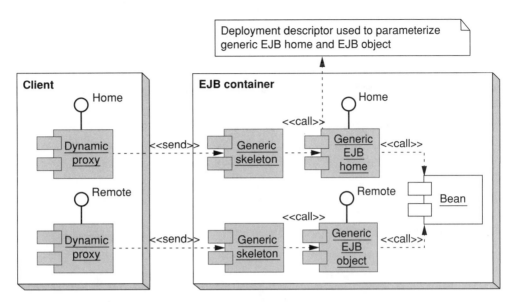

Figure 7–5 EJB without code generation

the name), but the former uses a static binding mode, and the latter uses a dynamic binding mode. Given that both designs accomplish the same thing, why go to the trouble of generating the additional classes shown in Figure 7–4?

There are two reasons why all containers will use at least some code generation and many containers will rely heavily on it. First, code generation is necessary to preserve Java syntax on the client. Clients expect to call methods on the home and remote interfaces, which means that stubs *must* be generated. The only real question is the binding time.

Second, code generation permits optimizations that are difficult or impossible with generic code. This is the crux of the matter. If the container provides a generic service layer for components, as in Figure 7–5, then the deployment descriptor must be bound into the code by passing parameters at runtime. Passing and interpreting these parameters takes time, possibly on every method invocation. If the container generates the code instead, then it has to deal with the specifics of the component only once, at generation time.

Actually writing performance tests to compare different techniques for implementing an EJB container would be an interesting task, but it would take us very far afield. Instead, the next examples will evoke similar issues within a scope amenable to some simple performance tests. You will see techniques to statically bind strongly typed collections and serialization, both of which are normally dynamically bound in Java. In both of these examples, code generation will replace generic code with code specifically tuned to the task at hand. This will boost performance by eliminating repetitive tasks at runtime.

If you plan to use code generation to improve the performance of an application, you should beware of the possible tradeoffs. In theory, generated code can run faster because you can hard-code values that might otherwise be parameters, or remove levels of indirection that would otherwise be implemented as virtual methods. However, these benefits must be offset against the additional effort to generate code, and the increased memory footprint if you generate several blocks of very similar code. Which of these factors will predominate is project and virtual machine dependent, but for many simple tasks code generation provides a clear performance advantage. Also, it is often easier to generate a specific solution than to code the logic needed to implement a generic solution.

7.7 Generating Strongly Typed Collections

As a simple example of the performance tradeoffs that drive a GP design, consider the collection classes in the `java.util` package. The various collections (`ArrayList`, `HashMap`, etc.) are all of type `Object`—in other words, the collections are entirely generic. If you want to use a collection in a type-safe fashion, then you must write additional code to enforce type safety at runtime, as shown here:

```
// Must pay runtime cost of casting to String
// also possible that cast might fail
String value = (String) stack.pop();
```

One workaround to this problem is to write your own strongly typed collections, such as hand-coded `StringStack`, `IntStack`, and so on. Such work is tedious, error-prone, and better suited to code generation. Since all the conceivable strongly typed `Stack`s look mostly the same, it is straightforward to generate the source code for them. One approach is to write a JSP page based on the source code for the generic version of the collection. Listing 7–8 shows a JSP page that extracts parameters from an HTTP query string and uses them to generate a specific stack class. Because the source code for different stack classes is similar, most of the JSP page is simply static text.

Listing 7–8 JSP Page That Generates Strongly Typed Stack Classes

```
<%
response.setContentType("text/plain");
String packageName = request.getParameter("package");
String type = request.getParameter("type");
String name=request.getParameter("name");
if ((packageName == null) || (type == null) || (name == null)) {
  throw new Error("must specify package, name, and type");
}
%>
package <%= packageName %>;

import java.util.*;
/**
 * This stack class was generated by StronglyTypedStack.jsp.
 *
 * @author  Stuart Halloway
 */
public
class <%= name %>Stack extends Vector {
    public <%= name %>Stack() {
    }

    public <%= type %> push(<%= type %> item) {
    addElement(item);
    return item;
    }
    public synchronized <%= type %> pop() {
    <%= type %> obj;
    int len = size();
    obj = peek();
    removeElementAt(len - 1);
    return obj;
    }
    public synchronized <%= type %> peek() {
    int len = size();
    if (len == 0)
        throw new EmptyStackException();
```

COMPONENT DEVELOPMENT FOR THE JAVA™ PLATFORM

```
    return (<%= type %>) elementAt(len - 1);
    }
  public boolean empty() {
  return size() == 0;
    }
  public synchronized int search(<%= type %> o) {
  int i = lastIndexOf(o);
  if (i >= 0) {
      return size() - i;
  }
  return -1;
    }
}
```

The specification that drives this generator is simply three text strings: the package name, the new class name, and the name of the class that the stack holds. To generate a `StringStack` class in the `com.develop` package, you would install the JSP page in a JSP engine, and then browse to the site with the following HTTP request:

```
http://yoursite/yourwebapp/StronglyTypedStack.jsp?
package=com.develop&type=java.lang.String&name=String
```

Then, you would simply paste the text content of your browser into a Java source code file and compile. To complete this example, you would want to automate the entire process from a build tool. You could eliminate the browser from the equation by writing your own simple HTTP client that automates connecting to the server, retrieving the source code, and saving it to file.

Strongly typed stack classes have two potential advantages over the generic `java.util.Stack` class. First, they enforce correct usage at compile time by type-checking the references involved in the `push` and `pop` operations. Second, the generated classes can be made more efficient than the generic `Stack` class. The generator shown in Listing 7–8 can provide the former, but not the latter. The generated code leverages the weakly typed `Vector` class so that it still has to execute a type cast for every `pop` operation.

Of course, nothing limits you to a single flavor of generator. Now that you have defined a specification, you could create a second generator that provides both advantages. This second generator would generate a strongly typed

`Vector` base class that uses a strongly typed array as its backing store. This would avoid type casts and provide a slight performance advantage over the standard API classes. Of course, the advantages of the generated code must be weighed against increased memory usage. The generated `Stack` and `Vector` classes take extra space in memory, possibly quite a bit of space if you generated dozens or hundreds of different varieties.

I am not going to evaluate the various arguments for and against strongly typed collections here. The weight you give to the various pros and cons will depend strongly on the specifics of your project. The important issue here is not which option you choose, but rather that you have multiple options available. Code generation makes it easy to try the various possibilities without having to hand code them all. The JSP example shown earlier generates only a single class, but you could design an entire project to include a parameterized generation step as part of the build process. If you have a compiler available, you could even generate different versions of your component at runtime based on the specifics of the current environment.

7.7.1 Code Generation Language versus Target Language

The environment you use to generate code need not have anything in common with the environment you are generating code *for*. In this example, using JSP as the generator language for Java code has several advantages. JSP has a well-known syntax, and implementations are freely available.[7] Also, JSP is more convenient than using Java to generate code, especially when the generation is driven mostly from a static template.

JSP also has several noteworthy disadvantages stemming from the fact that the language was not originally intended for code generation. As used here, JSP requires a separate server process, expects arguments to be passed as HTTP `GET` parameters, and returns a single source file. For generating source code, you might prefer to have a tool that runs as part of a build process, provides a convenient (or even customizable) syntax for the specification, and returns an entire collection of files. With additional effort you could coerce a JSP engine to

---

7. The reference implementation of JSP is open source; see [Jakarta].

COMPONENT DEVELOPMENT FOR THE JAVA™ PLATFORM

do all of these things, or you might consider just writing your generator from scratch. The next section gives an example of a simple generator written in straight Java code.

7.8 Generating Custom Serialization Code

Serialization is the perfect example of a generic service. Simply mark your object as `Serializable`, and at runtime the `ObjectOutputStream` class and friends will use reflection to extract/construct your object's instance state. Unfortunately, default serialization's heavy use of reflection imposes a performance penalty that is noticeable in some situations. In Chapter 4, you saw several options for manually customizing serialization. Some of these options could be used to improve serialization performance, but they would require you to hand-author the serialization code.

Generative programming offers an attractive middle ground. A generator can use reflection to generate custom code that is more efficient than default serialization. If done properly, this provides the best of both worlds. The serialization code is fast because it is compiled into the object, and it is error-free because it is generated directly from type information.

Consider the `Externalizer` class shown in Listing 7–9. `Externalizer` uses reflection to analyze a preexisting class and generate appropriate source code for `readExternal`, `writeExternal`, and `serialVersionUID`. The `serialVersionUID` is calculated trivially by calling an accessor method on serialization's `ObjectStreamClass` representation of the class. The `readExternal` and `writeExternal` methods are calculated by iterating over a class's serializable fields to produce the appropriate calls to read and write methods. The base class `GeneratorBase` (not shown in the listing) provides helper methods that open a Java file and insert the generated code.

Listing 7–9   The Externalizer

```
package com.develop.generators;

import java.io.*;
import java.lang.reflect.*;
```

```java
public class Externalizer extends GeneratorBase {

    public String primitiveName(Class cls) {
        if (!cls.isPrimitive()) {
            throw new IllegalArgumentException(cls +
                    " is not primitive");
        }
        String name = cls.getName();
        return name.substring(0,1).toUpperCase() +
                            name.substring(1);
    }

    public void readExternal(Class cls, Field[] fields) {
        indentPrint("public void readExternal(ObjectInput oi) " +
                "throws ClassNotFoundException, IOException {", 0);
        if (cls.getSuperclass() != Object.class)
            indentPrint("super.readExternal(oi);", 1);
        for (int n=0; n<fields.length; n++) {
            Field f = fields[n];
            if (0 != (f.getModifiers() &
                    (Modifier.STATIC + Modifier.TRANSIENT)))
            continue;
            Class fldClass = f.getType();
            if (fldClass.isPrimitive()){
            indentPrint(f.getName() + " = oi.read" +
                        primitiveName(fldClass) + "();", 1);
            } else if (fldClass == String.class) {
            indentPrint(f.getName() + " = oi.readUTF();", 1);
            } else {
            indentPrint(f.getName() + " = oi.readObject();", 1);
            }
        }
        indentPrint("}", 0);
    }

    public void writeExternal(Class cls, Field[] fields) {
        indentPrint("public void writeExternal(ObjectOutput oo) "+
                "throws IOException {", 0);
        if (cls.getSuperclass() != Object.class)
            indentPrint("super.writeExternal(oi);", 1);
        for (int n=0; n<fields.length; n++) {
            Field f = fields[n];
            if (0 != (f.getModifiers() &
                    (Modifier.STATIC + Modifier.TRANSIENT)))
```

```
      continue;
    Class fldClass = f.getType();
    if (fldClass.isPrimitive()){
    indentPrint("oo.write" + primitiveName(fldClass) +
            "(" + f.getName() + ");", 1);
    } else if (fldClass == String.class) {
    indentPrint("oo.writeUTF(" + f.getName() + ");", 1);
    } else {
    indentPrint("oo.writeObject(" + f.getName() + ");", 1);
    }
  }
  indentPrint("}", 0);
}

public void serialVersionUID(Class cls) {
  ObjectStreamClass ocs = ObjectStreamClass.lookup(cls);
  indentPrint("private final static long serialVersionUID="
            + ocs.getSerialVersionUID() + "L;", 0);
}

public void generate(Class cls, PrintStream out) {
  this.out = out;
  beginGenerated();
  serialVersionUID(cls);
  Field[] fields = cls.getDeclaredFields();
  writeExternal(cls, fields);
  readExternal(cls, fields);
  endGenerated();
}
}
```

Listing 7–10 shows a simple SerializeMe class after it was modified by the Externalizer. The code generated by the Externalizer is shown here in bold. The modified version of SerializeMe will serialize and deserialize more efficiently than the original version because there is no need to use reflection at runtime to access the class's type information or instance fields. At the same time, you can rely on the correctness of the code because it is generated directly from type information. If you want to use a large number of Externalizable classes in your application, you should take the Externalizer (or something like it) and make it part of your build process.

Listing 7–10 SerializeMe after Modification by Externalizer

```java
import java.io.*;

public class SerializeMe implements Externalizable {
  public SerializeMe() {
    i = 1;
    f = 10;
    l = 100;
    d = 1000;
    s = "serialize me ";
  }

  int i;
  float f;
  long l;
  double d;
  String s;

  //{{@@ BEGIN CODE GENERATION BY class Externalizer @@}}
  //edit at your own risk...
  private final static long serialVersionUID=
                       -2726536721571465800L;
  public void writeExternal(ObjectOutput oo) throws IOException {
      oo.writeInt(i);
      oo.writeFloat(f);
      oo.writeLong(l);
      oo.writeDouble(d);
      oo.writeUTF(s);
  }
  public void readExternal(ObjectInput oi)
            throws ClassNotFoundException, IOException {
      i = oi.readInt();
      f = oi.readFloat();
      l = oi.readLong();
      d = oi.readDouble();
      s = oi.readUTF();
  }
  //{{@@ END CODE GENERATION BY class Externalizer @@}}
}
```

Another approach to generating serialization code is shown in Listing 7–11. This version of SerializeMe contains serialization code from a different generator.

The UnreflectiveSerialize generator[8] uses the GetField and PutField hooks to modify default serialization. With these hooks, metadata is included in the stream format just as if the class had been serialized using the default mechanism.

Listing 7–11   SerializeMe after Modification by UnreflectiveSerialize

```java
import java.io.*;
public class SerializeMe implements Serializable {
  public SerializeMe() {
    i = 1;
    f = 10;
    l = 100;
    d = 1000;
    s = "serialize me ";
  }

  int i;
  float f;
  long l;
  double d;
  String s;

//{{@@ BEGIN CODE GENERATION BY class UnreflectiveSerialize
//edit at your own risk...
private final static long serialVersionUID=
                         -2726536721571465800L;
private static final ObjectStreamField[] serialPersistentFields =
{
    new ObjectStreamField("i", int.class),
    new ObjectStreamField("f", float.class),
    new ObjectStreamField("l", long.class),
    new ObjectStreamField("d", double.class),
    new ObjectStreamField("s", java.lang.String.class),
};
private void writeObject(ObjectOutputStream oos)
                    throws IOException {
    ObjectOutputStream.PutField pf = oos.putFields();
    pf.put("i", i);
    pf.put("f", f);
```

---

8. The UnreflectiveSerialize generator is not shown here for brevity, but it is included with the book's source code.

```
        pf.put("l", l);
        pf.put("d", d);
        pf.put("s", s);
        pf.write(oos);
    }
    private void readObject(ObjectInputStream ois)
                throws ClassNotFoundException, IOException {
        ObjectInputStream.GetField gf = ois.readFields();
        i = gf.get("i", 0);
        f = gf.get("f", 0.0f);
        l = gf.get("l", 0L);
        d = gf.get("d", 0.0);
        s = (java.lang.String) gf.get("s", null);
    }
    //{{@@ END CODE GENERATION BY UnreflectiveSerialize @@}}
    }
```

The `UnreflectiveSerialize` generator is helpful if you need to support multiple versions of a class over time. Imagine that you have a large data class with a few dozen fields. If only a few fields change, most of the code in `readObject` and `writeObject` will look exactly like the code generated by `UnreflectiveSerialize`. You could generate the basic code, and then hand-edit only the few lines that need to change. This demonstrates a general principle: Code generation during development is flexible because you can fix problems by hand. Therefore, a 90 percent solution is far better than nothing at all. By contrast, code generation at runtime must be exact, since no developer is present to adjust it.

7.9 Onward

In this chapter you have seen several widely different examples of generative programming. In all the examples, the goal is to reuse your knowledge of the problem domain. GP works in tandem with, not in opposition to, traditional OO techniques for reuse. Some generative schemes build bytecode, like dynamic proxies. Others build source code, like the serialization example. Some code generation tools bind your choices at runtime, like JSP. Others bind at deployment time or compile time, like the RMI stub compiler.

Sometimes your commitment to generative programming is pervasive and tied into special support libraries. For example, a component either is an EJB, and it requires all the associated container goo, or it is not. On the other end of the spectrum, you may use simple code generation helpers like interface wizards at the level of a single file, without any implication for your overall application architecture. Code generation inputs range from existing Java classes (dynamic proxies), to classes plus additional metadata (EJB), to custom languages (JSP).

Given the wide array of options, you need some way to impose order onto chaos and choose generative techniques that are appropriate for your own applications. This section will make some suggestions as to when code generation is useful, and how you should decide which types of tools to employ.

The most obvious example of when code generation is useful is in providing *generic service components*. A generic service component is a component that can add functionality to other components without having compile-time knowledge of the components that it will be working with. Many of the examples in this chapter fit this description. Dynamic proxies are generated at runtime to implement interfaces that were not previously known. Serialization streams the state of an object without advance knowledge of the object's fields. EJB containers add transactional semantics to objects without knowing in advance what methods the objects may have.

Consider EJB first. EJB requires code generation in order to ensure type safety. Refer back to Figure 7–4. Without the generated stubs, clients would be forced to use some sort of generic invocation mechanism. With the generated stubs, clients are able to communicate via a well-known interface instead.

EJB code generation tools can be used at any time during the component lifecycle. Depending on your container, you might generate the support classes during development, at deployment, at runtime, or some combination of all three. The reason for this flexibility is that EJBs are server-side code. The only client-side components are stubs, which can be downloaded dynamically from the server anyway. Because EJB is a server-side technology, you can reasonably expect access to a compiler and whatever other tools you may need to generate the stubs, EJB home, and EJB object. These tools are available throughout the component lifecycle, up to and including runtime. Since a compiler is available, you do not have to worry about generating bytecode directly. You can generate source code and then run it through the compiler.

Dynamic proxies, by contrast, are much more constrained. Because they are part of the core API, proxies must work in all sorts of Java environments. A compiler will not always be available, so proxies cannot count on compiling source code. Instead, they must generate bytecode directly. This makes dynamic proxies much more difficult to generate than the EJB support classes.[9] Also, dynamic proxies must be generated at runtime since they are created in response to an API call at runtime. Generating code later in the development cycle is more flexible for the user but more difficult for the developer.

As another example of this principle, consider the simple serialization code generators shown in §7.8. In all likelihood, you would use these tools at development time. This is more convenient for the developer since the generated code does not even have to be 100 percent correct—you can always edit it to fix small problems. However, it is less flexible for users of the object because serialization semantics are frozen into the object during development. By contrast, JSP code generators often execute at runtime. This allows even a web administrator to make cosmetic changes to the appearance of a page, without shutting down the web server.[10]

Another issue to consider is the type of inputs required by a code generation scheme. Many of the examples in this chapter require only the type information that is available to any Java object. However, some of the examples add their own metadata as well. EJB functionality is controlled by external XML deployment descriptors, and JSP provides an entire separate syntax with occasional escapes to Java code. In general, code generation schemes that build Java code from non-Java data have one or more of the following properties:

1. A problem domain that is well understood and repetitive
2. Syntaxes more expressive than Java in solving the problem
3. Special support libraries that are called from generated code

---

9. Consider how many programmers write in bytecode instead of Java. Or, compare the number of dynamic proxy implementations with the number of EJB implementations.
10. Whether this is a good idea or not is a site management decision.

Both EJB and JSP have the first property. EJBs repeat the same sequence over and over: check security, acquire transaction, use data, commit/abort. All of the steps other than "use data" are well understood and repetitive to code. JSP pages tend to do the same things again and again, such as generating a standard HTML structure to fill in with user-requested content. JSPs are also a good example of the second property. If most of the work on a page is static content, then Java code degenerates into a boring sequence of write instructions. EJB exemplifies the third property. You do not need to explain *how* the support libraries should implement transactions or security checks; instead, you need only *declare* the parameters to be used. Switching from a functional to a declarative approach also changes the locus of decision-making. Changing a declarative setting does not require a programmer since no code changes.

7.10 Resources

The examples in this chapter only scratch the surface of generative programming. Moreover, they are biased toward services that can leverage type information. For a gentle, general introduction to generative techniques using Java and XML see [Cle01]. For a more complete treatment not limited to Java, see [CE00].

Chapter 8

Onward

Java provides a solid infrastructure for component development and deployment. The next challenge for the software industry is to build a higher-level component infrastructure using standards such as XML.

8.1 Where We Are

This book explains how to develop components and assemble them within a Java virtual machine. Viewed at this level, component development is driven by two key concepts: loaders and types.

Java's class loader architecture provides the means to locate and load components into a process. When they are used carefully, class loaders guarantee security, manage versioning, prevent name collisions, and enable side-by-side deployment of changing components. Loaders also provide a hook from which custom behavior or metadata can be extracted from or added to classes. Even JNI is just a special loader that loads non-Java components in a local process.

Loaders use Java's type information to validate dependencies between classes at runtime. Equally important, containers and other service code can manipulate components via their type information, in order to provide services such as serialization, object/relational mapping, XML data binding, and dynamic proxies.

Taken together, loaders and type information provide great control over the bind mode of application decisions. In addition to compile-time binding and run-time dynamic binding, you can generate the bindings you need, which will give you runtime flexibility and static-bound performance.

8.2   Where We Are Going

Enterprise applications span multiple processes and machines, and they must be able to communicate with disparate hardware and software over the Internet. The current buzzword in enterprise application development is "web applications." Just like standalone Java applications, web applications need to be assembled from components. Therefore, all of the concerns of this book apply to web applications, but with a new twist: web applications need a longer reach.

Web applications must enable communication that reaches all products, and all vendors. No one vendor will define the protocols of web applications; they require industry standards implemented atop solid component platforms. XML will provide the standards, and Java will provide the platform.

As a Java developer, there are several things you should do to prepare for a web application world:

1. Learn servlets. A Java servlet is a network class loader. Servlets load code in some other process across the network in response to a request.

2. Learn XML and the Infoset. XML provides the conceptual model and the serialization format for web application data.

3. Learn XML schemas. Schemas add type information to XML data.

4. Learn XPath. XPath will be the query language of web applications.

5. Learn the Web Services Description Language (WSDL). Along with schemas, WSDL is the other half of XML type information. Where schemas describe data, WSDL describes functionality, that is endpoints and message formats.

6. Participate in the Java Community Process (JCP). Most of the technologies of web applications are too new to have standard Java APIs, but that will change swiftly. The JCP will define APIs so that web applications do not have to be programmed directly.

Java is well positioned to be a dominant platform for web applications. Java's class loaders, type information, and security model will map well to the loaders and type systems of web applications, however those may evolve.

8.3 Resources

There are a huge number of XML books already in print. However, the ways in which XML technologies will combine to enable web services are not completely understood at the present time. To keep track of the XML world, begin at the home page for the World Wide Web Consortium [W3C]. To join in the discussion of how Java and XML should work together, begin with the home page for the Java Community Process (JCP).

Appendix A

Interop 2: Bridging Java and Win32/COM

This chapter introduces Jawin, an open source architecture for Java/Win32/COM interop designed by the author.

A.1 Overview

The Java platform standardizes the services and data formats that you need to assemble an application from separate components. The class loader architecture, type information, and reflective services, such as serialization, provide the infrastructure to load component code, configuration information, resources, and component data from disparate sources at runtime.

When you need to assemble applications across *different* component platforms, things fall apart. All platforms take their own approach to component services, and the differences from Java can be daunting. In the case of Microsoft's Win32 API and the Component Object Model (COM), the problems are not merely of academic interest. Win32 and COM are associated with the dominant Microsoft Windows family of operating systems. Because the Windows family is so prevelant, most organizations will need to deal with code written for these systems, even if they have made a strong commitment to Java.

One approach to calling Win32 and COM components is to use the Java Native Interface (JNI), as described in Chapter 6. JNI does provide the necessary tools, but it is tedious to use for any but the smallest projects. When you use raw JNI, you have to write a large amount of infrastructure code every time you want to cross the boundary between Java and Win32 or COM. Moreover, JNI is a generic architecture for calling native code, and therefore it does not include any features that deal with the specific problems of the Win32 platform. For these two reasons, organizations that need to implement substantial communication between Java and Win32/COM components will want to look for other answers.

This appendix will demonstrate an alternative to JNI by describing a higher-level strategy for in-process interoperation between Java, Win32, and COM components. This strategy uses translucent stubs (introduced in §A.2) that bridge the differences between component platforms. These stubs are important because they sit between components from different platforms and hide the details of cross-platform communication. §A.3, §A.4, and §A.5 present the key differences between Java, Win32, and COM as component platforms and describe how translucent stubs might resolve these problems.

Most of a marshalling layer implementation is generic and can be shared by all components. However, each component interface will need its own interface stub, which must either be developed manually or generated from type information. §A.7 discusses how to generate stubs for Win32 and COM interfaces.

For concrete examples, this chapter uses Jawin, an open source Java-to-Win32/COM marshalling layer developed by the author. However, the emphasis here is on general concepts, not on the specifics of the Jawin implementation. For a list of other Java/Win32 interop solutions, see [JavaWin32].

A.2 Translucent Stubs

A translucent stub is the visible part of a marshalling architecture. A marshalling architecture moves a method call from one environment to another by executing the following series of steps.

1. Convert a method invocation into a request message.
2. Deliver the request message to a target environment.
3. Convert the request message into a method stack in the target environment.
4. Invoke the method.
5. Convert the return value(s) or exception(s) into a response message.
6. Deliver the response message to the source environment.
7. Convert the response message back into the types expected by the caller.

Figure A–1 illustrates these steps.

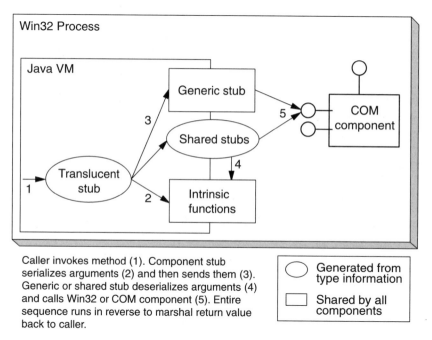

Caller invokes method (1). Component stub serializes arguments (2) and then sends them (3). Generic or shared stub deserializes arguments (4) and calls Win32 or COM component (5). Entire sequence runs in reverse to marshal return value back to caller.

⬭ Generated from type information

▭ Shared by all components

Figure A–1   Marshalling a call from Java to COM

Stubs vary in how well they hide the details of the steps listed above. JNI stubs are very simple, leaving the programmer explicitly aware of all of the steps listed above. On the other hand, you can define a *transparent* stub as one that completely hides the details of communication. Transparent stubs might seem ideal, but they are usually difficult (or impossible) to implement. A *translucent* stub fits somewhere between the extremes. It hides the details of communication that are easily hidden, but exposes the communication layer in some places.

JNI provides only a minimal interface for communicating between Java and native code. As Chapter 6 demonstrated, you must write hand-tuned code to deal with such basic issues as converting parameter types, manipulating arrays, and reporting errors. Worse, you must duplicate this code for every single native method. When you write JNI code, you are always acutely aware that you are working near the boundary of the Java platform, and because of this, you must be skilled in both Java and the native platforms.

If transparent stubs could be created easily, the problems of JNI would be neatly solved. Clients would not have to write any additional code to call Win32/COM components. More importantly, clients would not have to know any details about the Win32/COM platforms or even be aware that these platforms were in use.

How hard is it to create a transparent stub? There are three things to worry about when you are creating transparent stubs between Java, Win32, and COM:

1. Platform impedance. Each platform makes certain fundamental assumptions that are not valid elsewhere, thus forming an "impedance mismatch" between the platforms. Transparent stubs must hide these differences. For example, COM components indicate errors with numeric codes, which a transparent Java stub would hide by translating the error codes into Java exceptions.

2. Generating per-interface stubs. Each different "interface," however that concept maps to a particular platform, implies a different stub. These stubs are very similar to RMI stubs. Therefore, an interop solution needs to include a code generator. This could be a developer tool similar to `rmic`, or a runtime API akin to dynamic proxies.

3. Performance. The stubs have to meet performance criteria, which are specific to an application.

To determine whether transparent stubs are worth the effort, compare the costs of building the stubs with the benefits they provide. Is it easier to efficiently generate stubs that cope with various platform impedance issues, or is it easier to just brute-force your way with raw JNI?

Translucent stubs are based on the observation that some platform impedance problems are more difficult to solve than others. The stubs are called translucent because they hide *most* of the details of calling into native code. When an idiom has an obvious mapping from one platform to another, such as the error codes and exceptions mentioned previously, then it should be hidden in the stub layer. When an idiom does not translate well to another platform or you must understand it to use the component, it is more appropriate to expose the idiom directly.

Java RMI provides a good example of translucent stubs. RMI stubs hide the details of calling an object in another virtual machine, usually over a network. Using RMI is much easier than manually converting method invocation into socket communication. However, RMI stubs are not completely transparent. Object parameters passed to RMI methods must be serializable so that they can be transmitted over the network. RMI stubs will enforce this rule by throwing an exception, which breaks transparency and reveals to the client that RMI is involved.

In another case, the designers of RMI deliberately broke with transparency. They made it so all remote methods must be declared to throw the checked exception `java.rmi.RemoteException`. This reflects the underlying reality that even if the method succeeds, the stub communication may fail. Because the exception is checked, all clients must deal with it, which makes the presence of RMI obvious. It would have been just as easy to make `RemoteException` unchecked, which would have been more transparent. However, this would only have lulled developers into a false sense of security. The possibility of communications failure is so important that it outweighs the convenience of simpler, more transparent clients.

§A.3 describes the sources of platform impedance between Java, Win32, and COM. In this discussion, you will see how one particular stub architecture [Jawin] deals with these issues. The particular choices made in this implementation are reasonable, but not inevitable. Different development teams will assign different weights to the issues.

A.3 Platform Impedance

This section describes the facets of the COM and Win32 platforms that make interoperation with Java difficult. Table A–1 summarizes the chief sources of platform impedance. The COM approach is explored in more detail in §A.4, and the Win32 approach is discussed in §A.5. This is obviously not a complete introduction to these complex technologies. For more on COM see [Box98]; for more on Win32 see [Ric99].

Table A–1 Platform Impedance: Java, Win32, and COM

Concern	Java Approach	Win32 Approach	COM Approach
Loader architecture	Class loaders	Explicit paths	Registry lookup
Metadata/ Type info	Extensive	Minimal	Partial
Object lifecycle management	Implicit, GC	Explicit and ad hoc	Explicit and reference-counted
Type discovery	Per-class	Ad hoc	Per-instance
Error reporting	Throwable	GetLastError et al.	HRESULT et al.
Thread affinity	Explicit	Explicit	Apartments
Security model	Code source and signer	User principal	User principal

The examples in §A.4 and §A.5 show client-side syntax for dealing with these problems from Java, and subsequent sections show one approach to implementing this client-side syntax.

A.4 The Component Object Model

The Component Object Model (COM) defines a binary representation for interface contracts between components. Above that core level, COM includes a runtime with many services that are useful in assembling applications from components. Where the emphasis in Java is one language for many platforms, COM aims at many languages running on one platform.

Different languages use the COM runtime in different ways, which makes learning COM arduous. If you look past the trappings of particular languages, the COM specs and API docs define a set of core services analogous to many of those described in this book:

- COM defines a local loader based on lookup information stored in the Windows Registry.
- COM defines two different type information formats that are not entirely compatible.
- COM defines a reflection-like API for accessing type information.

While these services fill similar roles to their Java counterparts, they are different enough to introduce quite a bit of platform impedance.

A.4.1 The COM Loader

The COM loader loads COM objects by their unique name, which is a 128-bit identifier called a GUID (Globally Unique ID). The loader uses this name to locate the appropriate binary by consulting the Windows Registry. The Registry typically also contains a human-friendly name called a ProgID.

GUIDs and ProgIDs do not have an obvious analog in Java. The GUIDs do not map well to class names, and the ProgIDs may not be unique. Most importantly, any name mapping would replace a name that has some meaning in the COM world with a new name that has meaning only as defined by the stub architecture. The most appropriate thing to do is to expose these constructs directly to Java clients as shown here:

```
//create an instance of MS-Word from Java, using the ProgID:
WordApp wd =
        (WordApp) Ole32.CoGetObject("new:Word.Application", …);

//using the GUID:
GUID wordGUID = new GUID
                ("{000209FF-0000-0000-C000-000000000046}");
WordApp wd =
        (WordApp) Ole32.CoCreateInstance(wordGuid, …);
```

`WordApp` is a generated stub for the top-level COM interface to Microsoft Word. The `Ole32` class is a hand-coded API stub that is part of Jawin.

A.4.2 COM Type Information

Type information poses a trickier problem. COM type information comes in two important formats, the Interface Definition Language (IDL), and the type library. C and C++ developers use IDL to describe interfaces, as shown in Listing A–1.

Listing A–1   A Simple IDL Fragment

```
HRESULT
CrunchArray([in] int sizeIn, [in, size_is(size] int* in,
[out] int* sizeOut, [out, size_is(1,sizeOut)] int** out);
```

IDL method declarations include method names, return types, and argument types. A tool that could read the IDL text file could use this information to generate Java stubs.

There are two problems with using IDL files to generate stubs. First, many COM implementation languages do not use IDL files at all; instead, they describe interfaces with a *type library*. Type libraries are not as expressive as IDL and support only the most commonly used types. Type libraries can be stored standalone in type library (TLB) files or bound into the application binary as resources. The `ITypeLib` and `ITypeInfo` interfaces, COM's version of reflection, can be used to extract the information from a type library. This turns out to be a much easier approach to stub generation than parsing IDL. You do not need to write a parser, and type libraries are much more widely available. Even if there is only an IDL file available, you can use the `midl` compiler to generate a type library.

The second problem with IDL is that the vocabulary is too flexible. Because it can describe interfaces for pointer-based languages such as C and C++, IDL includes a number of constructs that do not have any trivial mapping to Java— or to most COM languages, for that matter. For example, the `CrunchArray` method in Listing A–1 uses two `out` parameters to "return" multiple values to the caller. A straight translation to Java will not work since Java does not support `out` parameters. In this example, the right thing to return would be an array, but IDL can express even more complex signatures that have no obvious Java mapping.

Most integration tools deal with the complexity of IDL by avoiding it. They support only the subset of types that can be expressed in a type library. Many tools handle an even smaller subset of types, those that are VARIANT-compatible. The VARIANT data type is a union of types that are available to scripting languages. Although VARIANT-compatible types are a small subset of full IDL, this limitation is not as bad as it seems. A large fraction of all COM interfaces voluntarily limit themselves to these types anyway so that they can be used from scripting languages. The Jawin architecture is capable of supporting all IDL types, but the implementation is complete only for the most commonly used types.

A.4.3 COM Object Lifecycle

COM uses reference counting to manage object lifecycle. All COM interfaces extend the base interface IUnknown, which has two reference counting methods:

```
ULONG AddRef();
ULONG Release();
```

When clients acquire an interface pointer, they must call AddRef. When they are finished with the interface, they must call Release. COM objects manage their own lifetime based on these hints. The most common approach is for the object to maintain a reference count and delete itself when the count reaches zero, although more esoteric approaches are possible. The client does not care what the object actually does in response to these methods; it simply must follow the rules in calling them. There are three ways that a Java client might deal with reference counting COM components:

1. Java stubs could implement the finalize method, which would call Release when triggered by the garbage collector.
2. Java stubs could provide an explicit Release method that clients must remember to call.
3. Stubs could provide both finalize and an explicit Release.

Option 1 is the most transparent. Java programmers are not used to reference counting, so why make them remember this detail? Unfortunately, this does not have acceptable performance. Garbage collection is not deterministic, so there is no guarantee when `finalize` will run, if ever. COM objects would be held in memory for an indeterminate amount of time, even after they were no longer needed. Worse yet, `finalize` might be called on the wrong thread.

Option 2 requires that clients remember to call `Release` when they are finished using a Java stub. This is the most efficient approach. However, if the client forgets to call `Release`, the object will be leaked. With option 3, `finalize` serves as a backup in case clients forget. This two-pronged approach is standard throughout the core Java API where native resources are used. In the core API, Java classes that manipulate sockets, files, database connections, or other native resources provide a well-known method, typically named `close`, which clients call to free the native resource. Jarwin provides a `close` method, but does not use `finalize` because of the threading issue.

A.4.4 COM Type Discovery

In COM, type is a property of a particular instance, not of an entire class. A particular instance can implement one or more interfaces. Interfaces are uniquely named by 128-bit GUIDs called IIDs. To discover whether an object supports a particular interface, you call the method

```
HRESULT QueryInterface(REFIID iid,
                        [out, iid_is(riid)] void *ppvResult)
```

Based on their responses to `QueryInterface`, different instances of the same class may implement different interfaces. This is the opposite of Java, in which the list of implemented interfaces is a fixed property of the binary class format.

Java's cast operator relies on the fixed nature of the binary class format, and therefore cannot work with transparent COM stubs. There are two options: Hack a virtual machine to change the semantics of casting, or simulate casting with a method call. The former option violates the Java license,[1] so there is no hope for modifying the virtual machine. Casting from one interface to another requires a method call:

```
SomeComInterface itf1 = getSomeComInterface();

//this won't work:
//OtherComInterface itf2 = (itf2) itf1;

//you must explicitly call COM's QueryInterface
OtherComInterface itf2 = (itf2)
                         itf1.QueryInterface(itf2.class);
```

Notice that this notion of "casting" also muddies the concept of identity. The variables itf1 and itf2 refer to the same COM object, but they are different stubs. The expression (itf1 == itf2) will evaluate to false.

A.4.5 COM Error Handling

COM provides several levels of support for error reporting. All COM interface methods return an unsigned 32-bit type called an HRESULT to indicate success or failure. The significant HRESULT values have an associated text message that can be retrieved via the Win32 API call FormatMessage. Applications that want to provide more specific information about an error can populate an "error object" which can be placed in thread local storage by calling SetErrorInfo. Clients can then "catch" the error object by calling GetErrorInfo.

All of COM's error information can be mapped into Java by simply creating a subclass of Exception that has data members for the HRESULT, text message, and any data from the error object. As a result, Java programmers can handle exceptions from Java/COM stubs just like they would for any other Java class. The COMException class in Listing A–2 is a simple wrapper for COM error information. The interesting design decision is whether to make the COMException class a checked or unchecked exception. In Jawin, COMException is a

---

1. This was one of the elements of Sun's lawsuit over the Microsoft VM, which modified casting to transparently support COM semantics.

checked exception. This design choice is based on the similar decision in the design of `RemoteException` for RMI. Even if the method itself succeeds, there may be communication errors in the stub layer.

Listing A–2   COMException

```
package com.develop.jawin;

public class COMException extends Exception {
  public final int hresult;
  public static final int E_UNEXPECTED = 0x8000ffff;
  public COMException() {
    this(E_UNEXPECTED);
  }
  public COMException(int hresult) {
    //code to get error string not shown
    this.hresult = hresult;
  }
  public COMException(int hresult, String text) {
    super(text);
    this.hresult = hresult;
  }
  public COMException(String text) {
    this(E_UNEXPECTED, text);
  }
  public String getMessage() {
    return Integer.toHexString(hresult) + ": "
            + super.getMessage();
  }
  public COMException(Throwable t) {
    this(E_UNEXPECTED, t.getMessage());
  }
}
```

A.4.6 COM Thread Affinity

From a Java programmer's perspective, the most unusual feature of COM is its built-in support for thread-affine components. Java, Win32, and COM all define some resources as thread-affine—those resources that can be used only from a subset of the threads in the process. There are two historical reasons for this:

1. User-interface subsystems are often built to run on a single thread to simplify the programming model for UI developers.

2. Some components do not use the concurrency protection mechanisms of the underlying platform, and therefore they are unsafe when called from more than one thread at a time. Most C++ and Java programs suffer from this problem.

In Java and in Win32, there is no special support for thread-affine components. You simply have to be careful. If you break the rules and call a component from the wrong thread, the resulting behavior is typically undefined. You might get lucky and crash your application, or you may get unlucky and have data corruption that goes unnoticed.

COM provides apartments to deal with thread affinity. An *apartment* is a logical subspace of a process within which all objects expect the same thread semantics. Method calls *across* apartments go through stubs[2] (called proxies in the COM world) that do any extra work necessary to guarantee the correct thread semantics, such as switching calls onto an appropriate thread. Objects can live in a single-threaded apartment (STA) if they want to be called from only one thread throughout their lifetime; or, they can live in a multi-threaded apartment (MTA) if they want to be called from multiple threads and might execute blocking calls. If an object knows that it will never need to make a blocking call, it can safely "visit" either an STA or the MTA and have no thread affinity. COM objects with no thread affinity are called agile, or are said to "aggregate the free-threaded marshaller."[3]

With COM+ 1.0, the apartment story is even more complex. The apartment model is extended to a more general *context model*. Objects can request that they live in a particular context, and inbound method calls will pass through a proxy that sets up the required context. This is very similar to EJB, where

---

2. These stubs are very similar to the stubs that are the subject of this chapter. They are generated from type information and exist to bridge between incompatible components—in this case *within* a single component platform.

3. This technology describes how an object implementor defeats thread affinity. Aggregation is a reuse mechanism in COM, and the free-threaded marshaller is a component that prevents the creation of cross-apartment stubs. This causes an object to belong to all apartments (or none) depending on your perspective.

method calls pass through container-generated code that sets up the transaction and security context. The addition of contexts necessitates yet another apartment type. The thread-neutral apartment (TNA) is home to objects that do not have thread affinity but need to have stubs to initialize their context.

Apartments are quite complex, and many trees have been felled describing them. There are three possible approaches to take when dealing with this complexity from Java:

1. Require that Java clients understand COM apartments and use them correctly.

2. Require that Java clients treat all COM components as thread-local.

3. Build logic into the stub layer that analyzes the current thread on each method call, and uses an appropriate COM proxy.

None of these options is perfect. Option 1 is a non-starter; it is completely unrealistic to expect that Java programmers learn the details of COM apartments just to use a COM object. Option 2 provides a very simple rule that Java clients can deal with, but it is overly restrictive in many cases. Option 3 is entirely transparent to Java clients, but the performance hit is significant in some cases.

Since none of the three options is perfect, Jawin supports more than one. Option 3 is the default: Stubs always guarantee that COM threading rules are followed. This will work correctly in all cases but may be slow. If you know that you plan to make repeated calls from the same thread, Jawin provides a helper method called `contextLocalize`. Calling `contextLocalize` turns off a stub's built-in apartment support. Calls through the stub will execute more quickly, but they are only guaranteed to work from the current thread.

A.4.7 COM Security

The security architecture is the most troubling source of impedance mismatch between COM and Java. COM security is based on the user identity currently associated with a thread. Java assigns permissions based on the code source, that is, the location (URL) that code came from and the signers of the code (if any). In theory, there is no problem with securing COM objects using Java permissions. It is simply a matter of defining some appropriate `Permission` subclasses, and calling `checkPermission` inside the generated stubs. But, you would have to write this code by hand. There is no straightforward way to *generate* security-aware stubs because there is no security metadata. Because there is not a good solution, most interop products (including Jawin) either ignore security or build special cases by hand.

A.5 Win32 Dynamic Link Libraries

Dynamic Link Libraries (DLLs) are the basic mechanism for component reuse in the Win32 family of operating systems. DLLs have been around much longer than Java or COM, so when I describe the DLL architecture as a component platform, I am fitting new terms to an old technology. While the goals of component programming are less fully realized in the DLL architecture, the key elements are still visible.

A.5.1 The DLL Loader

The loader architecture for DLLs is quite simple. First, call `LoadLibrary` to locate a binary by its name and location in the file system. Then, call `GetProcAddress` to locate a particular function entry point in the library, either by name or by ordinal (numeric address). Cast the result of `GetProcAddress` to an appropriate function pointer, and off you go, as shown in Listing A–3.

Listing A–3 Dynamic Loading of a DLL Entry Point

```
//dynamically loading and calling MessageBoxW:
typedef WINUSERAPI int  WINAPI
        MBFUNC(HWND, LPCWSTR, LPCWSTR, UINT);
HMODULE hm = LoadLibrary("USER32.DLL");
MBFUNC* MsgBox = (MBFUNC*)GetProcAddress(hm, "MessageBoxW");
MsgBox(0,L"Hello",L"Dynamically Loaded", 0);
```

The important difference from Java is that DLLs deal in functions, not objects. Since Java does not allow freestanding functions, the obvious mapping is to represent these functions as static methods on some Java class. This is Jawin's approach.

How should DLL entry point functions be grouped into Java classes? One approach would be to have a single Java class with all the stub functions for a particular DLL. For example, User32.java would contain stubs for all the functions from User32.dll. This approach leads to very large stub classes—User32.dll contains around 700 function entry points. An alternate approach is to group smaller sets of related functions under some meaningful name. Jawin usually takes the latter approach; for example, all the Registry functions are grouped in Registry.java.

A.5.2 DLL Type Information

A compiled DLL does not expose any useful type information other than the names of methods. In this respect DLLs are very primitive compared to either COM or Java. If you look back at Listing A–3, you will see that loading the `MessageBoxW` function is not type-safe. All DLL entry points look the same until you cast them. If you cast wrong, chaos ensues.

Java clients expect and deserve more type safety than this. In order to generate strongly typed stubs, you must obtain type information from somewhere. There are several possibilities:

- IDL files
- Type libraries (TLBs)
- Header (`.h`) files
- Custom type formats

IDL files and type libraries you remember from the discussion of COM type information. Both IDL and type libraries can describe DLL entry points. However, few DLLs actually ship with this information. Indeed, most DLLs are described by header files. The C/C++ header files ship with the Windows SDK, but they are more difficult to parse.

Even if you have successfully obtained and parsed an IDL, TLB, or header file, you may have trouble generating a Java-friendly signature for some Win32 functions. Consider the Win32 API `GetTokenInformation` shown in Listing A–4.

Listing A–4   Win32's GetTokenInformation

```
BOOL GetTokenInformation(
    HANDLE TokenHandle,                // handle to access token
    TOKEN_INFORMATION_CLASS TokenInformationClass, // token type
    LPVOID TokenInformation,           // buffer
    DWORD TokenInformationLength,      // size of buffer
    PDWORD ReturnLength                // required buffer size
);
```

Logically, this function returns an object whose type is determined by the `TokenInformationClass` flag. However, this "object" takes the form of an opaque array of bytes copied into the `TokenInformation` argument. A Java client would expect to see not these raw bytes, but instead an instance of a Java class. Because the information needed to make this conversion is not part of the method signature, a simple type library would be inadequate. You would need to customize the type information to describe this conversion, which the method signature does not capture.[4] Given these issues, it might be easier to enter the type information by hand, using a custom format.

Most interop products fail to support any of these options and are unable to generate stubs for Win32 DLLs. The current version of Jawin requires that you write Win32 stubs by hand, although a future version may utilize a custom XML-based type format.

A.5.3 DLL Object Lifecycle

Many DLL entry points define some notion of an "object" whose lifecycle needs to be managed. For example, the Registry function `RegOpenKey` returns an opaque handle that represents a key in the Registry. When you are finished with the key, you should call `RegCloseKey` to release the resource. Java stubs could hide this detail from clients by implementing `finalize` to release the resource, but this is a bad idea. As mentioned earlier in the discussion of COM lifecycle, `finalize` is unreliable. Even though it makes the programming model more

---

4. Neither COM nor Java metadata captures this sort of information either, so aren't all the component technologies equally vulnerable to this problem? In theory, yes; but in practice, no. The coding style (modulo syntax) used in `GetTokenInformation` is legal in Win32, Java, or COM, but though it is very common in the Win32 API, it is frowned upon in both the Java and COM worlds.

difficult, clients should be forced to call the lifecycle management APIs for such objects. These calls can be exposed directly, which is how Jawin handles the problem. If the stub layer manufactures a Java object to wrap the handle, then the lifecycle management API call should be hidden behind a `close` method. In the latter case, `finalize` can be used as a failsafe.

A.5.4 DLL Type Discovery

Because DLL entry points are not objects, they do not implement interfaces or support any notion of inheritance.[5]

A.5.5 DLL Error Reporting

DLLs do not enforce a standard scheme for reporting exceptional conditions. In the Win32 SDK, API calls report errors in several different ways:

- Some functions return zero on failure. A numeric code with more information is available by calling `GetLastError`. After calling `GetLastError`, you can obtain a string describing the error with `FormatMessage`. `GetTokenInformation` is one example of this approach.
- Some functions return zero on *success*. Again, more information is available through `GetLastError`. `RegCloseKey` is one example.
- Some functions return an error code such as an `HRESULT` directly. Most of the support API for COM fits in this category.

To add to the confusion, third-party DLLs are free to invent more unusual schemes. It should be straightforward to convert any documented exception reporting scheme into an exception for Java clients. Jawin handles the three standard types shown above, and it is extensible to deal with others.

A.5.6 DLL Thread Affinity

DLLs do not provide any special support for thread affinity, and neither does Java, so there is no impedance mismatch here.

---

5. DLL entry points into C++ libraries may provide access to C++ objects that *do* implement multiple interfaces. Jawin does not directly support non-COM C++ objects because there is relatively little demand for this ability. It would be straightforward (but tedious) to extend Jawin's COM support to also provide direct C++ support.

A.5.7 DLL Security

The issues with the DLL security model are the same as with COM; see §A.4.7.

A.6 Marshalling Architecture

A marshalling architecture ships method calls from one environment to another and provides some degree of help with the platform impedance issues discussed earlier. As mentioned in §A.2, marshalling involves seven steps:

1. Convert a method invocation into a request message.
2. Deliver the request message to a target environment.
3. Convert the request message into a method stack in the target environment.
4. Invoke the method.
5. Convert the return value(s) or exception(s) into a response message.
6. Deliver the response message to the source environment.
7. Convert the response message back into the types expected by the caller.

In order for this communication to occur inside a single process space, the marshalling layer must be built on top of JNI. There are two distinct approaches to marshalling a message from Java into native code. The shared stub approach, discussed in §A.6.1, lets JNI do the marshalling, but it requires that each unique method signature be manually coded in JNI. A generic stub, described in §A.6.2, marshals method calls and results in an opaque array of bytes. All method calls can then be implemented by a single native method.

A.6.1 Shared Stubs

The idea behind shared stubs is simple. Although the theoretical number of different API signatures is practically infinite, most APIs actually use one of a very small number of signatures. For example, you have probably coded a method that takes an `int` and returns an `int`. However, have you ever written a method that takes `int, float, int, int, int` and returns `double`? Probably not.

If the total number of different API *signatures* is small relative to the total number of different API *methods*, then it makes sense to develop and test a small set of native entry points, one for each signature. Once these entry points are in place, then you can add new methods without having to develop or test any new native code.

For example, consider the Win32 APIs listed in Listing A–5. These functions, selected from several different areas of the Win32 API, all appear to have different signatures. However, the `HGDIOBJ`, `int`, `LPVOID`, `HRESULT`, `BOOL`, `HWND`, `HANDLE`, `LONG`, and `HKEY` types all could be represented by the Java type `int`. As a result, these APIs could all share a single native stub method.

Listing A–5 Many APIs Can Share Stubs.

```
HGDIOBJ GetStockObject(int fnObject);
HRESULT CoInitialize(LPVOID reserved);
BOOL UpdateWindow(HWND hwnd);
BOOL DeregisterEventSource(HANDLE hEventLog);
LONG RegCloseKey(HKEY hKey);
```

Listing A–6 shows two shared stubs: one that handles one `int` argument, and a similar method that handles a single `String` argument. These stubs use a naming convention of `invoke{X*}_X`, where each x is replaced by a letter indicating the argument type, in this case `I` for `int` and `G` for `String`. Each stub takes zero or more parameters for the method arguments, plus the two special arguments `flags` and `func`. The `flags` control interpretation of the return value, and they correspond to the different error handling schemes for DLLs listed in §A.5.5. The `func` argument is the address of the API function.

Listing A–6 Shared Stub for Win32 APIs with a Single Integer Parameter

```
//Client code example: calling CoInitialize
Ole32.CoInitialize();

//Implementing the interface stub for CoInitialize
public class Ole32 {
  public static void CoInitialize() throws COMException {
    FuncPtr fp = new FuncPtr("OLE32.DLL", "CoInitialize");
    SharedStubs.invokeI_I(0, fp.getPeer(), CHECK_HR);
  }
  //etc.
}
```

```
//implementing the interface stub for the Registry APIs
public class Registry
{
  static private final FuncPtr fpCK;
  static {
    fpCK = new FuncPtr("ADVAPI32.DLL", "RegCloseKey");
  }
  public static void CloseKey(int key)
    throws IOException, COMException
  {
    SharedStubs.invokeI_I(key, fpCK.getPeer(), CHECK_W32);
  }
  //etc.
}


//excerpt from com.develop.com.marshal.SharedStubs;
public class SharedStubs {
    public static native int invokeG_I(int arg0, String arg1,
                                       int func, int flags);
    public static native int invokeI_I(int arg0,
                                       int func, int flags);
  //etc.
}
```

The native implementations of the shared stubs, shown in Listing A–7, are tedious but straightforward. Each stub executes the same basic series of steps:

1. Convert arguments to Java types if necessary.

2. Cast the `peer` to a function pointer and invoke the function.

3. Do any special processing of the return value.

4. Free any resources allocated in step 1.

Listing A–7 Implementation of Shared Stubs' Native Methods

```
typedef HRESULT (__stdcall * FTYPE1)(int);

inline bool checkRet(int ret, int flags) {
  switch (flags) {
    case 0:
    return true;
    case 1:
    if (!ret) {
      JNIComException::SetLastError();
```

```
          return false;
      }
      return true;
       case 2:
      if (FAILED(ret)) {
        JNIComException::SetContextException(ret);
        return false;
      }
      return true;
       case 3:
      if (ret != ERROR_SUCCESS) {
        JNIComException::SetContextException(ret);
        return false;
      }
      return true;
       default:
      JNIComException::SetContextException(
                        "Invalid code in checkRet");
      return false;
    }
}
JNIEXPORT jlong JNICALL
Java_com_develop_com_marshal_SharedStubs_invokeI_1I
  (JNIEnv * pEnv, jclass, jint arg0, jint peer, jint flags)
{
  int ret = ((FTYPE1)peer)(arg0);
  checkRet(ret, flags);
  return ret;
}
JNIEXPORT jlong JNICALL
Java_com_develop_com_marshal_SharedStubs_invokeG_1I
(JNIComUtil * pEnv, jclass, jstring arg0, jint peer, int flags)
{
  CComBSTR bs0;
  bs0.Attach(pEnv->jstobs(arg0));
  int ret = ((FTYPE1)peer)((int)bs0.m_str);
  checkRet(ret, flags);
  return ret;
}
```

For a stub that handles only primitive numeric types, steps 1 and 4 disappear and the implementation is entirely trivial. For slightly more complex types, such as strings, the marshalling layer uses a set of helper APIs called *intrinsic functions* to perform data conversions.

An intrinsic function is a hand-coded function that implements some atomic action inside the marshalling layer, such as streaming a particular data type or converting a numeric error code into a Java exception. The intrinsic functions get their name because they are built into the marshalling layer. More complex marshalling tasks, such as streaming a large `struct`, do not require hand-coded functions. They take the form of several intrinsic function invocations in sequence and are generated from type information.

In Listing A–7, the `invokeG_I` implementation uses a helper class `CComB-STR` as an intrinsic function. In this case, the "function" is actually a class because `CComBSTR` is already available as part of the Active Template Library (ATL), which Jawin uses. The `CComBSTR` class automates converting a Java string into a `BSTR`, which is the most common string format in COM programming.

When does a particular marshalling task deserve its own intrinsic function, and when should it be composed from calls to lower-level intrinsic functions? The boundary is arbitrary. High-frequency data types, such as strings and arrays, deserve custom functions both for convenience and for performance reasons. However, there is a strong motivation to minimize the number of intrinsic functions, since some human must write each one. Most intrinsic functions come in pairs: a Java function to convert from Java to Win32/COM, and a native function to go in the other direction, from Win32/COM to Java. Never having to hand-code a native function is a key goal of building a marshalling layer in the first place. Wherever possible, Jawin executes more complex marshalling tasks by calling preexisting intrinsic functions.

For all their value, shared stubs are unlikely to handle every possible API. Methods with a large number of arguments, or with more complex structured types, require more complex stubs—and are therefore likely to not have shared stubs at all. Of course, some stubs are better than no stubs. If nine of ten needed APIs can be accessed through a preexisting shared stub, then you have achieved a 90 percent reduction in the native code that you have to write.

A.6.2 A Generic Stub

Shared stubs implement one specific signature per stub. An alternate approach is to use a generic stub that can marshal any method call. A generic stub converts a method call into a serialized request message, which is then transmitted to the destination object. In addition to the request, the generic stub must also transmit some instructions that describe the method signature to be called. Using the request and the instructions, the generic stub builds the native call stack and invokes the method. Return values and exceptions are then serialized into a response, and returned to the client.

In theory, a generic stub could encode everything about the method call into a single array, and be declared like this:

```
public native byte[] genericInvoke(byte[] request);
```

In practice, the method call is likely to be encoded into more than one argument, for the convenience of the developer. Jawin's generic stub has this signature:

```
package com.develop.com.marshal;

public class GenericStub {
  public static byte[] win32Invoke(int peer, String inst,
                      int stackBytes, int totalBytes,
                      byte[] request, Object[] ObjectArgs);
  //remainder omitted for clarity
}
```

The `request` array is the serialized call, `totalBytes` is the number of relevant bytes in `request`, and the `peer` is the native function pointer to invoke. The separate array for Java object arguments is necessitated by JNI. JNI requires that objects passed to native code must be passed as object references, so the objects travel in their own separate array `ObjectArgs`. The object array also does double duty for any Java objects to be returned to the caller. The `StockBytes` and `inst` arguments are described in the next section.

A.6.3 Instruction Strings

The other two parameters, `stackBytes` and `inst`, tell the marshalling layer how to build the native call stack. The `stackBytes` value is the size of the call stack. The implementation of `win32Invoke` will allocate a call buffer of this size on the stack. Then, the `request` array must be unmarshalled into the buffer. The `inst` argument is an *instruction string* that tells the marshaller how to copy the `request` array into the call buffer.

An instruction string is a sequence of characters that drives a state machine inside the marshaller. The state machine processes the instruction string to create a call stack. If all the arguments to a method are primitive types, then the instructions are trivial: Simply copy the request directly into the call buffer. If the arguments to a method are COM interface pointers or data structures, then the instructions get more complex. For example, consider the Jawin code to call the `MessageBoxW` function that appears in Listing A–8.

Listing A–8   Marshalling MessageBoxW

```
//the MessageBoxW signature in C:
WINUSERAPI int
WINAPI MessageBoxW(HWND, LPCWSTR, LPCWSTR, UINT);

//Client code: calling MessageBoxW from Java
User32.MessageBoxW("Hello World", "Jawin");

//Implementing the interface stub. This code might be
//hand-written or generated from type information.
public class User32 {
  static final int mstackMessageBoxW = 16;
  public static void MessageBoxW(String msg, String title)
        throws COMException
  {
    FuncPtr fp = new FuncPtr("USER32.DLL", "MessageBoxW");
    NakedByteStream nbs = new NakedByteStream();
    LittleEndianOutputStream leos = new
                          LittleEndianOutputStream(nbs);
    leos.writeStringUnicode(msg);
    leos.writeStringUnicode(title);
```

```
GenericStub.win32Invoke(fp.getPeer(),
                        "kGGk:T1:",
                        mstackMessageBoxW,
                        leos.size(),
                        nbs.getInternalBuffer(),
                        null);
  }
  //etc.
}
```

The `User32` stub for `MessageBoxW` executes the following steps:

1. Create an instance of the `FuncPtr` helper class. Behind the scenes, this helper calls `LoadLibrary` and `GetProcAddress` to load the function.

2. Create a `LittleEndianOutputStream` to hold the request message. (Win32 and COM expect bytes to be in little-endian order).

3. Write the string arguments into the stream.

4. Call the method, passing in the request and the instruction string.

The instruction string `kGGk:T1:` is interpreted as follows:

- The characters before the first colon are the instructions for converting the message into a call buffer. The letter `k` means "skip this argument on the stack" and the letter `G` means "read a string from the message and write its address onto the stack." In this example, the first and last arguments are skipped because the entire call buffer is zero-filled, and these arguments need to be zero.

- The characters between the colons are the instructions for writing the return value into the response buffer. The characters `T1` mean "write the return value into the response buffer *and* raise a `COMException` if the function returned zero."

- The characters after the second colon are instructions for writing any `out` parameters into the response buffer. `MessageBoxW` does not have any `out` parameters, so this part of the string is empty.

Jawin supports a large number of different instructions which are documented at [Jawin] and can be extended to support arbitrarily complex API signatures.

Jawin's character encodings for the instruction strings are arbitrary and can be quite complex. The purpose of the generic stub is to replace raw JNI for complex method signatures. However, one could make the argument that learning to use encodings such as kGGk:T1 is just as difficult as writing raw JNI, so why bother? The answer, of course, is that you will not be writing the encodings directly. Classes such as User32 should be generated from type information, as discussed in the next section.

A.7 Generating Stubs

Consider again the marshalling architecture diagram, shown in Figure A–1. The intrinsic functions and other marshalling infrastructure code must be developed by hand. However, they are developed only once to be shared by all interface stubs. Each particular COM interface or set of DLL entry points will need its own interface stub. These interface stubs vary only by differences in type information, and they are ideal candidates for code generation. Jawin includes prototypes for generating both shared stubs and interface stubs.

A.7.1 Generating Shared Stubs

The com.develop.jawin.tools package, included with Jawin, is a pure Java implementation that builds the Java and native source code files for shared stubs. The COMSharedStubDriver class defines a set of argument types and a maximum number of arguments to generate. Then the COMSharedStubDriver iterates over every permutation of arguments, calling COMSharedStubBuilder to generate the Java declaration and native implementation. Listing A–9 shows the native stub declarations generated for two-argument methods with types int, float and String. Listing A–10 shows a small sample of the generated implementations.

Listing A–9 Stub Declarations Generated by COMSharedStubDriver

```
//stub declarations
package com.develop.com.marshal;import com.develop.com.*;import
com.develop.util.*;import java.io.*;import java.util.*;
    public class COMMarshal {    public static native void
    invokeII(int vtableIndex, int guidToken, int peer, int
    unknown, int arg0, int arg1);
    public static native void invokeIF(int vtableIndex, int
        guidToken, int peer, int unknown, int arg0, float arg1);
```

```
public static native void invokeIG(int vtableIndex, int
    guidToken, int peer, int unknown, int arg0, String arg1);
public static native String invokeIoG(int vtableIndex, int
    guidToken, int peer, int unknown, int arg0);
public static native int invokeIoI(int vtableIndex, int
    guidToken, int peer, int unknown, int arg0);
public static native float invokeIoF(int vtableIndex, int
    guidToken, int peer, int unknown, int arg0);
public static native void invokeFI(int vtableIndex, int
    guidToken, int peer, int unknown, float arg0, int arg1);
public static native void invokeFF(int vtableIndex, int
    guidToken, int peer, int unknown, float arg0, float arg1);
public static native void invokeFG(int vtableIndex, int
    guidToken, int peer, int unknown, float arg0, String arg1);
public static native String invokeFoG(int vtableIndex, int
    guidToken, int peer, int unknown, float arg0);
public static native int invokeFoI(int vtableIndex, int
    guidToken, int peer, int unknown, float arg0);
public static native float invokeFoF(int vtableIndex, int
    guidToken, int peer, int unknown, float arg0);
public static native void invokeGI(int vtableIndex, int
    guidToken, int peer, int unknown, String arg0, int arg1);
public static native void invokeGF(int vtableIndex, int
    guidToken, int peer, int unknown, String arg0, float arg1);
public static native void invokeGG(int vtableIndex, int
    guidToken, int peer, int unknown, String arg0, String arg1);
public static native String invokeGoG(int vtableIndex, int
    guidToken, int peer, int unknown, String arg0);
public static native int invokeGoI(int vtableIndex, int
    guidToken, int peer, int unknown, String arg0);
public static native float invokeGoF(int vtableIndex, int
    guidToken, int peer, int unknown, String arg0);
public static native void invokeI(int vtableIndex, int
    guidToken, int peer, int unknown, int arg0);
public static native void invokeF(int vtableIndex, int
    guidToken, int peer, int unknown, float arg0);
public static native void invokeG(int vtableIndex, int
    guidToken, int peer, int unknown, String arg0);
public static native String invokeoG(int vtableIndex, int
    guidToken, int peer, int unknown);
public static native int invokeoI(int vtableIndex, int
    guidToken, int peer, int unknown);
public static native float invokeoF(int vtableIndex, int
    guidToken, int peer, int unknown);
}
```

COMPONENT DEVELOPMENT FOR THE JAVA™ PLATFORM

Listing A–10   Native Stubs Generated by COMSharedStubDriver

```
JNIEXPORT void JNICALL
Java_com_develop_com_marshal_COMMarshal_invokeIF(JNIComUtil *
pEnv, jclass, jint vtableIndex, jint guidToken, jint peer, jint
unknown, jint arg0, jfloat arg1)
{
    CComPtr<IUnknown> cpUnk;
    try {
        getUnknown(guidToken, peer, unknown, &cpUnk);
        FTYPE3* vtable = (FTYPE3*) (*(int*)(cpUnk.p));
        int inv0 = arg0;
        float inv1 = arg1;
        JNI_HR(vtable[vtableIndex]((int)cpUnk.p, inv0, inv1));
    }
    HANDLE_JNI_EXCEPTIONS()
}
JNIEXPORT void JNICALL
Java_com_develop_com_marshal_COMMarshal_invokeIG(JNIComUtil *
pEnv, jclass, jint vtableIndex, jint guidToken, jint peer, jint
unknown, jint arg0, jstring arg1)
{
    CComPtr<IUnknown> cpUnk;
    try {
        getUnknown(guidToken, peer, unknown, &cpUnk);
        FTYPE3* vtable = (FTYPE3*) (*(int*)(cpUnk.p));
        int inv0 = arg0;
        CComBSTR temp1;
        temp1.Attach(pEnv->jstobs(arg1));
        int inv1 = (int)temp1.m_str;
        JNI_HR(vtable[vtableIndex]((int)cpUnk.p, inv0, inv1));
    }
    HANDLE_JNI_EXCEPTIONS()
}
```

The code for the actual generator is almost insultingly simple. That is one of the beauties of generative programming. There is often no need (or temptation) to optimize the generator because it is run only at development time. Also, the generator does not need to be particularly user-friendly since the target user is a developer. Of course, a very large, widely used generator might need to be developed and optimized like a "normal" program. Nevertheless, generators are often simpler than the same logic implemented dynamically at runtime.

One reason that the generator is simple is that "almost right is good enough." The `COMSharedStubDriver` makes several simplifying assumptions about `out` parameters:

- There is at most one `out` parameter per method.
- If there is an `out` parameter, it appears last.
- The `out` parameters should be translated to a Java return value.

None of these assumptions is entirely true, but they probably apply to better than 98 percent of actual COM interfaces. Many developers would consider it unwise to code these assumptions into an OO base class since they are not entirely accurate and might compromise the architecture. Nobody worries if a development-time generator is predictably inaccurate for some cases. You can always replace the generator with another generator, defer special classes to another generator, or simply code the outlying cases by hand.[6]

A.7.2 Generating Interface Stubs

Whether you use shared stubs or a generic stub, the front end of the marshalling layer is an interface stub that provides a Java representation of some COM interface or Win32 entry point. In general, the source code for an interface stub looks like this:

```
//pseudo-code
package <% =some.arbitrary.package %>;
import <%= some.standard.imports %>;

class <%= SomeStub %> {
  //Some per-class goo…

  <%= SomeReturnType %>
  <%= someMethod %>(<%=  someArgs %>) { //for each method
    SomeCallStackRep r = new SomeCallStackRep();
    r.addArg(<%= arg[n] %>); //for each arg
```

---

6. This entire argument is as much about culture as it is about technology. It is entirely feasible to code an inheritance-based solution that deliberately ignores special cases. However, many OO purists are obsessive about accurately modeling the problem domain. The recent rise of Extreme Programming (XP) is, in part, a rejection of this aspect of OO culture.

```
    ReturnRep ret = Stub.invoke(r);
    return <%= someReturnTypeConversionFunc %>(ret);
  }
}
```

Most of the text in this file is boilerplate; only the bolded portions need to change for different methods. Type information can be used to generate these replacements. The use of the `<%= expr%>` syntax implies an obvious approach, which is to use JSP or a JSP-like syntax to generate the source code for the stubs.

Because COM type information is already available through COM interfaces, Jawin uses a COM-based code generation language called X-Code[7] instead of JSP. Listing A–11 shows the method generation portion of the X-Code template, and Listing A–12 shows an example of a generated method.

Listing A–11   Method Generation Template from COMThunk.xjava

```
public <%= returnTypeName(method) %>
<%= method.Name %>(<%= argList(method,0) %>)
throws COMException, IOException
{
  int vtIndex = <%= method.VtableIndex %>;
  NakedByteStream nbs = new NakedByteStream();
  LittleEndianOutputStream leos =
        new LittleEndianOutputStream(nbs);
  //arg stream
<% for (i=0; i < method.ArgCount; i++) { %>
<%= marshalArg(method, i)%><% } %>
  //object args
<%= customObjArray(method) %>
<% for (i=0; i < method.ArgCount; i++) { %>
<%= marshalObject(method, i)%><% } %>
  byte[] result = GenericStub.comInvokeString(
                    "<%= marshalString(method) %>",
                  <%= method.ArgCount * 4 %>,
                  leos.size(),
                  nbs.getInternalBuffer(),
```

---

7. X-Code is part of Gen<X>, a commercial code general reaction tool developed by the author's employer. Jawin began as a proof of concept for X-Code, and Jawin itself is completely free and open source. For more information on Gen<X>, see [GenX].

```
                    objArgs,
                     vtIndex,
                    iidToken,
                    peer,
                    unknown);
<%= customMaybeStream() %><%= customMaybeReturn() %>
}
```

Listing A–12   Sample Generated Method: Saving a Word Document

```
public void Save(Object arg0, Object arg1)
        throws COMException, IOException
{
  int vtIndex = 16;
  NakedByteStream nbs = new NakedByteStream();
  LittleEndianOutputStream leos =
          new LittleEndianOutputStream(nbs);
  //arg stream
  Variant.marshalIn(arg0, leos);
  Variant.marshalIn(arg1, leos);
  //object args
  Object[] objArgs=null;

  byte[] result = GenericStub.comInvokeString("VV:H:ll",
                            8,
                            leos.size(),
                            nbs.getInternalBuffer(),
                            objArgs,
                            vtIndex,
                            iidToken,
                            peer,
                            unknown);
}
```

The Save method implementation shows both the benefits and limits of a type-
information driven approach. On the plus side, the generation of this method is
entirely automatic; all you have to do is run the template against the Microsoft
Word type library. However, the signature is not very informative. Many COM interfaces are designed primarily with scripting in mind, and they do not use
strong typing. The Save method uses VARIANT arguments, which can be any legal scripting type. As a result, the Java stub is weakly typed as well, taking arguments of type Object.

A.8 Onward

Interoperation between Java, Win32, and COM is an important aspect of most enterprise systems. Even organizations with a strong commitment to Java need access to the huge number of existing COM and Win32 DLL components.

There is no single solution to this problem, and the relationship between the key vendors makes it unlikely that there ever will be. [JavaWin32] summarizes the various third-party products that have appeared to fill this void. To varying degrees, each product hides the sources of platform impedance presented in §A.3.

The latter half of this appendix presented an example marshalling architecture. You have three important decisions to make in choosing the best marshalling architecture for your own use:

1. Decide which aspects of platform impedance need to be handled transparently, which ones to expose to Java clients, and how they should be exposed.

2. Find support for the type systems you need. If you only need to access scriptable COM components, there is no need to invest in a product that supports DLL entry points or complex IDL expressions.

3. Minimize the work that must be done by hand. Choose a solution that can automatically generate the interface stubs you need.

Many of the marshalling products will let you mix-and-match solutions to these three questions. For example, since Jawin is open source, you could easily use Jawin's intrinsic functions but replace its stub generators with your own.

This appendix has examined in-process communication. In-process solutions have several benefits. They are almost certain to be faster because they do not pay the penalty of crossing a process or network boundary. Also, they allow Java programs direct access to process-local resources. If you need access to process-local resources, in-process interop is your only choice.

Another possibility, beyond the scope of this book, is out-of-process techniques, using network communication to bridge between Java and native processes. Calling native code in another process provides some fault tolerance since the native process has no way to damage the Java process. On the other hand, out-of-process communication is slower and is completely unsuitable for some tasks, such as manipulating process-specific resources inside the virtual machine.

Index

Bootclasspath, 41–43
Bootstrap class loader, 36, 41–43, 48
Boss class, 141, 146

C

C++
   calling Java from, 208–217
   exception handling, 218–219
   method declarations, 196
   parameters with multiple levels of indirection,
      196
Call stack logging, 46
Callee class, 189
Caller class, 189
Caller class loader, 21
CallVoidMethod method, 213, 219
CallVoidMethodA method, 221
Capability, 16
CauseConfusion methods, 199
CComBSTR class, 307
Chars API, 239
checkPermission method, 299
Child loader and classes, 49
Circular reference problems during resolution, 141–
   142
Class class, 21, 67–68, 70, 123
Class loader architecture, 5, 11
   assembling applications, 14
   capability, 16
   configurability, 16
   explicit class loading, 19
   extensibility, 15–16
   goals, 14–17
   handling name and version conflicts, 16–17
   security, 17
   transparency, 15
Class loader delegation model, 5
Class loaders, 11, 14, 55, 281
   applet, 25
   caller's, 21
   choosing, 174–175
   configuration options, 36
   consistency rule, 23–24
   context, 5
   crossing boundaries, 72
   custom, 5, 153–190
   delegation, 24–25, 27

effective use of, 14
exotic designs, 15–16
explicit use of, 29
getting past security to, 175–177
hierarchy, 52
holding cache of classes, 35–36
hot deployment, 29–34
installing all classes under, 52
instantiating, 53, 177
interaction with, 36
inversion, 49-55
JNI (Java Native Interface), 202–204
keeping in memory, 36
limited sharing of classes, 25
loading arbitrary resources, 22–23
meeting common needs, 16
memory, 35
multiple versions of native code, 203
overriding findLibrary method, 202
parent, 24
role, 157–159
rules, 23–29
security hole, 177
since SDK 1.2, 160–162
source-aware, 23
system, 25
transforming, 162–167
visibility rule, 25–26
Class loading, 55
   capable, 16
   debugging, 43–49
   dynamic, 28–29, 251
   easily configurable, 16
   errors, 28
   explicit, 18–23
   implicit, 19–23, 24, 29
   name conflicts, 16–17
   reading attributes during, 183–188
   supporting flexible binding modes, 251
   version incompatibilities, 16–17
Class object, 18, 35
ClassCastException class, 144
Class-controlled object replacement, 137–139
Classes
   already-loaded, 23–24
   child loader, 49
   compatibility, 66
   compatible and incompatible changes, 117–118

G

Garbage collector, 35
  classes, 36–37
  encouraging, 132–133
  interacting with, 224–231
  local references, 224
gc method, 204
Generating stubs, 311–316
GeneratorBase class, 271
Generators, 247–248, 249
Generic collections, 267
Generic delegation and dynamic proxies, 84–85
Generic interceptors, 83
Generic services, XVI, 87–89
Generic skeletons, 256
Generic stubs, 308
get method, 72
GetAnswer method, 194, 197
getBadDateValue method, 90
getClass method, 35
getClassLoader method, 19, 35, 41
GetContentType method, 170
GetDate method, 170
getDeclared method, 72
getDeclaredField method, 70–71, 210
getDeclaredFields method, 69
getDeclaredXXX accessor method, 68–70
GetErrorInfo function, 295
getExpiration method, 170
GetField class, 121, 275
getField method, 70–71, 123–124, 210
GetFieldID method, 210
getFields method, 69
getGoodDateValue method, 90
getInputStream method, 170
GetIntArrayElements method, 236, 237
GetIntArrayRegion method, 235
getInterfaces method, 67
GetLastError function, 302
getMethod method, 73, 75
GetMethodID method, 213
getModifiers method, 69–70
getOutputStream method, 170
getParent method, 24, 44
GetPrimitiveArrayCritical method, 238
GetProcAddress function, 299, 310
getProtectionDomain method, 162

GetRegion method, 240
getResource method, 22, 165
getResourceAsStream method, 22
getResources method, 22
getSuperclass method, 67
getSystemClassLoader method, 25
getTargetException method, 82
GetTokenInformation Win32 API, 300–301, 302
getURLBase method, 165
getVersionInfo method, 187
getXXX accessor method, 68–70
Global references, 224–225, 226
GP (generative programming), 243
  binary classes, 252
  bind modes, 253–255
  bind times, 253–255
  class loading supporting flexible binding modes, 251
  code generation boosting performance, 252
  code generation language, 270–271
  custom serialization code, 271–276
  domain analysis, 250
  ease of generating Java source code, 251
  EJB (Enterprise JavaBeans) code generation, 260–267
  generating stubs, 311–316
  inputs and outputs, 254–255
  JSP (Java Server Pages) code generation, 257–260
  levels of commitment to code generation, 252–253
  marshalling architecture, 303–311
  reasons for generating code, 243–250
  strongly-typed collections, 267–271
  target language, 270–271
  type information as free specification document, 250–251
GUID (Globally Unique ID), 291

H

Handler class, 169, 174
hashCode method, 86
HashMap class, 24
Header files, 300
Hello.jsp servlet, 257, 258–259
Helper components, 253

JNIEXPORT macro, 197
JNI_OnLoad method, 212, 220–221, 222, 226
JNI_OnUnload method, 226
JNI_VERSION_1_2 method, 212
jobject references, 224
jobject type, 197, 208, 210
JSP (Java Server Pages), XVII, 251, 253, 254
   code generation, 257–260
   generator language for Java, 270–271
   strongly-typed stack classes, 268–269
_jspService method, 258

L

Late binding, 252
Launcher and command line processing, 39
LaunchVehicle interface, 98–99
LD_LIBRARY_PATH environment variable, 201
LICENSE file, 49
LineNumberTable attribute, 101
Linking
   application correctly, 13–14
   methods at runtime, 59
   native libraries, 199-202
   with full paths, 200
ListBaseTypes class, 67
ListByLastName console client, 2
ListMostFields class, 69–70
LittleEndianOutputStream, 310
load method, 200-202
loadClass method, 21, 47, 159–161
LoaderDemo class, 19, 27–28
Loading native libraries, 199–202
LoadLibrary Win32 function, 310
loadLibrary method, 200–202, 205–206, 299
LoadMe class, 19, 20, 27–28
LoadMeAlso class, 20
LoadMeBase class, 20
LoadMeThree class, 20
LoadMeToo class, 20
LoadNonExistentLibrary class, 205
LoadTheWrongLibrary class, 206
Local references, 224, 226, 227
LocalVariableTable attribute, 101
Locating components, 12
logConstructor method, 46
Logging call stacks, 46
LoggingHandler class, 85–86

M

-m switch, 95
MadScientist class, 58–61
Main class, 49
Mars singleton, 138
MarshalledObject class, 150
Marshalling architecture, 6, 286–287
   generic stubs, 308
   instruction strings, 309–311
   shared stubs, 303–307
Message object, 149
MessageBoxW function, 300, 309–311
Metadata, 57, 66
   abandoning, 124–130
   accessing from packages, 96
   binary classes, 63–64
   binary compatibility, 58–62
   class-level, 94
   correct units for numeric arguments, 98
   custom, 98–102
   externalizable classes, 125–127
   overwriting, 122–123
   reading custom, 177–189
   serialization, 105–106
   setting for packages, 95–96
   skipping, 127
   supplementing, 197
   tables of allowable state transitions, 98
   version information, 94
Method class, 71, 72–73, 77, 256, 257
Methods
   call forwarding, 87
   converting to network messages, XVI
   invalid arguments, 81
   invisible, 60
   linking at runtime, 59
   nonexistent, 60
   overloaded, 198
   reflection, 71–72
   small-grained, 211
   throwing exception, 82
   virtual and non-virtual invocation, 215
midl compiler, 292
Mobile components, 105
Modifying applications, 12
Money class, 263
Moving corrected PointImpl, 33

MTA (multi-threaded apartment), 297
Multiple inheritance, 83, 196

N

Name conflicts, 16–17
Name mappings, 195
Namespaces, delegations as, 27–28
Naming rule, 16–17
Native code
    bypassing language protection modifiers, 193
    calling Java constructor, 216
    dangers of, 193–194
    failures, 217–218
    finding and loading, 194–208
    global references, 224–225
    handling Java exceptions, 219–222
    loading, 204
    reflective access, 209
    throwing Java exceptions, 222–223
    type-safety, 193
native keyword, 194
Native libraries
    common errors loading, 205–207
    loading, 199–202
    loading old version, 204
    troubleshooting loading, 207
    visible across all class loaders, 203
Native methods
    instantiating Person class, 79
    loading, 200
    populating fields, 81
    shared stubs implementation, 305–306
Native resources, managing, 231–232
Native singleton implementation, 29
nativeMove method, 209–212
NativePoint class, 208–209
neverLoaded method, 206
NewGlobalRef method, 224–226
newInstance method, 176, 177, 216
NewObject method, 216
newProxyInstance method, 85
Non-Java components, XVI
NoOpResourceTransformer class, 165
NoSuchFieldException class, 71
NoSuchMethodError class, 60
not handler, 174
not protocol and protocol handlers, 169–170

Not referencing type dynamically replaced, 33
not stream handler, 168
NotConnection class, 174
NotInputStream class, 170–171, 174
NotSerializableException class, 131, 135
NotURLReader class, 172–173

O

obj reference, 20
Object approach, 3
Object class, 86
Object graphs, 130
    controlling ordering, 145–147
    custom serialization hooks, 145
    encouraging garbage collector, 132–133
    preserving identity, 131–132
    pruning, 131
    serializing more data than wanted, 131
Object replacement
    class-controlled, 137–139
    ordering rules, 139–144
    stream-controlled, 134
ObjectArgs array, 308
ObjectInputStream class, 112, 115, 118, 124, 134, 145
    defaultReadObject method, 112
    GetField method, 119, 120–121
ObjectInputValidation class, 145, 146–147
Object-oriented approach, questions raised by, 3
Object-oriented design, 3, 5
Object-oriented languages modeling problem domain, 3
ObjectOutputStream class, 108, 133, 134, 271
    GetField method, 119
    PutField method, 119
Objects, XV, 3
    deserializing, 113
    dynamically instantiating, 66
    explicitly destroying, 35
    preserving identity, 131–132
    serializing state of, XVI
ObjectStreamClass class, 123, 271
ObjectStreamField class, 123
OpenConnection method, 169
Optimization, 20
OSDeallocResource method, 231
out variable, 258

los angeles · boston · london · portland, OR

A DEVELOPER SERVICES COMPANY

developmentor®

develop.com

ABOUT DEVELOPMENTOR

DevelopMentor is a distinct educational resource providing advanced technical information through training, publications, conferences, and software. DevelopMentor is comprised of passionate developers who offer insight and leadership in areas such as .NET, XML, JAVA, and COM. The DevelopMentor Technical Staff have authored over 24 technical books and are regular contributors to *MSDN, Java Pro, Visual Basic Programmer's Journal*, and other publications. DevelopMentor training facilities are located in Los Angeles, Boston, London, and Portland.

HELPING DEVELOPERS WITH TRAINING, SOFTWARE, PUBLICATIONS, AND CONFERENCES.

COM+ · VB.NET · XML · Java
ASP.NET · OLE DB · J2EE · C++
.NET · C# · COM+ · XML
Web Services · EJB · CLR · C#

FOR MORE INFORMATION:

develop.com

IN THE US
800.699.1932

WITHIN THE UK
0800.056.22.65

WITHIN EUROPE
+44.1242.525.108

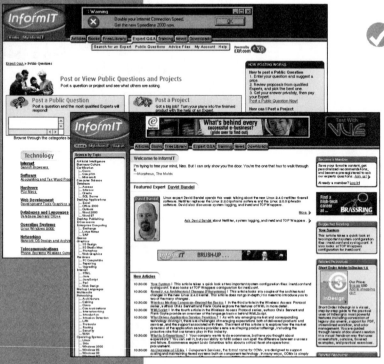